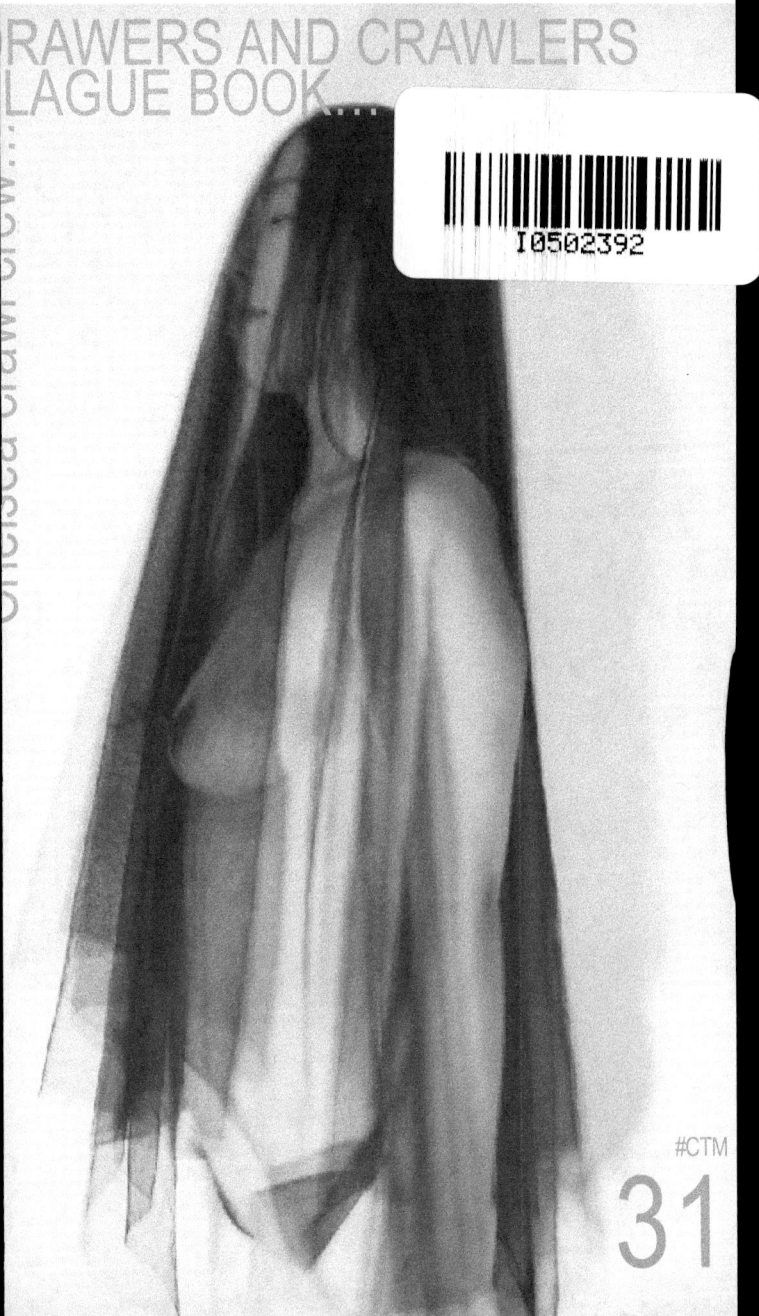

#CTM

31

drawers, crawlers, and lurkers

S.M. Sullivan
Iris Johnson
Patrisha Holly Zabrycki
Philipp Kuecuekyan
David Turner
Victor Harshbarger
elizabeth popiel
Leah Aschkenasy-Reid
Dr. Paul Martin
Tina Ball
Joan Marie Kelly
Ariel Revan
Sal Trapani
Jim Roderick
Jung Nam Lee
Phillip Baldwin

'The figure, Modernity, and Resulting Abstraction'

The hustle:

until the invention of the camera, we assumed that 'progression' in painting had much to do with verisimilitude, academic figures, and even the invention of the one-point perspective as a contrived 'immersion device'. This grew with 'bourgeois culture'....whatever that might be now.....With many variation including most African art works, ancient cave painting (with flourishes of academic finesse) Tantric 17thc Painting...(looking a lot like af Klint), and most of non-western art, there was little concern for blending abstraction with the academic figure....modernity as a global movement (of 'self liberatory' practices) in combination with the camera, and certainly now in the digital age, the modernist imperative ramped this up: to sweat over the 'academic figure' was to be 'a petite bourgeois stooge'. And what about 'abstract choices executed as academic tropes?'

For the drawers, and the crawlers, and the drinkers send in your ideas of this contrived syllogism of modernity: modernism means and results in abstraction. Please send in one or a few hooks on this jive.

Mine:

figurative....Jean-Jacques Lequeu having a great show at the Morgan this spring.
Lebbeus Woods, modern architect of fantasy, fantastic draughsperson like Lequeu, my favs, Ledoux, and master Boullee

...hard transitions into modernity: Kollwitz, Malevich,

out the other side: Sarah Sze (on platonic caves), Mark Tansey, Geoff Chadsey,

rock and roll...send your images to draw....
see you 7 30 on zoom....byob. Add more people if you want...i liked that JN just phoned in and breathed hard on the mystery line. turned me on. loved the final drawing of 'the Hoff'.

Note_55, 3 June 2020

Drawing in the age of Internet. Or rather drawing in the age of Instagram.

it's funny, 100 hundred years ago almost everyone a middle-class and was trained in to play the piano and to draw. Drawing was based on some sort of Academic Way... first with a figure... than wood Landscapes, and then with architecture. but almost everyone had that skill. This Was the decline of this skill caused by the mechanical reproduction reality in cameras? I think it was. It's so easy to do. Push the Button. Yet now, strangely, drawing is back in the era of Instagram.

I belong to a number of academic and drawing sites and Instagram. I look at these things. Turn off my Instagram feed and summer extremely interesting very well done and it would lead me to believe that there's a Resurgence of this... of hand drawing. something even in an academic sense, but certainly it seems in any abstract works. Why is this the case? There was a decline and drawing certainly through the television era and then with the return of the internet we see many people enjoying the DIY aspect of their lives.... Down in the beautiful cafe table. it is not all about photographing everything, but about drawing. The bodily process. And there's the other 'in-body thing' about bringing in the reality into your eyes and having it come out through your hands to paper. I think this is a Nostalgia for the body as not a machine, but the body is an emotional thing, able to take in reality and express it in any way.

Yet, we used to do these things in my generation and unless you were a famous Gallery artists you felt like you were in a vacuum. No one would see that stuff. I think now with the motivation of 'likes' we've achieved another culture where someone could just sit in their backyard and draw the trees, sit in the backyard and draw an abstraction, (either) and take a photograph of it, both, on their iPhone or a Samsung and then posted the Instagram it immediately get 40 50 60 likes. It's strange that we're re-motivated to play, to return to an older technology that never really died but the newer technology and the likes have brought this again to the Forefront. Much like the paleolithic caves. But also, very different from them.

Instagram has reinvented drawing.
And I am

AN COMPUTER INTERFACE AND PERFORMANCE

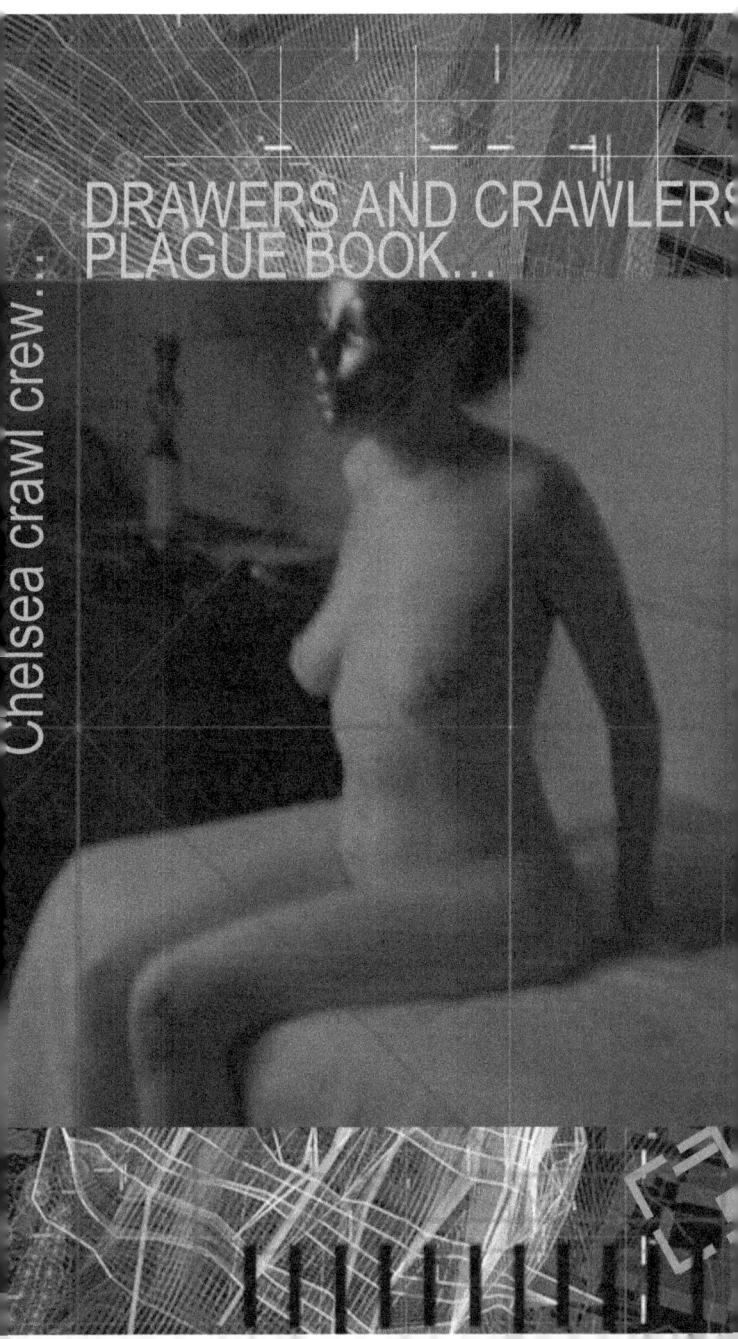

DRAWERS AND CRAWLERS
PLAGUE BOOK...

Chelsea crawl crew...

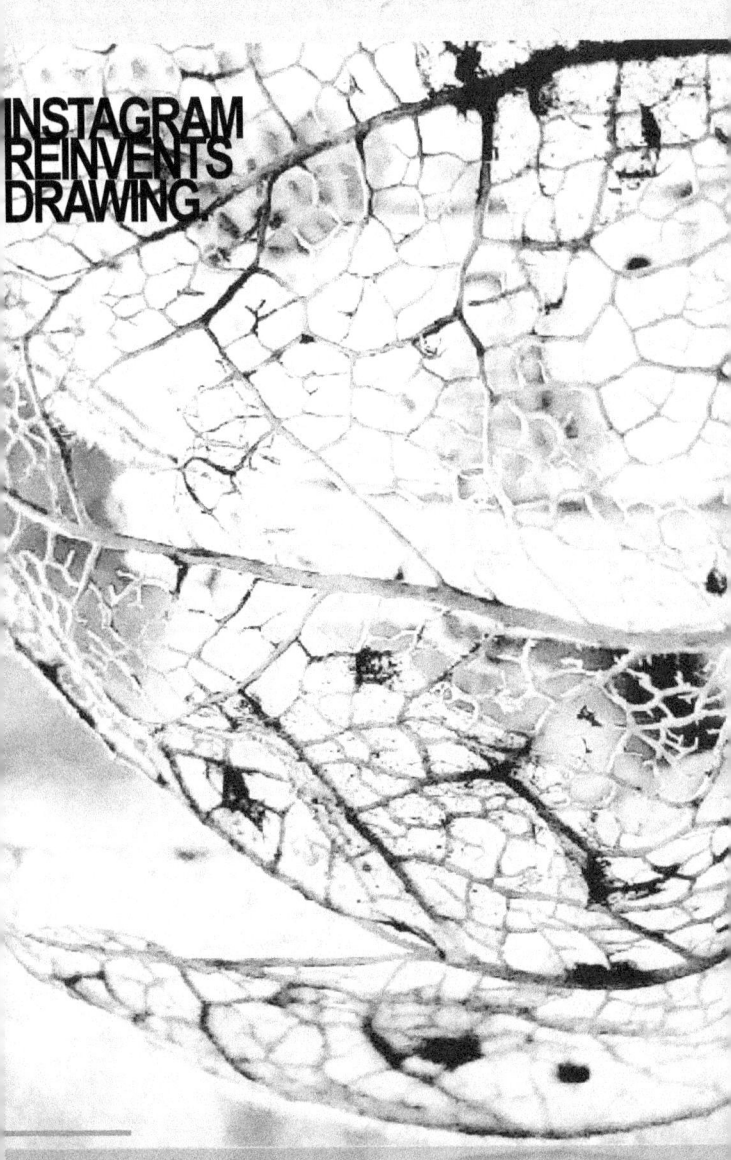

INSTAGRAM
REINVENTS
DRAWING.

AN COMPUTER INTERFACE AND PERFORMANCE

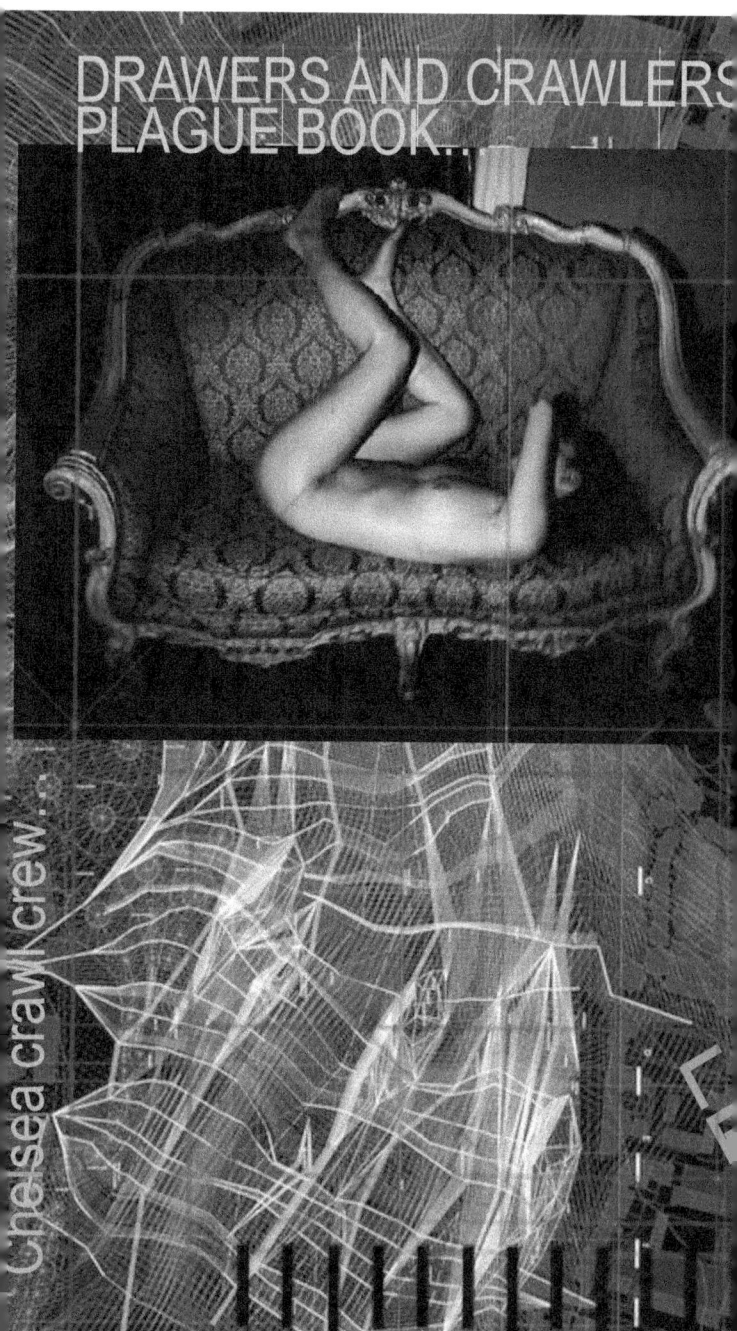

DRAWERS AND CRAWLERS
PLAGUE BOOK...

chelsea crawl crew...

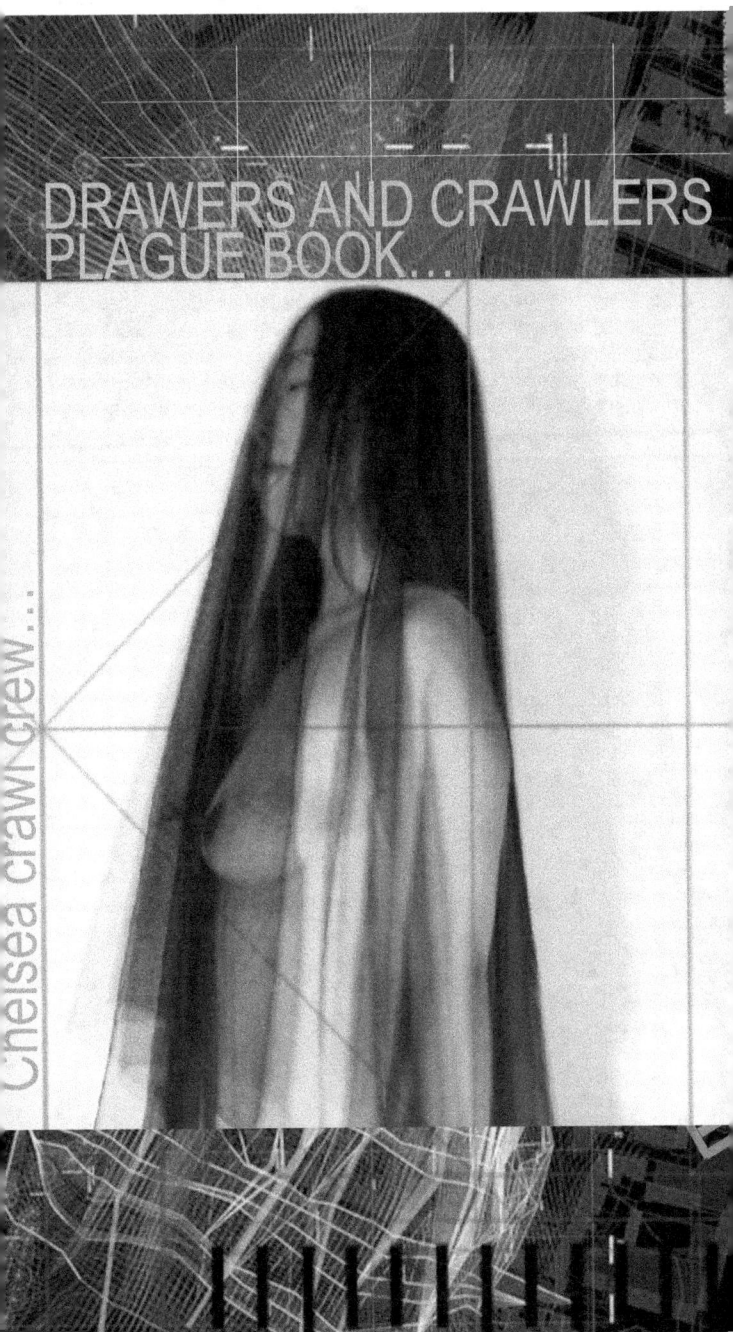

DRAWERS AND CRAWLERS
PLAGUE BOOK...

Chelsea crawl crew...

'The figure, Modernity, and Resulting Abstraction'

The hustle:

until the invention of the camera, we assumed that 'progression' in painting had much to do with verisimilitude, academic figures, and even the invention of the one-point perspective as a contrived 'immersion device'. This grew with 'bourgeois culture'....whatever that might be now.....With many variation including most African art works, ancient cave painting (with flourishes of academic finesse) Tantric 17thc Painting... (looking a lot like af Klint), and most of non-western art, there was little concern for blending abstraction with the academic figure....modernity as a global movement (of 'self liberatory' practices) in combination with the camera, and certainly now in the digital age, the modernist imperative ramped this up: to sweat over the 'academic figure' was to be 'a petite bourgeois stooge'. And what about 'abstract choices executed as academic tropes?'

For the drawers, and the crawlers, and the drinkers send in your ideas of this contrived syllogism of modernity: modernism means and results in abstraction. Please send in one or a few hooks on this jive.

Mine:

figurative.....Jean-Jacques Lequeu having a great show at the Morgan this spring.
Lebbeus Woods, modern architect of fantasy, fantastic draughsperson like Lequeu, my favs, Ledoux, and master Boullee

...hard transitions into modernity: Kollwitz, Malevich,

out the other side: Sarah Sze (on platonic caves), Mark Tansey, Geoff Chadsey,

rock and roll...send your images to draw....
see you 7 30 on zoom....byob. Add more people if you want...i liked that JN just phoned in and breathed hard on the mystery line. turned me on. loved the final drawing of 'the Hoff'.

Note_27, 13 May 2020
The death of the object the birth of the other.

Drawers and crawlers meet for the fifth week, or is it the 6th? by the time we get out of prison we should have a book. Get ready to photograph your work....and keep sending those nudes. So if you have essays, verse, short stories, and all of your drawings we can compile it and put it in a book. Just to remember the big house by. First baked potato on me.

'The death of the object': Starting with Bruegel's the 'death of Icarus' we move back to Hieronymus Bosch. Examining the many creatures as 'objects' in a Bosch canvas we get a real feeling for 16th century surrealism. During these troubled times moral action is judged as a place, and a vidid Disneyland, resulting in heaven or Hell. In each of these places objects attended. I have recently seen The Garden of Earthly Delights about a year ago in The Prado Museum in Spain. Amazing. It is an overwhelming canvas, and an overwhelming departure into imaginary objects that inhabit both Heaven and Hell. Where did this this popular and successful wacko find his inspiration?

Jumpcut up to Moholy-Nagy and the Bauhaus. In the design based objective of the Bauhaus (the first NIMBY liberals posing as Commies), the bourgeois individualistic painters experience a fine art creation, but the higher calling was design and the 'useful object'. Gropius, and his architecture and product design cohorts are talking about 'social utility' on the collective to raise the masses with good design of objects. Moholy-Nagy took this for a turn with his automatic photography and direct photo emulsion shots....objects leave and image shadow. objects he laid accross and emulsion. Again we see a modernist trend to make an object even more surreal by mechanically portraying it in its most direct form. Given these two strange directions into the creation of objects, from an individualistic painters such as Hieronymus Bosch, to a collectivist marxist such as Moholy-Nagy, we arrive at an implication of what the 'other' should be. In all cases of the other, who is your family, stranger, lover, you will individually amass over 1 million things in your lives. This is a strange psychology to which the things themselves take on a life and seduce you into a fetish.

Hope to see your Inspirations on this theme, prepare some of the sketches you would like to have included in the book, tell other friends to come along. It will be 2 minute quick sketches in the beginning to limber up. As always, potty talk is encouraged, but the coin jar exist to balance out that equation. as in life.
Aloha.

On Wed, May 6, 2020 at 6:00 PM Phillip Baldwin
<phillip.baldwin@gmail.com> wrote:

On Wed, May 6, 2020 at 6:00 PM Phillip Baldwin
<phillip.baldwin@gmail.com> wrote:

DRAWER'S AND CRAWLER'S

if you still up for it. Drawin', drinkin' discussin'....coin jar fully
operational...

thursday....7:30-9:30 zoom

try to get some watercolor or something into it.

The drift: BODY AS POWER, BODY AS EXPLOITED FORM.

From the Venus of Willendorf (conjectured as a totemic object
made by a woman in the 200,000 year matriarchy) to the greek
representation of the nude male form as high civilization, athletic
standard, and warlike threat to all, we see body portray riding a
thin line between power and powerlessness. My trajectory will go
from that groovy first Venus, through the greeks, Romans (who
put up statues to threaten their new colonies) , Pompeian erotic
frescos (painted by slave owners to slaves as a gift in their
rooms), Titian, Bernini, Munch, 30's german and Italian body on
the left and right. John Berger made that pop-Marxist statement:
'Men watch, women watch themselves being watched'....but what
if, in our surveillance culture of the precariate, we want to be
unwatched? I will go into anti-face detection surveillance, face
alteration, into the Nudie apps that undress everybody, I will
explore the power in the overexposed body of Bu-tho, Exotic
dance, and Singapore transexuals. I will end with the late Peter
Beard and his work onstage and offstage of the power of
physical beauty. And yes, I recycle this lectures for the kiddies
but I am done for the summer!

Hope to see ya. Come armed with your media of choice and
drink....Add more friends for the potty talk....and the drawin'.

Pb

DRAWERS AND CRAWLERS
SEND YOUR STUFF! ORIGINAL OR INSPIRED!

I think this has been 8 or 9 weeks....beautiful days. But as the crawl might
not open until 2027 will rock on with drawing.....

curation I suggest: THE ARCHITECTURAL BODY. As I was prepping' a lecture on this I came up with some interesting data on the relationship of Josephine Baker, and Le Corbusier! They were BFFs! They would travel down to Rio in Airships and he (of the ultra NIMBY 'hygienic modernity for the unwashed working class) and Adolf Loos (ornament as crime, fame) would try to box their sexy, poor St. Louis glam girl into boxes (she became one of the wealthiest black women   of the 30's) spy, and humanitarian.... She would escape with her 20 adopted kids to a castle with her rich gay, (Cor-bu was also gay) Jewish husband and even Hitler made a stab at them in Mein Kampf as 'decadent Negroid-ism' ....but Adorno (on the left) also hated jazz.

Be that as it may, do we make spaces or do spaces make us? Please send your lurid examples of the body in spaces to draw. Quick sketches in the beginning, potty talk encouraged as this is brought to you by the coin jar. Hope Bob Ross shows up again. Onward, spring is here. Zoom from outside! pB

Hey
pb,

Thanks for putting me in the loop. Although pretty talentless in the visual art dept. I've been trying to sketch in my journal freely + unapologetically, as regularly as possible, and I love it. Feel like Picasso. I look forward to whatever this turns out to be.....

Xo,

BODY/CITY

gang....smoke em if you got em. I think this is week 9! the weather is getting so nice. Tomorrow   drawers   and   crawlers   meet at 7:30-9:30 ...Liz sent to me and said she had walked the high line with a plein air watercolor and the city looks groovy from all angles up there. I included these and her idea of Yugoslav brutalism....great show at the MOMA on this a couple of years ago.... ....i got this non-pedantic jive on BODY/CITY: inserting the human body into spaces, crime and forensic shots of 1909, Greek statuary, mob hits, city mood views in watercolor, Penn, Man Ray, and a whole lot more. If you could bring a cheapo watercolor set with your beverage and your potty talk, that would be excellent. See ya tomorrow. Gonna slap that book together soon, so pick out your favs from the past 9 weeks! pb.

The body, the room, and its Prosthetics.

The great science fiction writer JG Ballard stated that the 'invention of the 20th century was automobile. The invention of the 21st Century will be the room.' This led me to consider, during this lock down under covid-19, under the curfew, after the explosive events Minneapolis, that the room has got to become more. The room now is almost like an Infinity space, or should. And that other prosthetic devices should or would or could be attached to the body, the senses, to achieve some sort of Transportation, and even release.

In drawers and crawlers, we should approach our 10 week, do you believe it!, as the notion of the agoraphobic body is put under strain by the hors d'oeuvres of covid-19, and the main course of revolution. It's dangerous out there. We knew it was going to bust open.

Just as the black movement catalyzed and transfigured the anti-Vietnam protests, and second wave feminist protests in the late 60s and early 70s, certainly the Death of George Floyd in Minneapolis added the spark to the combustive mix of 500 years of race problems, fifty years of post-industrialism, and three months of covid lock down.... we are all a gigantic agoraphobic nation of 'precariate's. Will our rooms follow us? Are the rooms really safe? Is this the end of travel and public space as we know it?

Liz added some incredible inspirations from the scenographic world, and I'm following up on this notion of the 'room as Prosthetics' and other things to attach to your imploded narratives. Hope to see your work and your Inspirations also. send em! See you for drinks under curfew now! 730 9:30, come on in and be prepared for a lot of potty talk.

sorry dawgs! i must have felt that the screen shot of liz making out with her dog was one of the most porno things we have done. the coin jar floweth over.....Mr. Marylin Chambers agrees....

see ya next week. weather is fine! pb

if you are still cooped up and missin' the crawl, we start at 730 and go to 9 30. nock on the door hard. 917 385 2446.

same Bat time: THE AMERICAN BODY AND THE TERROR OF SOLIPSISM....
what makes the american body so special? so in denial to the forces around it....? we will have a line up. please send some. SS sent us some shots hot off the press last time and they were wunderbar.

we have gone weeks with the body and, when Phillippe comes in later from LA, if we are caught dead drawing a bridge or a building we quickly switch to a nude and ramp up the potty talk so we can get a finger wagging.   dont let him down!   ...ten weeks strong.   choose your medium and elixir well....mine is oxytocin...the cuddle drug.

see ya then, if you are in the park or doing the lone crawl, we understand. i will be in my back yard with bbq. if you have a proposal for the Bioscleave house in East Hampton, let me know. ....pb.

almost a semester class....!   send your photos!   THE DOCILE BODY, LIBIDINAL ECONOMIES.

all that great medical stuff from Eatkins, body charts, the invisible bodies. ming told me there might be an opening tomorrow night in lower east side. but if you are at home, tuuuuune in. the coin jar is waiting....i've got 200 pages in the book....send if you want more stuff in.

onward
pb

IF YOU WANNA meet and sketch tonight 7 30 - 9 let me know.   i will check in with zoom.   if you wanna big up for the next free stay session and swim in east hampton lemme know.   we had a great weekend this past one.   its all about the body....site of reversible destiny....all that with Gins Arakawa...but they both died....

PENCIL NUDE/PENCIL CITY. TONIGHT...if you wanna.

PLEASE SEND EXAMPLES!

BOOK IS COOKIN'.

found a very adept pencil nude guy on instagram....sending....i also made a round of Fellow Rome Prize ladies and gentlemen who did their travel sketches of cities.   Zaha hadid, Louis Kahn, Koohass, Corbu, graves, phillip guston, and a lot, lot more!

at 9 sharp i am going to a zoom Tantra meetup club meeting....yall invited ....it should be a hoot.   its fully clothed, clean (too), and hygenic....it covers a further platonic and carnal depth with your significant, or self! remember, Autoerotica doesnt happen in cars...

get out there and drink in the streets...pb

The face in ecstasy, the mysteries c the micro-gesture, and the rise of th psychotic.

DRAWERS AND CRAWLERS WEEK 14

Theme: The face in ecstasy, the mysteries of the micro-gesture, and the rise of the psychotic.

Evolutionary biologist Robin Trivers has said 'Deception AND self-deception are both evolutionary strategies. ' We think lairs, psychotics, and hustlers don't believe their own bull shit....but many of them do and are successful by this1....they get to pass their genes along into infinity!...like the psychotic Jeff Koons with Cicolinna. Trump? Warhol? And even Picasso...big egos...but Warhol was characterized by Lou Reed as a vampire. We think of people on the specturm as having little integration into our world of networks of deceptions..... In some primate societies and early humans the psychotic was dispatched post haste. Killed by all of the beta males as a fake alpha......How can we read/draw a face, see the micro-gestures (especially on zoom and in the body) and do you really need to be a self-deluding psychotic to 'win'?

We will first examine the face that doesn't lie (or does it?) the face of the big O. Sufi trance, club kids, and people who broadcast 'I am immersed in it'. But even a method actor can fake tears....so we will 'fake it till we make it'. ...through the difficult terrain of micro-gestures and the lack of mirror neurons, to the cynical aspects of the art world that seems to favor the self deluding psychotics....just like politics. While the rest of the tribe sweats it out under covid with these little postage stamps...looking for faces as safe harbors....what is left of the body expression?

Smoke em if you got em....hope to see ya all there with some charcoal,....Tina just got some, and this is a designated safe space for potty talk....it is our sponsor.

Liz and I are wrapping up a 300 page lulu book on this lock down and draw....hope you can hit the charrette when the wheelbarrow comes around.

pb

17

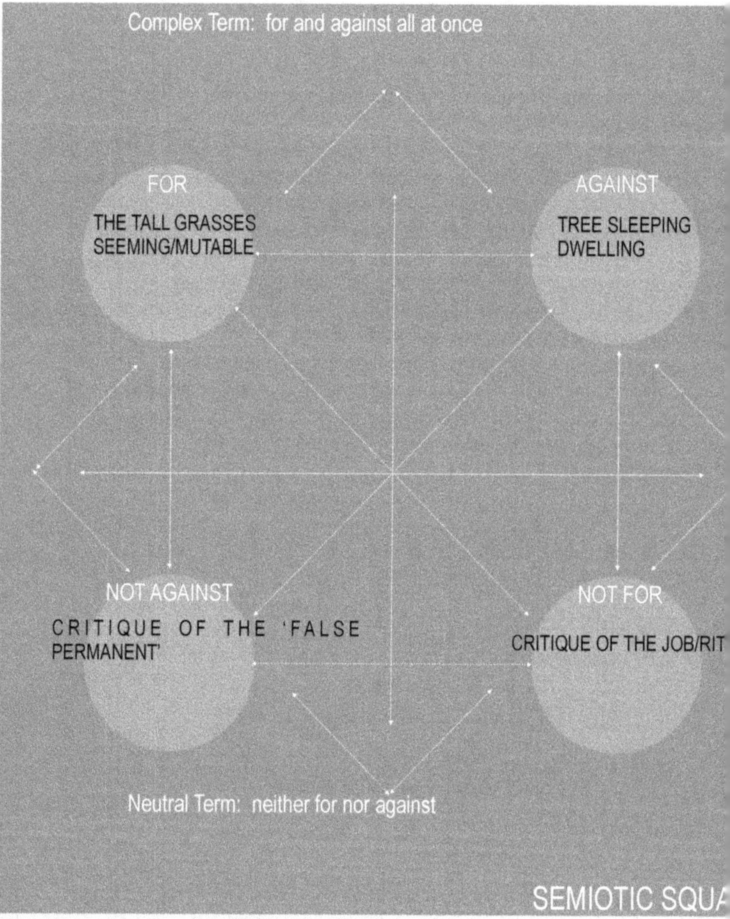

Complex Term: for and against all at once

FOR
THE TALL GRASSES
SEEMING/MUTABLE

AGAINST
TREE SLEEPING
DWELLING

NOT AGAINST
CRITIQUE OF THE 'FALSE PERMANENT'

NOT FOR
CRITIQUE OF THE JOB/RIT

Neutral Term: neither for nor against

SEMIOTIC SQUA

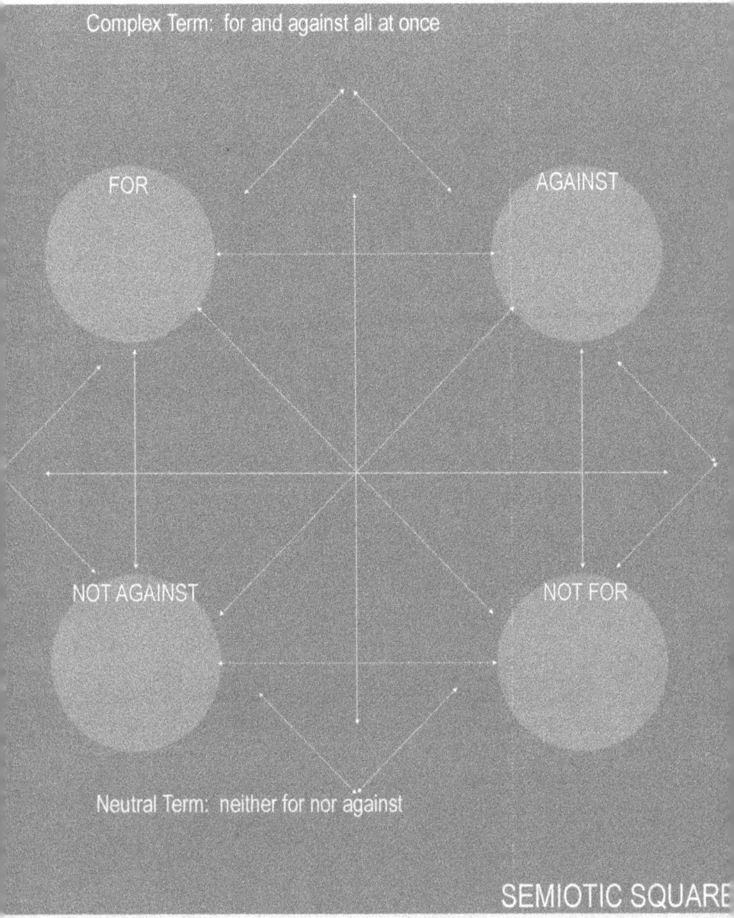

Complex Term: for and against all at once

FOR

AGAINST

NOT AGAINST

NOT FOR

Neutral Term: neither for nor against

SEMIOTIC SQUARE

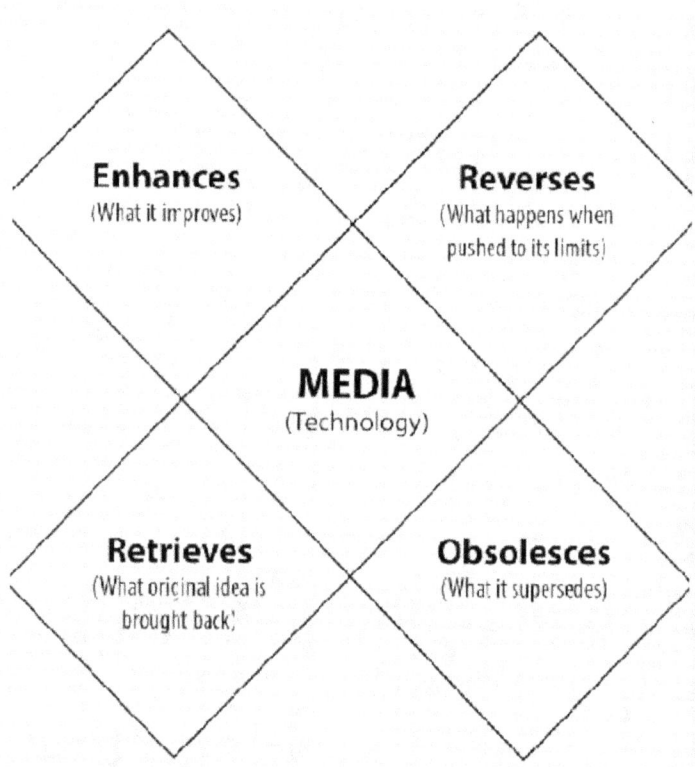

GRAB AN OAR, END OF
PETTY-BOURGEOIS
INDIVIDUALITY.

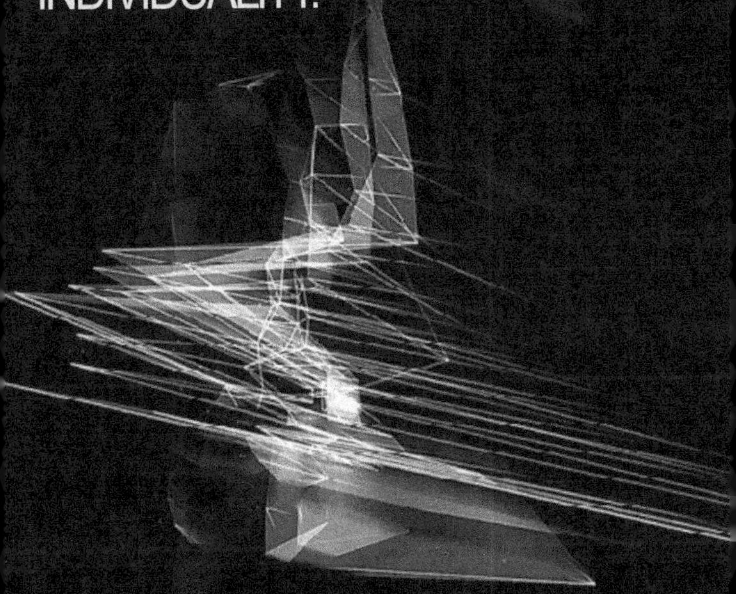

PROJECTS IN HCI

vers and crawlers

Joan Marie Kelly
Senior Lecturer, Nanyang Technological University Art Design and Media,
81 Nanyang Drive, Singapore 637458
Email: jmkelly@ntu.edu.sg
tel: (65) 81260134, WhatsApp
https://joanmariekelly.net

YouTube: Joan Marie Kelly

https://www.youtube.com/channel/UCMfltPHq7kMYKD1B3nr5j_w?
view_as=subscriber

Words: 1204
All drawings by Joan Marie Kelly

Title: 3rd Month of Lockdown: Remembering Run-ins with the Police in the USA

I am a foreigner teaching at a university in Singapore. I have lived in Singapore for 14 years but still feel like a foreigner. It's a very formal society that does not allow itself to get close to outsiders. Although I truly love my job I count on getting out of the tiny, very hot nation state as soon as I turn in my grades. All Singaporeans including myself depend upon the exuberance and vitality of the world and the rest of Southeast Asia to stimulate us, and keep our creativity nurtured. Summer of 2020 brought an amazing line-up of invitations to artistic events all of which were canceled. I didn't spend too much time mourning the death of my

summer plans because I quickly became preoccupied with the news and covid deaths in China and Italy. At least I was safe, had food and an income. I began to fear what will happen to people living in very confined spaces with large numbers of people, who are vulnerable to the spread. My first thought was for the community of male migrant workers I work with in collaboration with my painting class. The men live sixteen to a room. I saw no movement or changes being made in the dormitory as I checked in on WhatsApp with various workers. I knew the Singapore government is not overlooking them but at the same time they are not taking action to prepare the men for the pandemic. I didn't feel sorry for my situation but simultaneously felt overwhelmed and tired. I had to drag myself around each day. I couldn't seem to accomplish anything.

The preoccupation of daily updates on Covid19 paralyzed me. I couldn't concentrate. On the rare occasions I face some kind of shock or sudden change my response is to simplify and don't make any decisions. I looked in front of myself and tried to figure out how I felt. Distressing news, came of my 85 year old father in the USA who is very ill, took a turn for the worse which brought my family to question if he would live much longer.

In the past as a way to navigate trauma, I felt better if I came up with a plan. Not knowing what news I would find happened in the night while I tried desperately to sleep I couldn't make plans. Confined

rawlers and crawlers

to my flat, going out only to purchase groceries, I began to reflect. I thought back on the sex workers I worked with for years in Kolkata who from year to year have no opportunities. The only notable events to mitigate their situations were new difficulties that came before them. Each day was the same. I tried to imagine how they feel. What it would mean to live a day to day reality where the future is not part of daily considerations? I spent so much of my life thinking about plans for the future. Those plans got me through each day, looking forward to events or something I was excited to achieve. Plans were the topic of conversations. My fantastic plans brought attention to me, by colleagues, peers and family. I could say I thrive on making plans.

Life would feel empty without opportunities for development and change.

But when I think back on the time in Kolkata, in the brothel hanging out in the rooms of sex workers, we had many serious talks. They discussed very clearly and frankly their situations and concerns. But we also spent a lot of time laughing. They were smiling most of the time.

How did they do it? It's like asking Billy Holiday how she kept singing beautiful music that show compassion while facing day to day oppression?

Pouring down torrential rains with cracking thunder made me feel better. I was able to sleep while it rained. The repetitious sound comforted me. Nothing else comforted me. Weather reports became interesting, I wanted to check what hour the rain would begin. 3am was my favorite time. It assured that I would sleep into the morning. The rain fell and I slept.

The dark mindset will never pass if I sit all day and toss and turn all night. I have to put down the news and read something else at night. I knew I had to start to move my body again. Each night I forced myself to run only a mile. There was still a remnant of the sunset left which made a back light to silhouetted clouds. The run did make me feel a little better.

Still the virus news preoccupied me. The inequities in societies all over the world were laid bare. A daily article in the international press about the poor conditions the wealthy nation of Singapore keep migrant workers, had Singaporeans debating heavily on social media. The virus was now inside the dormitories. I wrote friends inside the dormitories to hear of their conditions. Some were being moved. The occupancy in the rooms was seven and eight men instead of sixteen. They were told to stay in the rooms all day. Their food would be delivered. They slept and played games and stayed still. None of the men I spoke with complained. They spoke of worries they have for their families not of themselves. How did they do it? Each said the delivered food was good. "I gud ma'am."

In the USA a young black man was jogging. White guys followed him in a truck and shot him? Last week they were surrounding the Michigan state capitol, now they're hunting Black people down? Wait, Ahmaud Arbery was killed two months ago and they are just arresting the men now? I watched the videos. I watched Ahmaud in the abandoned house looking around. I do

that too. I've done that many times when I come across an abandoned house. No one ever tried to shoot me.

Disgust? Is that my biggest feeling? ...a mix of anger and disgust. Then all over social media was a video of a white woman getting hysterical over a black man who was watching birds asked her to leash her dog. She threatens him with the fact that she will call the police on him. I know that part of Central Park. It's called The Ramble. It's a rare part of the park that has no road access. Police can only access that area on

scooters. I know because I had an incident with a policeman in the Brambles. It wasn't dangerous, it's humorous. It's one of my favorite "police stories" that makes everyone laugh. I might even tell this at a party. You see, that's what I have, funny police stories from my past. Where I made a mistake or the police did and all is forgiven and the misunderstandings were laughed at. During none of these incidents did I have a passing thought of the possibility of my violent death. Witnessing the news in the USA from Singapore being so preoccupied with the catastrophic details I had not thought in comparison the details my own interactions with the police over the years and the way they function in my life as funny stories to tell at parties until now.

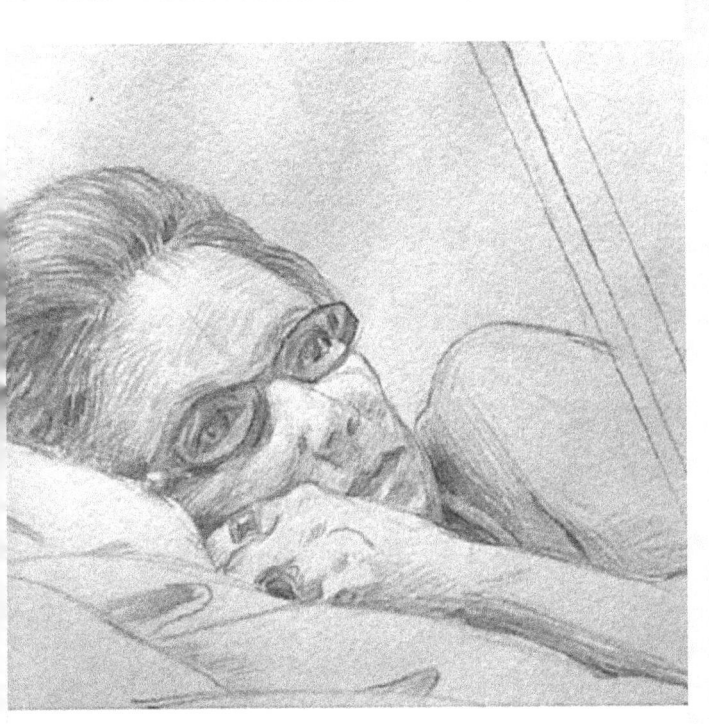

ers and crawlers

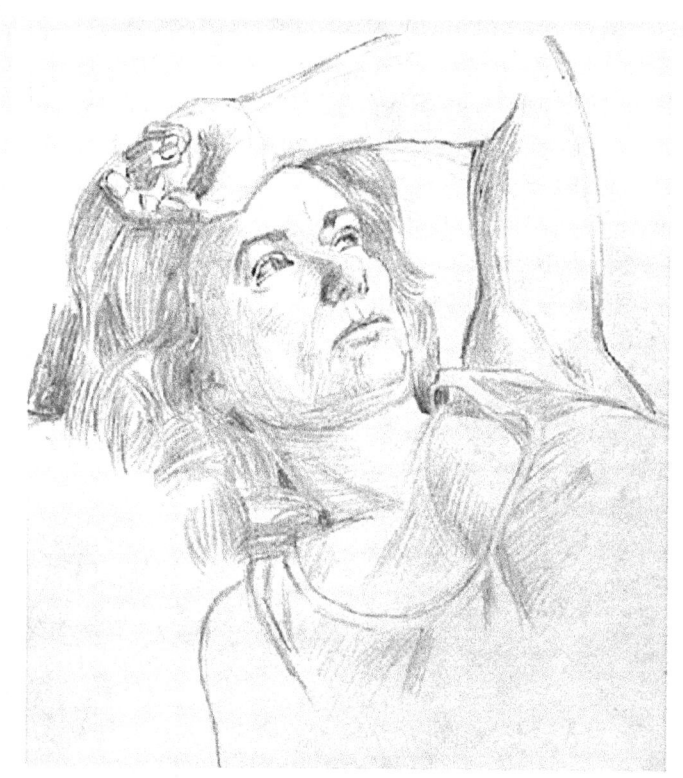

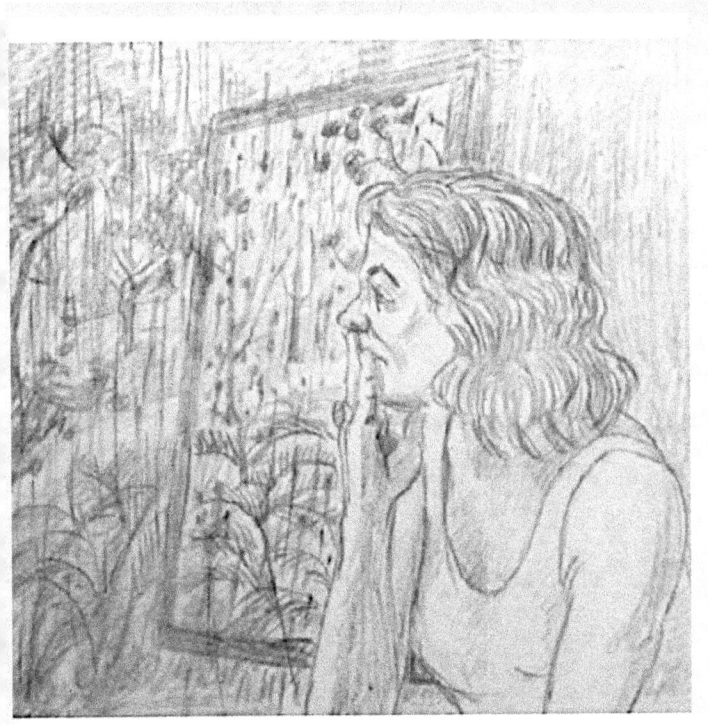

...ers and crawlers

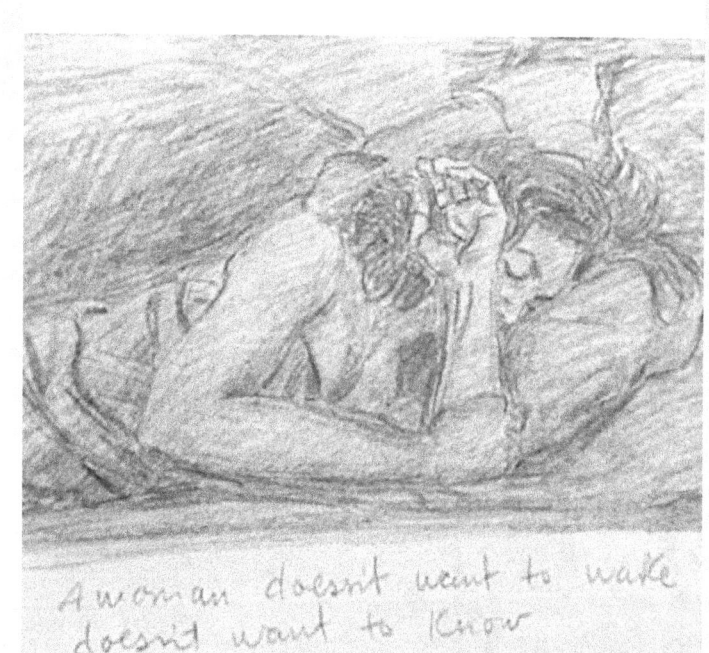

A woman doesn't want to wake
doesn't want to Know

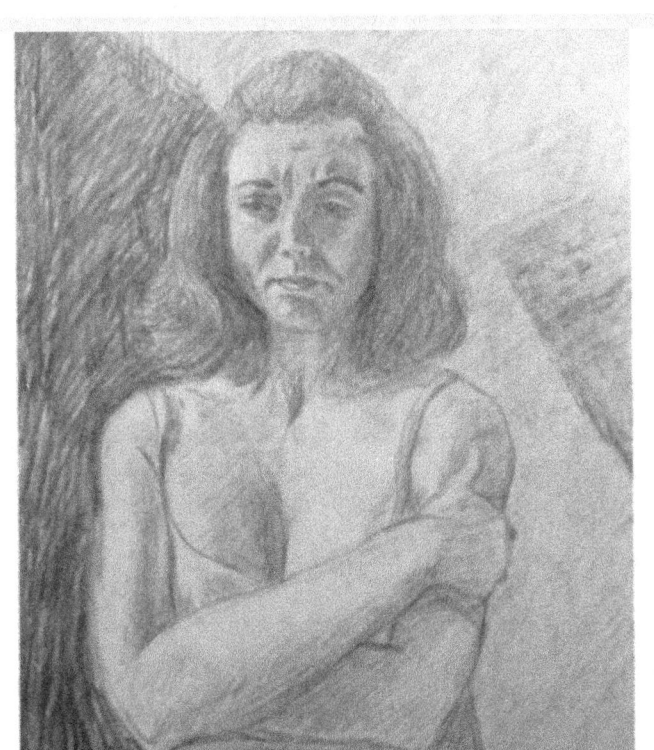

Complex term: THE SAVANNA, THE INTERNET

ASSERTION/FOR

The assertion:
In the quadrant of a certain danger, it is an infinite savanna. In it you can hid from your tribe and make love to the fertile alpha female. Your rite of passage is bringing her here and making her fertile without being eaten.....this is the place of people who watch and don't dwell. The modern male has his leisure colonized by 'entertainment' and 'facts'. For what? We have the dystopic ideas such as 'ready player one', those who looking for a safe place to learn, or being on the high grass Savanna in Africa finding the place to hide for the night. Feeding, breeding, protecting the young.... It is a place of other worlds. Is the place of the predator but less at daytime. It is Context that makes the story, and you can't dwell in drama. Drama is that narrative.
rama could be real at any moment.

NEGATION/AGAINST

The negation:
This is the reprieve, this could be deep erotica or Surface erotica, you don't have the time to determine either. It is a place of axis Mundi at night in the tree with your love and her other male lovers: possibly your seed with find the mark.... all are vying to get her fertilized for survival. There it's a type of axis Mundi in the trees. Only poisonous snakes and leopards would attack you at night. They have the night. So the night must be a type of axis Mundi. It is a safe place for now with your female. You hold, she might have your baby, or it is some other male's, you might dwell in the illusion of the secure.... watched for now. You are the unwatched.....The leopards and the others do not watch you. In the day earlier he would find time with her in the grasses to hide and make love. ....she might want to linger to see if you attend to her release and pleasure for the longest time....time before the tribe and its alphas notice, and the leopards notice..... And time to hide and make love hoping it is your seed that makes it in and through her.

NOT AGAINST/PARTS

The assertion:
I

NOT ASSERTION/EXCLUDE

WILL

TIME

SEMIOTIC SQUA

Neutral term: THE BASEMENT SHAPE-SHIFTER

SEMIOTIC SQUARE/GENERATING TERMS

Complex term: THE SAVANNA, THE INTERNET

ASSERTION/FOR
NOT AGAINST/PARTS

he non negation: This is a critique of the real,
ritique of the pleasant but dangerous night in
he tree with some temporary sense of
welling... a critique of that axis Mundi. This is
hat place in the suburbs, American suburbs,
where the parents have split their house into
ou live in the basement. They can barely
olerate each and their 'contract' is just left as a
red mortgage....they might say it is for
ou....you know better. others are living there
or the mortgage, although they say they're
ving there for you and your safety, and your
iblings, or the neighbors....this has been
ears. The sexual union is gone and you
ensed this as a young child....you father was
ery upset....you mother made a project of
ou..... This is the space of the discordant
Welling. This is the space are the young man,
nable to hunt during the day and avoid
anger at night becomes mutable, like a cell
hone case. A young man might play their
ames forever, change from boy to girl, I do
almost anything to help mutate to survive and
understand..... Mutates in that failed institution
n that discordant house.
he neutral term is the gender shape shifting.

NEGATION/AGAINST
NOT ASSERTION/EXCLUDE

Non assertion: This is a critique on the
sceneographic, critique of the context 'i'll be
online!' always... life is a place where you
found yourself in the Deep Savannan grasses,
it is the Oasis maze in the Maze of the grasses
which any danger can and destroy you. Or
destroy you slowly like the shadow of the
grasses....the internet. Endless rabbit
holes.....It is also a change of the surface of
the day, and the reality of camouflage. And not
the camouflage within Society of changing
from boy to girl (that is you) the Freudian
archetypes are gone. Both genders don't care
in that they fight against the grasses and what
is real there..... It is a space of binging Netflix,
as if this is a savanna, the Protector and the
Destroyer. This is the space of ADD or OCD.
This is the space of the confused boys who no
longer have the rite of passage to Danger, and
they become nerds in the Infinite Space of the
Savannah. They assumed the food will keep
coming and one day it will not. And they must
turn their 'play' and to the seriousness the
pyramid scheme: Making others play their
game. Imperative. But what cache? The
young male has a crisis....the young female
has her beauty. There's no ideal rite of
passage anymore. The Female is still Superior
in that she's still the only one who can give
birth. Who can further your tribe.

L

TIME

SEMIOTIC SQUARE

Neutral term: THE BASEMENT SHAPE-SHIFTER

IOTIC SQUARE/GENERATING TERMS

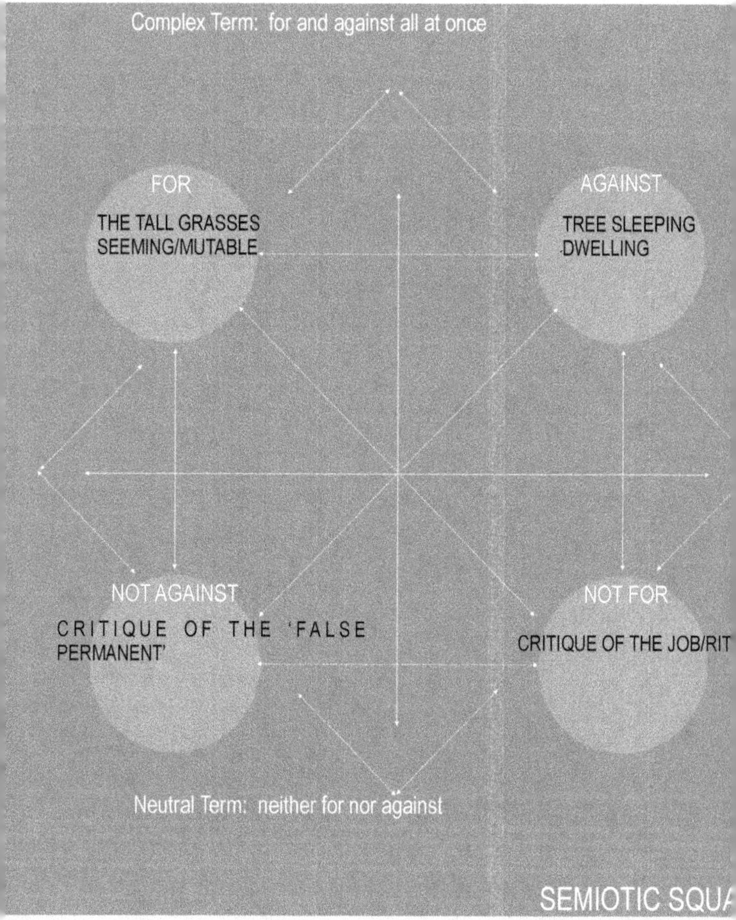

Complex Term: for and against all at once

FOR
THE TALL GRASSES
SEEMING/MUTABLE

AGAINST
TREE SLEEPING
DWELLING

NOT AGAINST
CRITIQUE OF THE 'FALSE
PERMANENT'

NOT FOR
CRITIQUE OF THE JOB/RIT

Neutral Term: neither for nor against

SEMIOTIC SQUA

SEMIOTIC SQUARE/GENERATING TERMS

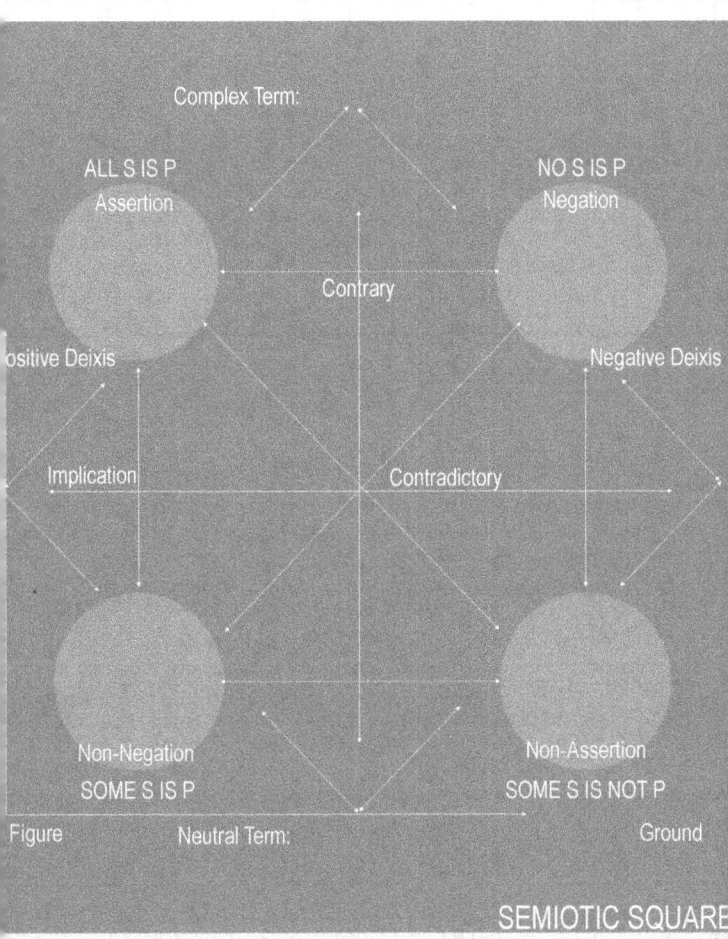

Complex Term:

ALL S IS P
Assertion

NO S IS P
Negation

Contrary

Positive Deixis

Negative Deixis

Implication

Contradictory

Non-Negation
SOME S IS P

Non-Assertion
SOME S IS NOT P

Figure

Neutral Term:

Ground

SEMIOTIC SQUARE

The assertion:

In the quadrant of a certain danger, it is an infinite savanna. In it you can hid from your tribe and make love to the fertile alpha female. Your rite of passage is bringing her here and making her fertile without being eaten.....this is the place of people who watch and don't dwell. The modern male has his leisure colonized by 'entertainment' and 'facts'. For what? We have the dystopic ideas such as 'ready player one', those who looking for a safe place to learn, or being on the high grass Savanna in Africa finding the place to hide for the night. Feeding, breeding, protecting the young.... It is a place of other worlds. Is the place of the predator but less at daytime. It is Context that makes the story, and you can't dwell in drama. Drama is that narrative.
rama could be real at any moment.

The negation:

This is the reprieve, this could be deep erotica or Surface erotica, you don't have the time to determine either. It is a place of axis Mundi at night in the tree with your love and her other male lovers: possibly your seed with find the mark.... all are vying to get her fertilized for survival. There it's a type of axis Mundi in the trees. Only poisonous snakes and leopards would attack you at night. They have the night. So the night must be a type of axis Mundi. It is a safe place for now with your female. You hold, she might have your baby, or it is some other male's, you might dwell in the illusion of the secure.... watched for now. You are the unwatched.....The leopards and the others do not watch you. In the day earlier he would find time with her in the grasses to hide and make love. ....she might want to linger to see if you attend to her release and pleasure for the longest time....time before the tribe and its alphas notice, and the leopards notice..... And time to hide and make love hoping it is your seed that makes it in and through her.

The complex: It is the Savannah.

The non negation:
This is a critique of the real, critique of the pleasant but dangerous night in the tree with some temporary sense of dwelling... a critique of that axis Mundi. This is that place in the suburbs, American suburbs, where the parents have split their house into you live in the basement. They can barely tolerate each and their 'contract' is just left as a tired mortgage....they might say it is for you....you know better. others are living there for the mortgage, although they say they're living there for you and your safety, and your siblings, or the neighbors....this has been years. The sexual union is gone and you sensed this as a young child....you father was very upset....you mother made a project of you..... This is the space of the discordant dWelling. This is the space are the young man, unable to hunt during the day and avoid danger at night becomes mutable, like a cell phone case. A young man might play their games forever, change from boy to girl, I do almost anything to help mutate to survive and understand..... Mutates in that failed institution in that discordant house.
he neutral term is the gender shape shifting.

Non assertion:
This is a critique on the sceneographic, critique of the context 'i'll be online!' always... life is a place where you found yourself in the Deep Savannah grasses, it is the Oasis maze in the Maze of the grasses which any danger can and destroy you. Or destroy you slowly like the shadow of the grasses....the internet. Endless rabbit holes.....It is also a change of the surface of the day, and the reality of camouflage. And not the camouflage within Society of changing from boy to girl (that is you) the Freudian archetypes are gone. Both genders don't care in that they fight against the grasses and what is real there..... It is a space of binging Netflix, as if this is a savanna, the Protector and the Destroyer. This is the space of ADD or OCD. This is the space of the confused boys who no longer have the rite of passage to Danger, and they become nerds in the Infinite Space of the Savannah. They assumed the food will keep coming and one day it will not. And they must turn their 'play' and to the seriousness the pyramid scheme: Making others play their game. Imperative. But what cache? The young male has a crisis....the young female has her beauty. There's no ideal rite of passage anymore. The Female is still Superior in that she's still the only one who can give birth. Who can further your tribe.

Complex Term: for and against all at once

Assertion: An action or Retreat Into The Enclave life. What the beatniks did for the urban setting, the hippies in their communes in new England and northern California, was also turned into middle class pastiche..... It is an attempt at the countercultural. ...devised networks amongst like minded people before the internet. Then came the internet. Some of this stopped short of sexual equality, and polyamory. Within them, One still the possessed woman, as an important as an outgrowth of Eisenhower era imprinting. Oedipal imprinting.

The valorization of production. This is an outgrowth of Schiller's take on Spiel or 'play'. Itself an outgrowth of Kant's division of faculties. Ruskin and Morris took this further into aesthetic non aliened. Labor based on design and not individualistic 'canvas art'.

FOR

Negation: The capitalist drive to hot glue together a bunch of Mcmansions as investment properties. The training, narrative is to 'live inside your investment'. The result is precarious relationship to employment, an alienation with labor not the least of which is is zero-sum hostility toward co-workers. It is an area of, commodity fetish not solidarity. I defers to the infantile, leisure is colonized by Hollywood, furthering infantile violence reflected back to the co-workers. It is a valorization of consumption. It is the training to live in your 'investment property' with the notion that someone richer in the future (if employment lasts) through the system would purchase it at a profit have driven 80s 90s and early aughts Up until 2008. it ignores the precarity of employment and UBI.

AGAINST

NOT AGAINST

Non negation: Aesthetic non-alienated labor. Non alienated labor. This is Ruskin and Morris. This is Marcuse aesthetics inspired by the art happenings of the 60s. This is the critique of the situationist in debord. Urban communes, anarchists, squaters, punks, New England slackers.

Non-assertion: This is The 'Curse Of The Lost Garden.' This is Weber's 'protestant ethic and spirit of capitalism' after Locke. Protestant abstract work ethic ignoring alienation...work in itself. This is the 'sweat of the brow', and compulsive Lockean liberalism guiding America in particular. The anti-royal, Lockean impulse is to despise those inclined to natural leisure, free sexual pleasure, spiel, and minorities from non-protestant cultures....so it abhors sloth and slackers. It is marxist son-in-law speaking of the 'virtues of idleness' against Leninist left and Gramsci's love of Ford and Taylor. It is embracing of both the conservative work ethic and the radical notion of non-alienated tools, products, and productivity. Non alienation from 'species-being' help dismissing compulsive work. hunter-gatherers.

NOT FOR

Neutral Term: neither for nor against

SEMIOTIC SQUARE

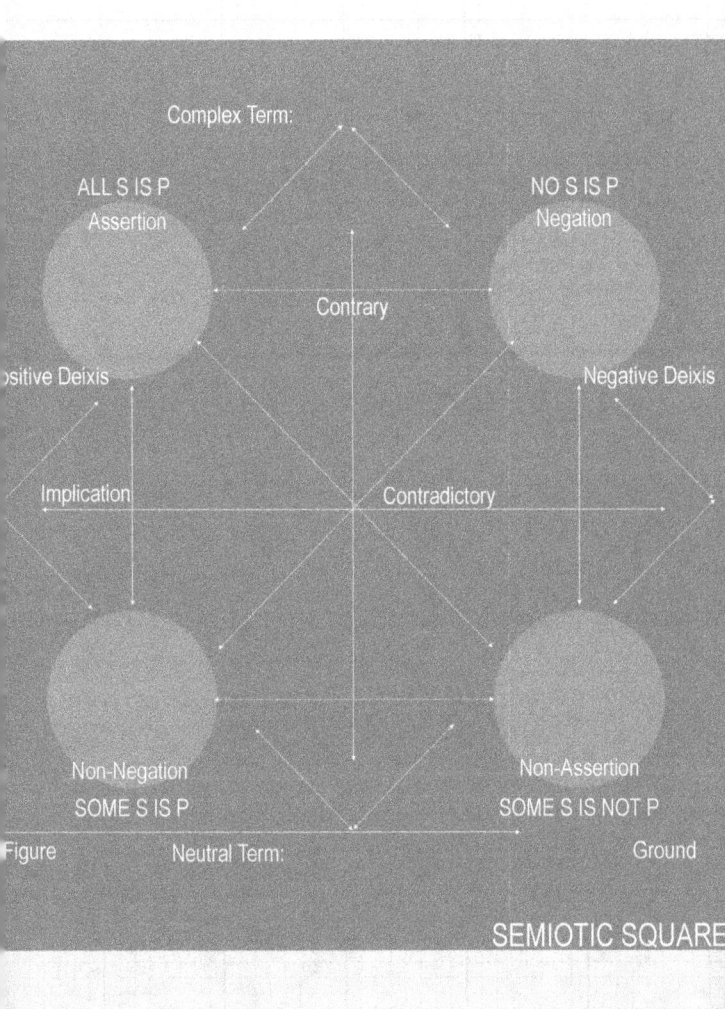

SEMIOTIC SQUARE

Complex term: Internet 'doppelganger'

ASSERTION/FOR

Assertion: An action or Retreat Into The Enclave life. What the beatniks did for the urban setting, the hippies in their communes in new England and northern California, was also turned into middle class pastiche..... It is an attempt at the countercultural. ...devised networks amongst like minded people before the internet. Then came the internet. Some of this stopped short of sexual equality, and polyamory. Within them, One still have the possessed woman, as an important as an outgrowth of Eisenhower era imprinting. Oedipal imprinting.

The valorization of production. This is an outgrowth of Schiller's take on Spiel or 'play'. Itself an outgrowth of Kant's division of faculties. Ruskin and Morris took this further into aesthetic non aliened. Labor based on design and not individualistic 'canvas art'.

NEGATION/AGAINST

Negation: The capitalist drive to hot glue together a bunch of Mcmansions as investment properties. The training, narrative is to 'live inside your investment'. The result is precarious relationship to employment, an alienation with labor not the least of which is is zero-sum hostility toward co-workers. It is an area of, commodity fetish not solidarity. It defers to the infantile, leisure is colonized by Hollywood, furthering infantile violence reflected back to the co-workers. It is a valorization of consumption. It is the training to live in your 'investment property' with the notion that someone richer in the future (if employment lasts) through the system would purchase it at a profit have driven 80s 90s and early aughts Up until 2008. it ignores the precarity of employment and UBI.

NOT AGAINST/PARTS

Non negation: Aesthetic non-alienated labor. Non alienated labor. This is Ruskin and Morris. This is Marcuse aesthetics inspired by the art happenings of the 60s. This is the critique of the situationist in debord. Urban communes, anarchists, squaters, punks, New England slackers.

NOT ASSERTION/EXCLUDE

Non-assertion. This is The 'Curse Of The Lost Garden.' This is Weber's 'protestant ethic and spirit of capitalism' after Locke. Protestant abstract work ethic ignoring alienation...work in itself. This is the 'sweat of the brow', compulsive Lockean liberalism guiding America in particular. The anti-royal, Lockean impulse is to despise those inclined to natural leisure, free sexual pleasure, spiel, and minorities from non-protestant cultures....so it abhors sloth and slackers. It is marxist son-in-law speaking of the 'virtues of idleness' against Leninist left and Gramsci's love of Ford and Taylor. It is embracing of both the conservative work ethic and the radical notion of non-alienated tools, products, and productivity. Non alienation from 'species-being' help dismissing compulsive work.
hunter-gatherers. SEMIOTIC SQUA

WILL

TIME

SEMIOTIC SQUA

Neutral term: 'slacker coder', 'cottage industry'

SEMIOTIC SQUARE/GENERATING TERMS

WORK, ALIENATION, AESTHETIC, AND CONSUMPTION.
Note_26, 13 May 2020

Terms.
Assertion: An action or Retreat Into The Enclave life. What the beatniks did for the urban setting, the hippies in their communes in new England and northern California, was also turned into middle class pastiche..... It is an attempt at the countercultural. ...devised networks amongst like minded people before the internet. Then came the internet. Some of this stopped short of sexual equality, and polyamory. Within them, One still the possessed woman, as an important as an outgrowth of Eisenhower era imprinting. Oedipal imprinting.

The valorization of production. This is an outgrowth of Schiller's take on Spiel or 'play'. Itself an outgrowth of Kant's division of faculties. Ruskin and Morris took this further into aesthetic non aliened. Labor based on design and not individualistic 'canvas art'.

Negation: The capitalist drive to hot glue together a bunch of Mcmansions as investment properties. The training, narrative is to 'live inside your investment'. The result is precarious relationship to employment, an alienation with labor not the least of which is is zero-sum hostility toward co-workers. It is an area of, commodity fetish not solidarity. It defers to the infantile, leisure is colonized by Hollywood, furthering infantile violence reflected back to the co-workers. It is a valorization of consumption. It is the training to live in your 'investment property' with the notion that someone richer in the future (if employment lasts) through the system would purchase it at a profit have driven 80s 90s and early aughts Up until 2008. it ignores the precarity of employment and UBI.

Non negation: Aesthetic non-alienated labor. Non alienated labor. This is Ruskin and Morris. This is Marcuse aesthetics inspired by the art happenings of the 60s. This is the critique of the situationist in debord. Urban communes, anarchists, squaters, punks, New England slackers.

Non-assertion: This is The 'Curse Of The Lost Garden.' This is Weber's 'protestant ethic and spirit of capitalism' after Locke. Protestant abstract work ethic ignoring alienation...work in itself. This is the 'sweat of the brow', and compulsive Lockean liberalism guiding America in particular. The anti-royal, Lockean impulse is to despise those inclined to natural leisure, free sexual pleasure, spiel, and minorities from non-protestant cultures....so it abhors sloth and slackers.

ers and crawlers

It is marxist son-in-law speaking of the 'virtues of idleness' against Leninist left and Gramsci's love of Ford and Taylor. It is embracing of both the conservative work ethic and the radical notion of non-alienated tools, products, and productivity. Non alienation from 'species-being' help dismissing compulsive work.
hunter-gatherers.

drawers and crawlers

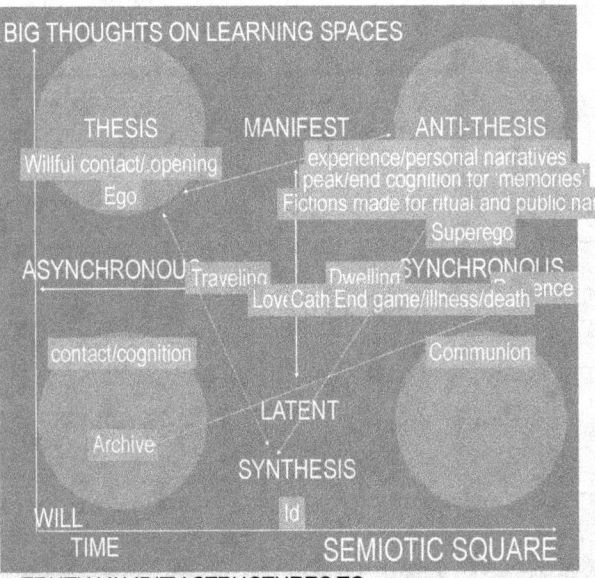

BIG THOUGHTS ON LEARNING SPACES

THESIS   MANIFEST   ANTI-THESIS
Willful contact/.opening   experience/personal narratives
        Ego   peak/end cognition for 'memories'
                Fictions made for ritual and public narratives.
                        Superego

ASYNCHRONOUS Traveling   Dwelling SYNCHRONOUS
                Love Cath End game/illness/death ence
contact/cognition   Communion

                LATENT

                SYNTHESIS

WILL   Id
        TIME   SEMIOTIC SQUARE

TRUTH VALIDITY STRUCTURES TO
STATEMENTS ABOUT VALUES
PHILLIP.BALDWIN@GMAIL.COM

SCENOGRAPHY

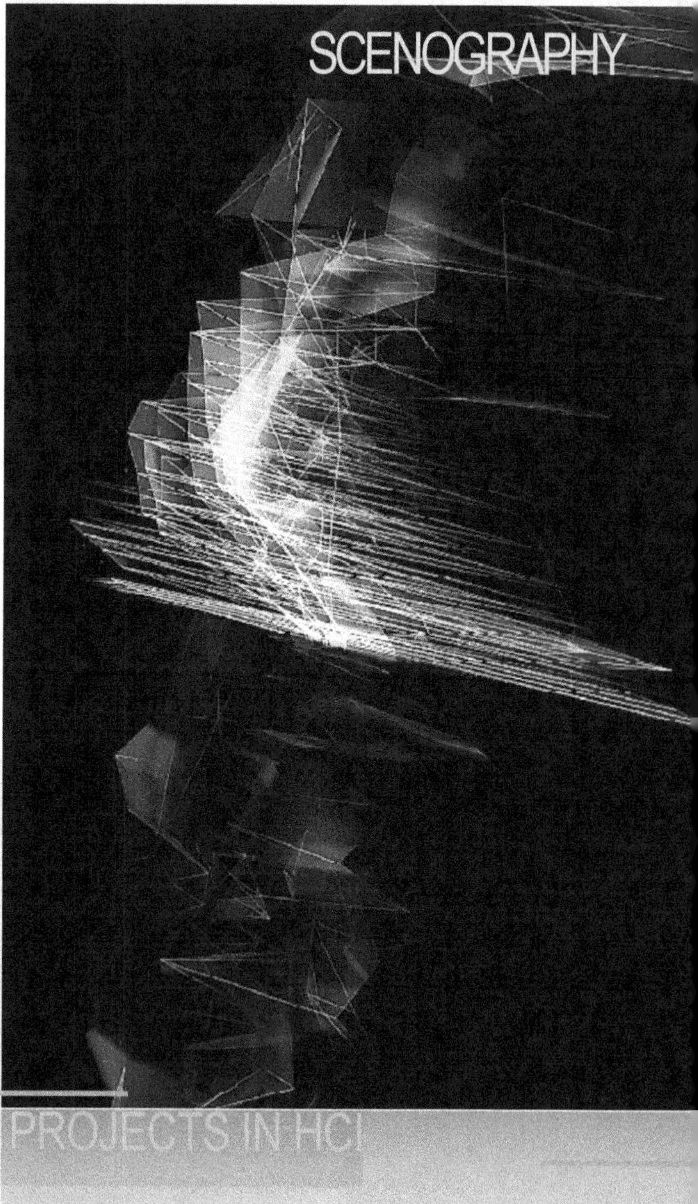

PROJECTS IN HCI

Drawers and crawlers

The assertion:

In the quadrant of a certain danger, it is an infinite savanna. In it you can hid from your tribe and make love to the fertile alpha female. Your rite of passage is bringing her here and making her fertile without being eaten.....this is the place of people who watch and don't dwell. The modern male has his leisure colonized by 'entertainment' and 'facts'. For what? We have the dystopic ideas such as 'ready player one', those who looking for a safe place to learn, or being on the high grass Savanna in Africa finding the place to hide for the night. Feeding, breeding, protecting the young.... It is a place of other worlds. Is the place of the predator but less at daytime. It is Context that makes the story, and you can't dwell in drama. Drama is that narrative.

rama could be real at any moment.

The negation:

This is the reprieve, this could be deep erotica or Surface erotica, you don't have the time to determine either. It is a place of axis Mundi at night in the tree with your love and her other male lovers: possibly your seed with find the mark.... all are vying to get her fertilized for survival. There it's a type of axis Mundi in the trees. Only poisonous snakes and leopards would attack you at night. They have the night. So the night must be a type of axis Mundi. It is a safe place for now with your female. You hold, she might have your baby, or it is some other male's, you might dwell in the illusion of the secure.... watched for now. You are the unwatched.....The leopards and the others do not watch you. In the day earlier he would find time with her in the grasses to hide and make love. ....she might want to linger to see if you attend to her release and pleasure for the longest time....time before the tribe and its alphas notice, and the leopards notice..... And time to hide and make love hoping it is your seed that makes it in and through her.

The complex: It is the Savannah.

The non negation:
This is a critique of the real, critique of the pleasant but dangerous night in the tree with some temporary sense of dwelling... a critique of that axis Mundi. This is that place in the suburbs, American suburbs, where the parents have split their house into you live in the basement. They can barely tolerate each and their 'contract' is just left as a tired mortgage....they might say it is for you....you know better. others are living there for the mortgage, although they say they're living there for you and your safety, and your siblings, or the neighbors....this has been years. The sexual union is gone and you sensed this as a young child....you father was very upset....you mother made a project of you..... This is the space of the discordant dWelling. This is the space are the young man, unable to hunt during the day and avoid danger at night becomes mutable, like a cell phone case. A young man might play their games forever, change from boy to girl, I do almost anything to help mutate to survive and understand..... Mutates in that failed institution in that discordant house.
he neutral term is the gender shape shifting.

Non assertion:
This is a critique on the sceneographic, critique of the context 'i'll be online!' always... life is a place where you found yourself in the Deep Savannah grasses, it is the Oasis maze in the Maze of the grasses which any danger can and destroy you. Or destroy you slowly like the shadow of the grasses....the internet. Endless rabbit holes.....It is also a change of the surface of the day, and the reality of camouflage. And not the camouflage within Society of changing from boy to girl (that is you) the Freudian archetypes are gone. Both genders don't care in that they fight against the grasses and what is real there..... It is a space of binging Netflix, as if this is a savanna, the Protector and the Destroyer. This is the space of ADD or OCD. This is the space of the confused boys who no longer have the rite of passage to Danger, and they become nerds in the Infinite Space of the Savannah. They assumed the food will keep coming and one day it will not. And they must turn their 'play' and to the seriousness the pyramid scheme: Making others play their game. Imperative. But what cache? The young male has a crisis....the young female has her beauty. There's no ideal rite of passage anymore. The Female is still Superior in that she's still the only one who can give birth. Who can further your tribe.

Assertion: An action or Retreat Into The Enclave life. What the beatniks did for the urban setting, the hippies in their communes in new England and northern California, was also turned into middle class pastiche..... It is an attempt at the countercultural. ...devised networks amongst like minded people before the internet. Then came the internet. Some of this stopped short of sexual equality, and polyamory. Within them, One still the possessed woman, as as important as an outgrowth of Eisenhower era imprinting. Oedipal imprinting.

The valorization of production. This is an outgrowth of Schiller's take on Spiel or 'play'. Itself an outgrowth of Kant's division of faculties. Ruskin and Morris took this further into aesthetic non aliened. Labor based on design and not individualistic 'canvas art'.

NOT AGAINST

Non negation: Aesthetic non-alienated labor. Non alienated labor. This is Ruskin and Morris. This is Marcuse aesthetics inspired by the art happenings of the 60s. This is the critique of the situationist in debord. Urban communes, anarchists, squaters, punks, New England slackers.

Neutral Term: neither for nor against

Negation: The capitalist drive to hot glue together a bunch of Mcmansions as investment properties. The training, narrative is to 'live inside your investment'. The result is precarious relationship to employment, an alienation with labor not the least of which is is zero-sum hostility toward co-workers. It is an area of, commodity fetish not solidarity. It defers to the infantile, leisure is colonized by Hollywood, furthering infantile violence reflected back to the co-workers. It is a valorization of consumption. It is the training to live in your 'investment property' with the notion that someone richer in the future (if employment lasts) through the system would purchase it at a profit have driven 80s 90s and early aughts Up until 2008. it ignores the precarity of employment and UBI.

Non-assertion: This is The 'Curse Of The Lost Garden.' This is Weber's 'protestant ethic and spirit of capitalism' after Locke. Protestant abstract work ethic ignoring alienation...work in itself. This is the 'sweat of the brow', and compulsive Lockean liberalism guiding America in particular. The anti-royal, Lockean impulse is to despise those inclined to natural leisure, free sexual pleasure, spiel, and minorities from non-protestant cultures....so it abhors sloth and slackers. It is marxist son-in-law speaking of the 'virtues of idleness' against Leninist left and Gramsci's love of Ford and Taylor. It is embracing of both the conservative work ethic and the radical notion of non-alienated tools, products, and productivity. Non alienation from 'species-being' help dismissing compulsive work.
hunter-gatherers.

SEMIOTIC SQUARE

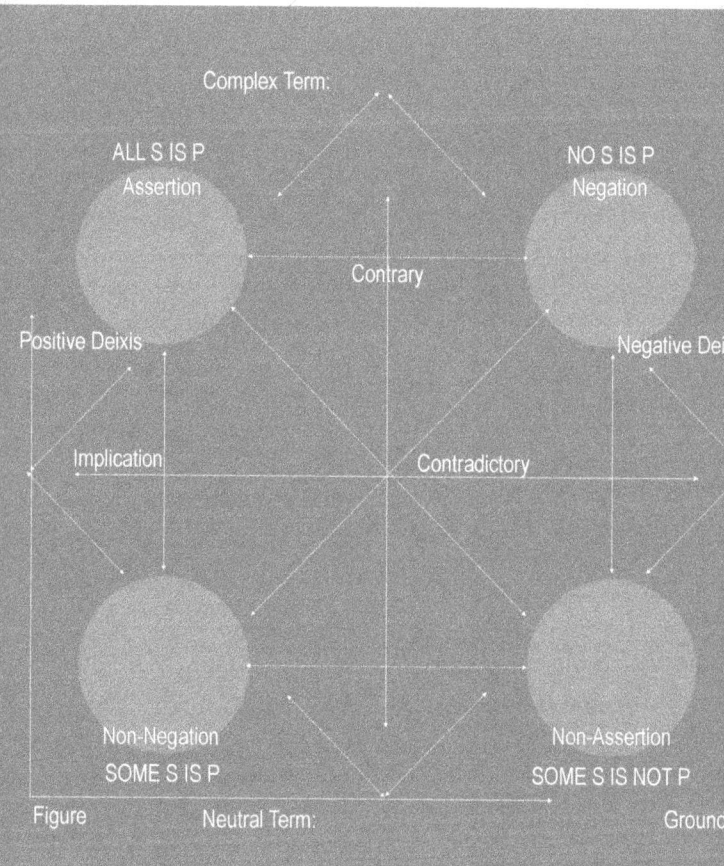

Complex term: Internet 'doppelganger'

ASSERTION/FOR

Assertion: An action or Retreat Into The Enclave life. What the beatniks did for the urban setting, the hippies in their communes in new England and northern California, was also turned into middle class pastiche..... It is an attempt at the countercultural. ...devised networks amongst like minded people before the internet. Then came the internet. Some of this stopped short of sexual equality, and polyamory. Within them, One still the possessed woman, as an important as an outgrowth of Eisenhower era imprinting. Oedipal imprinting.

The valorization of production. This is an outgrowth of Schiller's take on Spiel or 'play'. Itself an outgrowth of Kant's division of faculties. Ruskin and Morris took this further into aesthetic non aliened. Labor based on design and not individualistic 'canvas art'.

NEGATION/AGAINST

Negation: The capitalist drive to hot glue together a bunch of Mcmansions as investment properties. The training, narrative is to 'live inside your investment'. The result is precarious relationship to employment, an alienation with labor not the least of which is is zero-sum hostility toward co-workers. It is an area of, commodity fetish not solidarity. It defers to the infantile, leisure is colonized by Hollywood, furthering infantile violence reflected back to the co-workers. It is a valorization of consumption. It is the training to live in your 'investment property' with the notion that someone richer in the future (if employment lasts) through the system would purchase it at a profit have driven 80s 90s and early aughts Up until 2008. it ignores the precarity of employment and UBI.

NOT ASSERTION/EXCLUDE

Non-assertion. This is The 'Curse Of The Lost Garden.' This is Weber's 'protestant ethic and spirit of capitalism' after Locke. Protestant abstract work ethic ignoring alienation...work in itself. This is the 'sweat of the brow', and compulsive Lockean liberalism guiding America in particular. The anti-royal, Lockean impulse is to despise those inclined to natural leisure, free sexual pleasure, spiel, and minorities from non-protestant cultures....so it abhors sloth and slackers. It is marxist son-in-law speaking of the 'virtues of idleness' against Leninist left and Gramsci's love of Ford and Taylor. It is embracing of both the conservative work ethic and the radical notion of non-alienated tools, products, and productivity. Non alienation from 'species-being' help dismissing compulsive work. hunter-gatherers.

NOT AGAINST/PARTS

Non negation: Aesthetic non-alienated labor. Non alienated labor. This is Ruskin and Morris. This is Marcuse aesthetics inspired by the art happenings of the 60s. This is the critique of the situationist in debord. Urban communes, anarchists, squaters, punks, New England slackers.

L

TIME

SEMIOTIC SQUARE

Neutral term: 'slacker coder', 'cottage industry'

IOTIC SQUARE/GENERATING TERMS

WORK, ALIENATION, AESTHETIC, AND CONSUMPTION.
Note_26, 13 May 2020

Terms.
Assertion: An action or Retreat Into The Enclave life. What the beatniks did for the urban setting, the hippies in their communes in new England and northern California, was also turned into middle class pastiche..... It is an attempt at the countercultural. ...devised networks amongst like minded people before the internet. Then came the internet. Some of this stopped short of sexual equality, and polyamory. Within them, One still the possessed woman, as an important as an outgrowth of Eisenhower era imprinting. Oedipal imprinting.

The valorization of production. This is an outgrowth of Schiller's take on Spiel or 'play'. Itself an outgrowth of Kant's division of faculties. Ruskin and Morris took this further into aesthetic non aliened. Labor based on design and not individualistic 'canvas art'.

Negation: The capitalist drive to hot glue together a bunch of Mcmansions as investment properties. The training, narrative is to 'live inside your investment'. The result is precarious relationship to employment, an alienation with labor not the least of which is is zero-sum hostility toward co-workers. It is an area of, commodity fetish not solidarity. It defers to the infantile, leisure is colonized by Hollywood, furthering infantile violence reflected back to the co-workers. It is a valorization of consumption. It is the training to live in your 'investment property' with the notion that someone richer in the future (if employment lasts) through the system would purchase it at a profit have driven 80s 90s and early aughts Up until 2008. It ignores the precarity of employment and UBI.

Non negation: Aesthetic non-alienated labor. Non alienated labor. This is Ruskin and Morris. This is Marcuse aesthetics inspired by the art happenings of the 60s. This is the critique of the situationist in debord. Urban communes, anarchists, squaters, punks, New England slackers.

Non-assertion: This is The 'Curse Of The Lost Garden.' This is Weber's 'protestant ethic and spirit of capitalism' after Locke. Protestant abstract work ethic ignoring alienation...work in itself. This is the 'sweat of the brow', and compulsive Lockean liberalism guiding America in particular. The anti-royal, Lockean impulse is to despise those inclined to natural leisure, free sexual pleasure, spiel, and minorities from non-protestant cultures....so it abhors sloth and slackers.

It is marxist son-in-law speaking of the 'virtues of idleness' against Leninist left and Gramsci's love of Ford and Taylor. It is embracing of both the conservative work ethic and the radical notion of non-alienated tools, products, and productivity. Non alienation from 'species-being' help dismissing compulsive work.
hunter-gatherers.

N COMPUTER INTERFACE AND PERFORMANCE

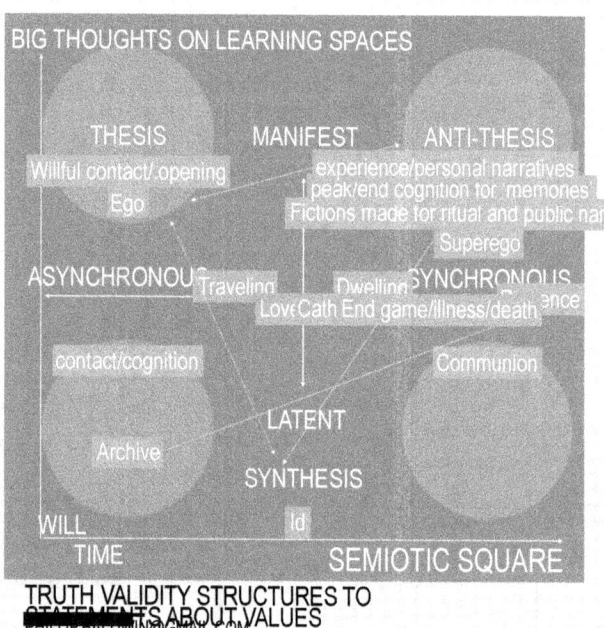

BIG THOUGHTS ON LEARNING SPACES

THESIS MANIFEST ANTI-THESIS

Willful contact/.opening
Ego

experience/personal narratives
peak/end cognition for memories
Fictions made for ritual and public narrati
Superego

ASYNCHRONOUS Traveling Dwelling SYNCHRONOUS
Love Cath End game/illness/death ance

contact/cognition Communion

LATENT

Archive SYNTHESIS

WILL Id
TIME SEMIOTIC SQUARE

TRUTH VALIDITY STRUCTURES TO
STATEMENTS ABOUT VALUES
PHILLIP.BALDWIN@GMAIL.COM

CONTACT, COMMUNION,

MOVEMENT4
SOMATIC
MECHANIC

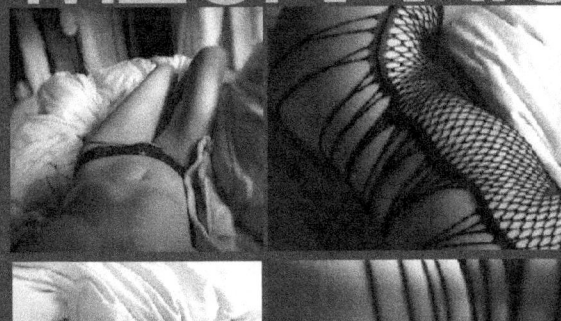

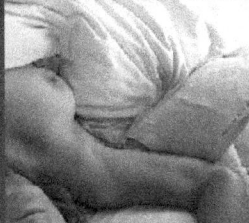

RSE YOURSELF....COMING BACK

P.BALDWIN@GMAIL.COM

SOMATIC MECHANIC

One of the things that we hit upon was the fact that the robotic eye became a type of prosthetic for these elusive mirror neurons. What are they? There were first detected in the 1970s though their perceived existence is known to be thousands of years old.... probably in many species on earth. What we were hitting on with the kinect camera that reads the motions and interface of the standing individual is that we can empathize more directly with a standing individual in front of a crowd like a shaman conjuring out bad spirits and brining in the new. This is not unlike Jimi Hendrix performances that we have from Woodstock and Monterey where he lights his guitar on fire and mimics the sound of a descending bomb while playing the national anthem. In this act of rock and roll he was a modern day shaman.... he was using his guitar to great effect to root out the evil feelings of the society and bring in.... what? The sound of the amped guitar. For a couple of generations after this young men and women mad attempts to mimic his virtuosic playing of the guitar as he was basically making his own language of play, electronic shamanism and catharsis. He capped this mimetic experience off by dying early. He inspired the next generations of young guitarists to amplify both the sonic and somatic languages of gesturing onstage in front of thousands and making a type of music that mixed with the somatic sonic excellence in something that was new and unique yet ancient. From these concerts forty years ago we still retain that feeling of the amplified 'big beat' of the music, coupled with the gesturing body showing us the cathartic performance of that music. Body and sonic released would be coupled forever with the legacy of Hendrix...even before this. What had become entangled with this expression in this immediate gratification generation was the fact that most didn't want to practice to train their bodies to play with that level of invention and virtuosity...it took too long and demanded discipline. Enter the guitar hero's and the air guitar.

The big beat is the heart of your mama inside her womb. There it is safe and there is no memory as there is no desire to become something else. All is present in side the womb and there is an overwhelming and almost oppressive sense of the continuous present. The only thing that would give you any sense of the temporal is the beat of your mother's heart. You can't even perceive of your own heartbeat. You kick and you react to the beautiful connection to it all. You grow and never dream of leaving the warm fluid that space of no space and yet all spaces. You have not mad that distinction between the temporal and the spatial. Your womb is all spaces. Your time is the datum beat of your mother's heart... outside of you but strangely inside of you. When you hear the large amped beat of the bass and drums you are transported back to this time. When you are in the large auditorium with many different souls all writing to the beat of the music you are shocked and pleased that these people are like one fluid.... there are no differentiated individuals. They are one. You are one. The beat grows louder and then the lights flicker. You are still in the moment. In the womb you recognize the bet of your mother's heart and you wish to see your will land desire become a part of that and fulfill this. You are not marking time because there is no time...all time is amniotic fluid and this is a time for reflection because you don't mix the battle between memory and desire. And then. And then...

The father…the shaman. From the unconditional time/space of the fluid there emerges some sort of joker…some comic insignificant creature far off but well lit. What is this you think? What is this thing, this joker on the edge of the stage? How dare…or how did he break from the mass of dark swelling timeless others…. perhaps the dark and swelling timeless billions who could have been born but who weren't and then he is taking he place upon the stage? Why is this? We were having such a fun timeless time without desire or even memory swimming in the dark big beat and now this comic shaman has usurped the main position in front of our…our…eyes! We have eyes. What happen to the sound without need of earths? What happened to hearing our voice through our bones or the rumble of the timeless outside world that came in through our loving mothers unconditionally loving body? This shaman who seems to be controlling the beat has destroyed our big beat! How dare he…yet…. yet this is the beginning of a time fullness. And now he takes the treble sound…amped…and he moves and writhes and starts to tell us how to be aware and deal with time. He is comic but he is magnificent in his irony…. he is graceful and comic like a peacock or a rooster. He has cleft both time and space with his treble line of will and making something of this dark morass. The unconditional dark amniotic fluids of yourself and those never born and yet to be born seem pathetic, boring, and dull. Yes. This is the father using the prosthetic of time and the treble line to show us how the world can be divided. He is there because he loves us and wishes us to be born out of the dark love and morass of the undivided others. Yes…these are our brother and sisters who will never be born because of luck and circumstance. We are the lucky to be born and then…when the music grows faint…we feel that we are unlucky and we curse the day that we were born. We threaten suicide when the music stops and we are in the desert of the bright and dry. Where and how did the cruel punch of the one two happen? First the mothers with the dark love over all of us in a timelessness. Then the father shaman standing up before us showing us how unfair the rest of the spit of time space can be. Then…then…

Then the prosthetic. It is an act of luck to be born. Yet. We need the prosthetic to help us back to those realms of the timeless fluid with our unborn brothers and sisters. Then we need the lit rooster shaman clown father to show us how to separate from the dark time space suffocation. And then we look to drug or alcohol for completion. And then we look for more music. Always music. And then we look for compulsive lists…things to do and lists to grow on. To subsume us. Then.

Then we mad a prosthetic. The music moves to your motion. Long live the rooster kings. Long live the guiding father…that doesn't have to collapse on authority but is the true mentor…this is the individual who is the guide…the one who can show us how life is unfair but it is also a gift…. we have left the thousands and billions of brothers and sisters who were never born because they didn't want to take on the lesson of the rooster shaman…they must trust. They must cleave space-time for now. With it is born memory and desire. This trick is a prosthetic as well as a trope. A trope for emancipatory time …for now. From here on in many cling to gimmicks to do this. This is all right. For now.

"Struggle for love in a dream,"

The title "Hypnerotomachia" is an invented word drawn from the Greek roots for "sleep" (as in "hypnotize"), "love/lust" (as in "erotic"), and "struggle/strife" (as in "naumachia," the mock sea-fights held by ancient Romans). The title thus literally means something like "Struggle for love in a dream," and describes what the main character, Poliphilo, spends the entire story doing: searching for his beloved in a dream.- Hypnerotomachia Poliphili from Wikipedia

BIG PICTURE:

-The old skool system was designed as a pyramid scheme where energies focused 'upward'

-this pyramid scheme did not focus on the 'usefulness' of current sustainable infrastructure, but became a type of 'futures speculation' of the self robbing from the future to pay the present.

-this system is not just industrial or post-industrial service economies...it retains the strong influence from the beginning of agrarian culture with toil, kings, priestly classes, necessity, and scarcity to conduct information.

-misinformation, coercion, herd mentalities, bullying, authority addiction, are the nodes of conduction of basic information.

-religions used to be an alternative system of communication of 'imaginary worlds' so that humans could endure the project with 'meaning' within an agrarian hierarchy, yet at times they collaborated with them.

-mobile telematics with a sense of autonomy can break this 5000 year old hierarchies. This is an imperative to conduct the 'long tail' of necessary infrastructure and resources.

-this is the life in the long tail after a 5000 year old cycle come to completion not through the tools itself, but through the comparison of lateral information...and information on how to sustain.

-this is life in the long tail of human dignity and possibility

-this will start with a new respect for lateral information in energy and education as the tools to dismantle the hierarchies.

my daily essay inspired by the idea, the fact of two people moving through the night at opposite ends of this simulacrum country....the beauty trying to find gas in the night with one mile to go....the contingency of caring....the desire to hear a mothers heart in the womb, the heart of a beautiful woman beating, the comingling....gorgeous photos...i knew you hade immense style in this puritanical 'fly over' country......there is so much behavoral conditioning now iin this country with the screen separating us....it is ironic that two found a way to 'suture' the empty expanse one night....reading a lot of jg ballard.

P.BALDWIN@GMAIL.COM

DRAWERS AND CRAWLERS
PLAGUE BOOK...

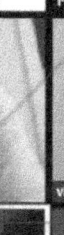

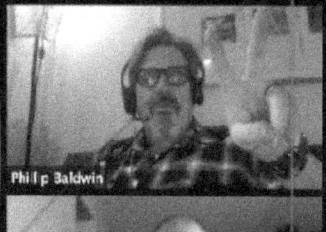

Phil p Baldwin

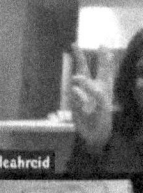

leahreid

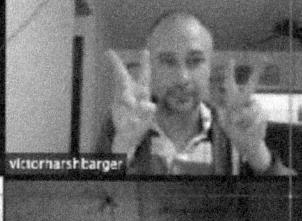

victorharshbarger

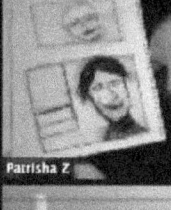

Patrisha Z

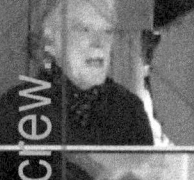

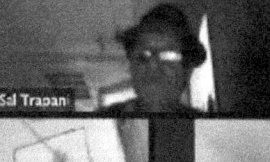

Sal Trapani

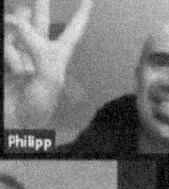

Philipp

Chelsea crawl crew...

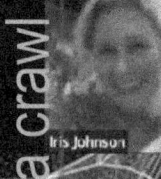

Iris Johnson

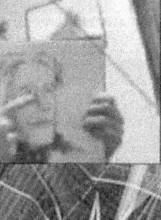

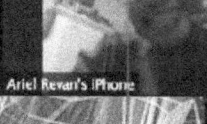

Ariel Revan's iPhone

ahreid

Phillip Baldwin

is Johnson

Patrisha Z

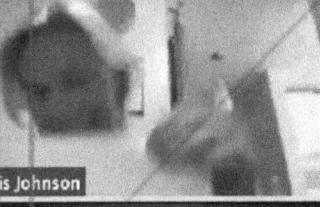

izabeth Popiel

victorharshbarger

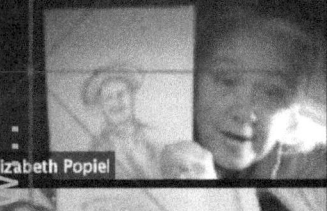

tephen's iPad

Philipp

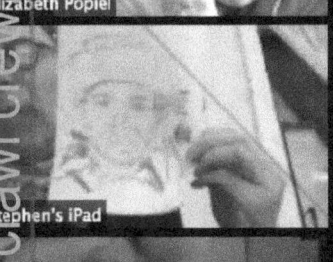

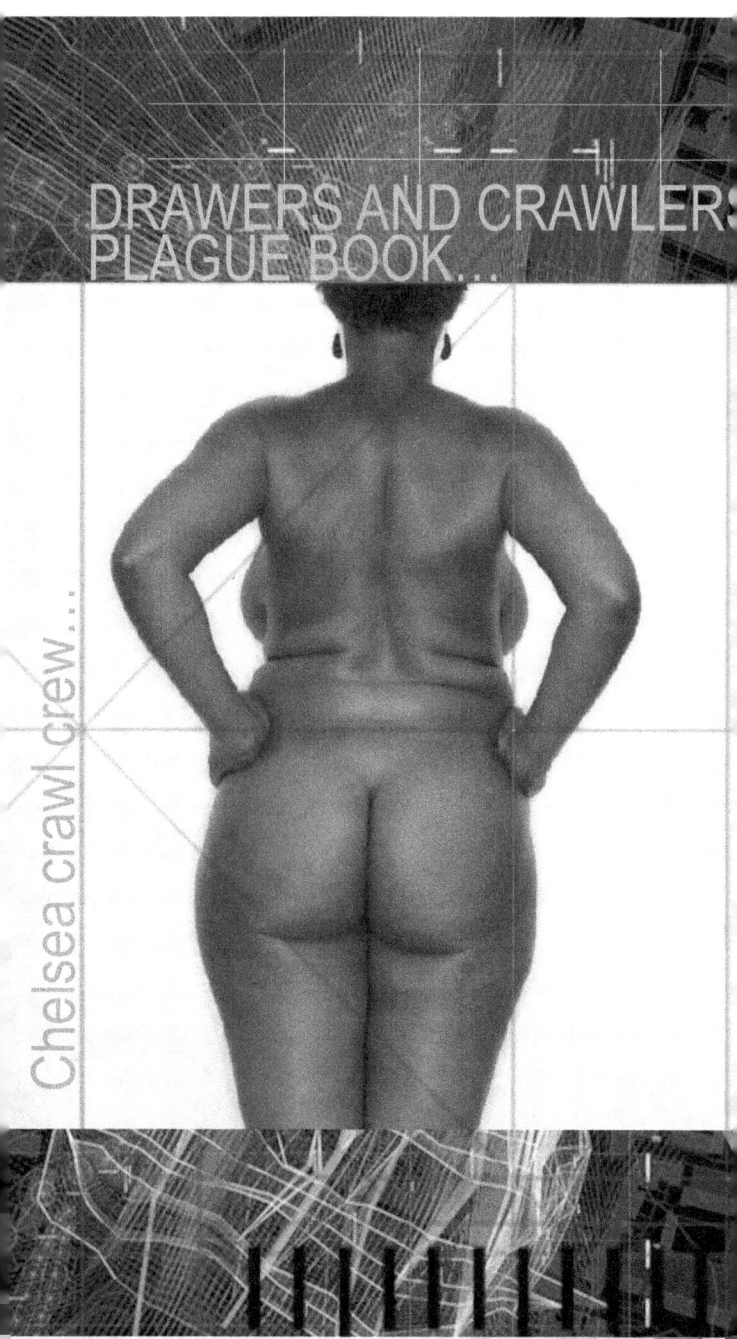

DRAWERS AND CRAWLERS
PLAGUE BOOK...

Chelsea crawl crew...

DRAWERS AND CRAWLERS
PLAGUE BOOK...

Chelsea Crawnview...

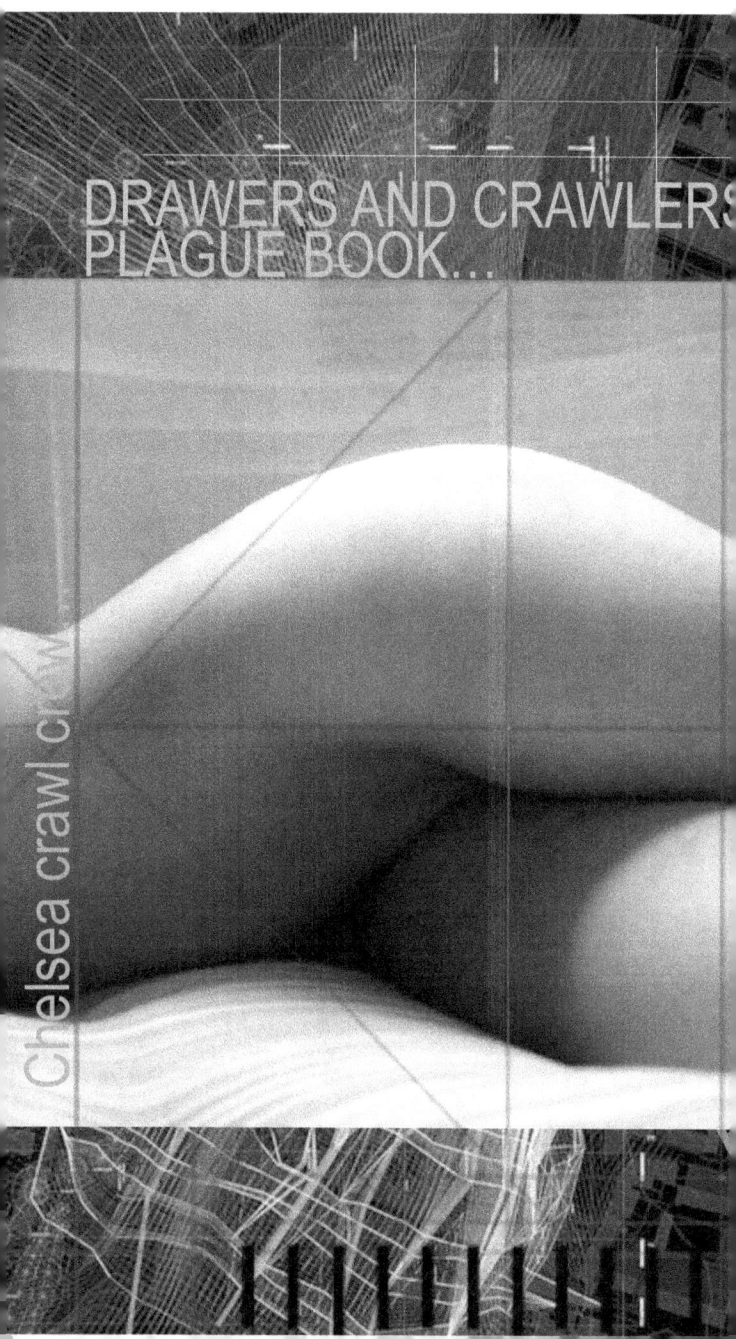

DRAWERS AND CRAWLERS
PLAGUE BOOK...

Chelsea crawl crawl

DRAWERS AND CRAWLERS
PLAGUE BOOK...

A Chelsea Crawl Crawler...

DRAWERS AND CRAWLERS
PLAGUE BOOK...

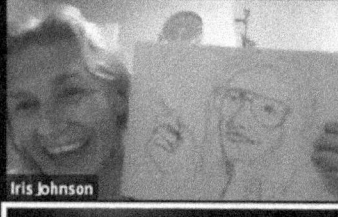

Iris Johnson

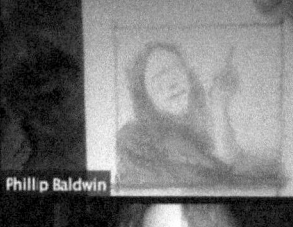

Phillip Baldwin

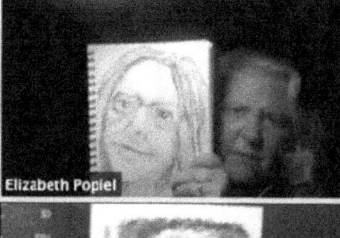

Elizabeth Popiel

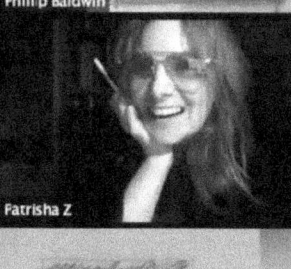

Patrisha Z

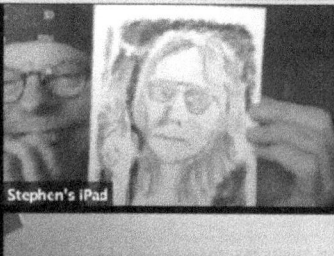

Stephen's iPad

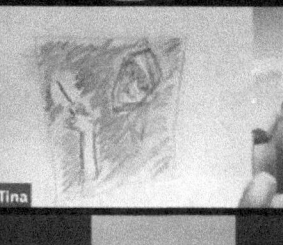

Tina

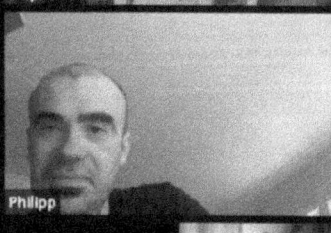

Philipp

Ariel Revan

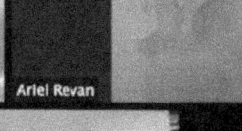

DRAWERS AND CRAWLERS
PLAGUE BOOK...

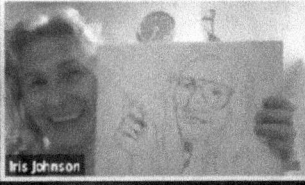

Iris Johnson

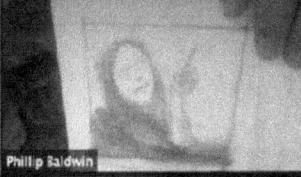

Phillip Baldwin

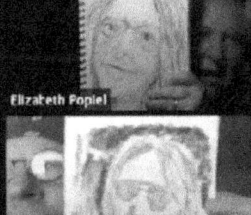

Elizabeth Popiel

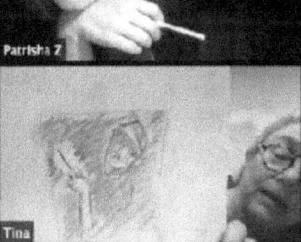

Patrisha Z

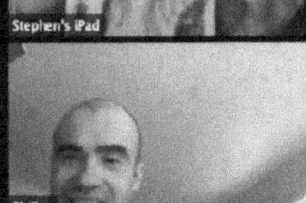

Stephen's iPad

Tina

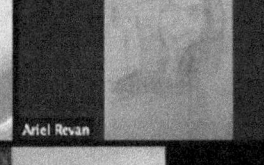

Philipp

Ariel Revan

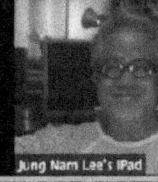

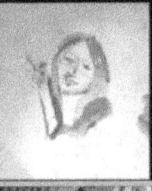

Jung Nam Lee's iPad

DRAWERS AND CRAWLER PLAGUE BOOK...

\\Chelsea crawl crew...

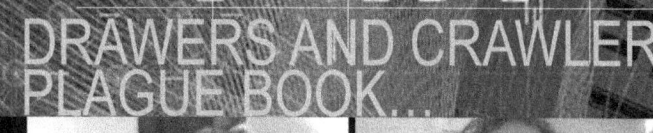

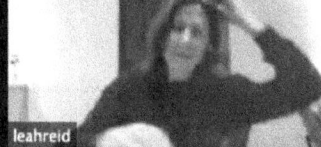

leahreid

Phillip Baldwin

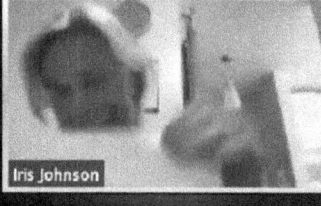

Iris Johnson

Patrisha Z

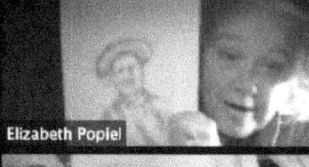

Elizabeth Popiel

victorharshbarger

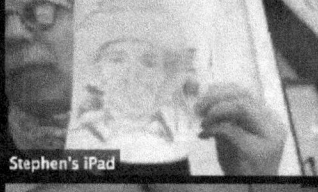

Stephen's iPad

Philipp

DRAWERS AND CRAWLERS PLAGUE BOOK...

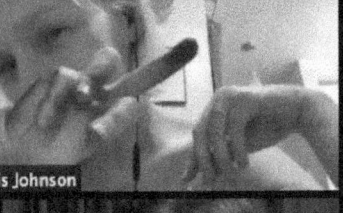

Iris Johnson

Phillip Baldwin

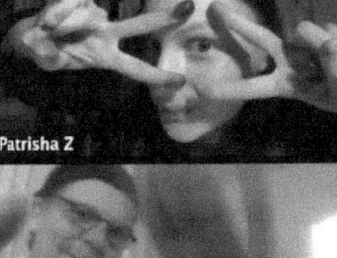

Patrisha Z

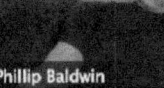

Elizabeth Popiel

Stephen's iPad

Philipp

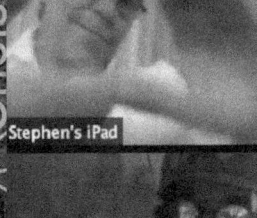

Sal Trapani

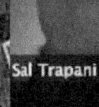

Ariel Revan's iPhone

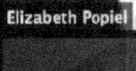

DRAWERS AND CRAWLER
PLAGUE BOOK...

Chelsea crawl crew...

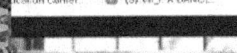

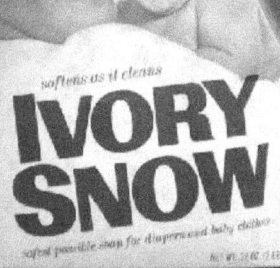

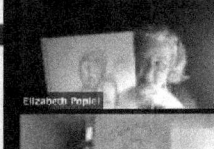

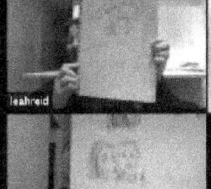

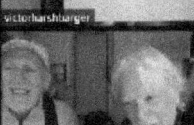

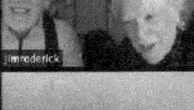

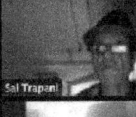

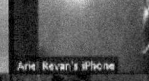

DRAWERS AND CRAWLERS
PLAGUE BOOK...

Chelsea crawl crew...

SELF

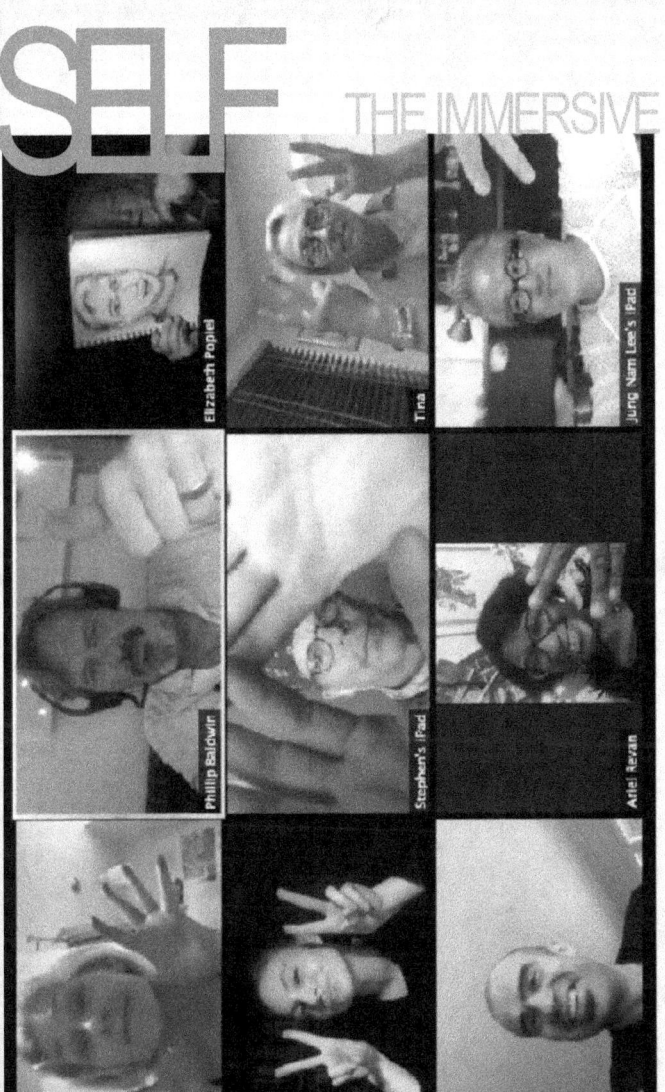

Elizabeth Popiel

Tina

Jung Nam Lee's iPad

Phillip Baldwin

Stephen's iPad

Ariel Revan

CHELSEA CRAWL CREW

DRAWERS AND CRAWLERS PLAGUE BOOK

PHILLIPBALDWIN@GMAIL.COM

SELF

THE IMMERSIVE

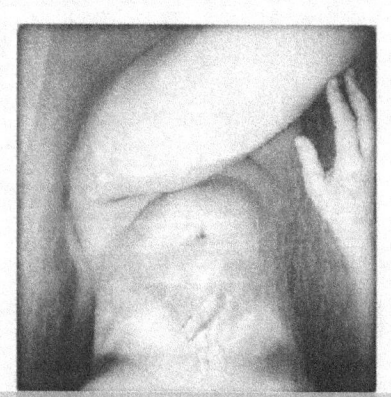

CHELSEA CRAWL CREW

DRAWERS AND CRAWLERS PLAGUE BOOK

PHILLIPBALDWIN@GMAIL.COM

SELF THE IMMERSIVE

CHELSEA CRAWL CREW

DRAWERS AND CRAWLERS PLAGUE BOOK
PHILLIP.BALDWIN@GMAIL.COM

SELF

THE IMMERSIVE

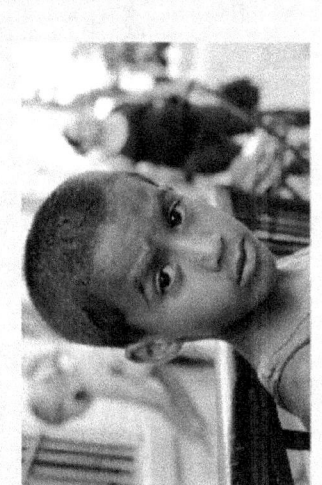

CHELSEA CRAWL CREW

DRAWERS AND CRAWLERS PLAGUE BOOK

PHILLIP.BALDWIN@GMAIL.COM

SELF

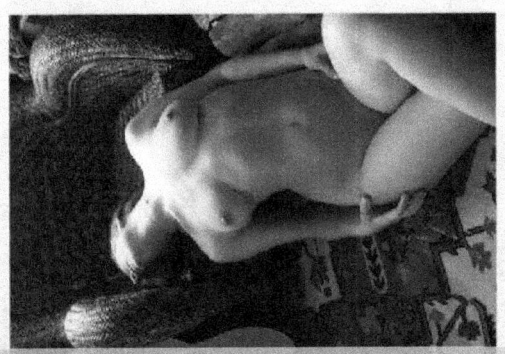

Phillip Baldwin

Patrisha Z.

Tina

Iris Johnson

Elizabeth Rupel

Stephen's iPad

Juno Nam Lee's iPad

CHELSEA CRAWL CREW

DRAWERS AND CRAWLERS PLAGUE BOOK

PHILLIP.BALDWIN@GMAIL.COM

SELF
THE IMMERSIVE

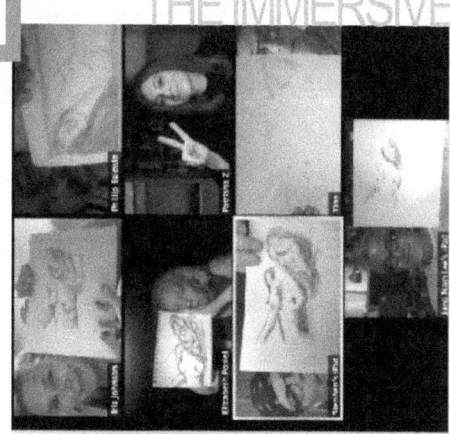

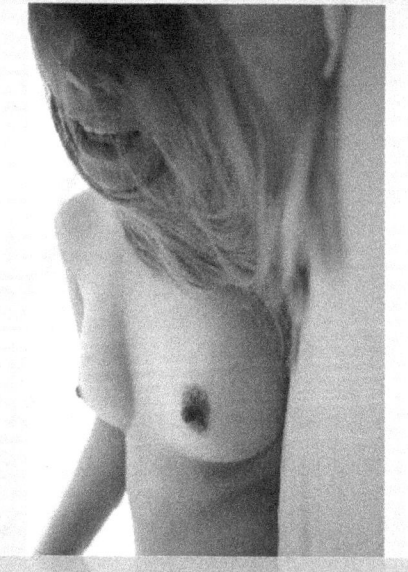

CHELSEA CRAWL CREW
DRAWERS AND CRAWLERS PLAGUE BOOK
PHILLIP.BALDWIN@GMAIL.COM

SELF

THE IMMERSIVE

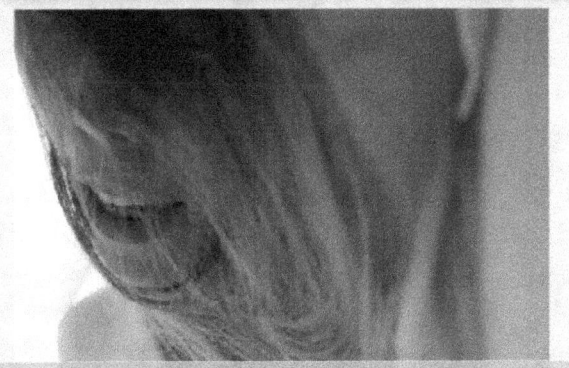

Philip Baldwin

Fatisha Z

Tina

Iris Johnson

Elizabeth Peplel

Stechen's iPad

CHELSEA CRAWL CREW

DRAWERS AND CRAWLERS PLAGUE BOOK

PHILLIPBALDWIN@GMAIL.COM

SELF

THE IMMERSIVE

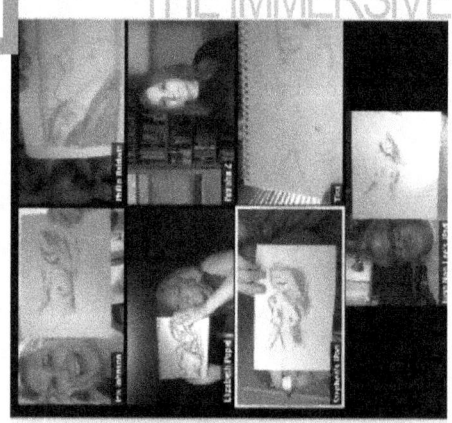

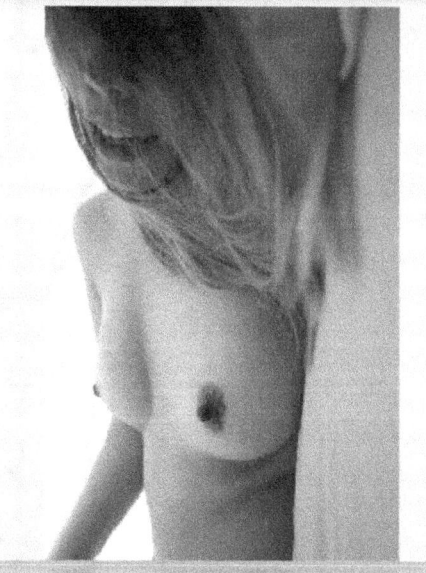

CHELSEA CRAWL CREW

DRAWERS AND CRAWLERS PLAGUE BOOK
PHILLIP.BALDWIN@GMAIL.COM

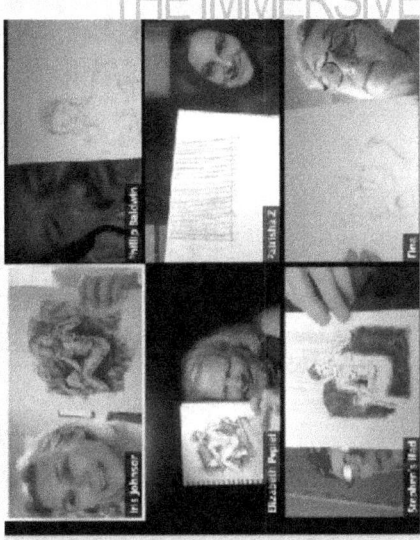

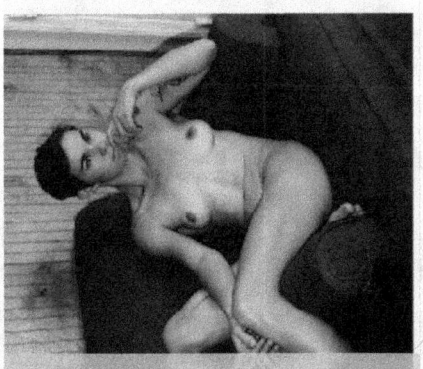

CHELSEA CRAWL CREW

SELF

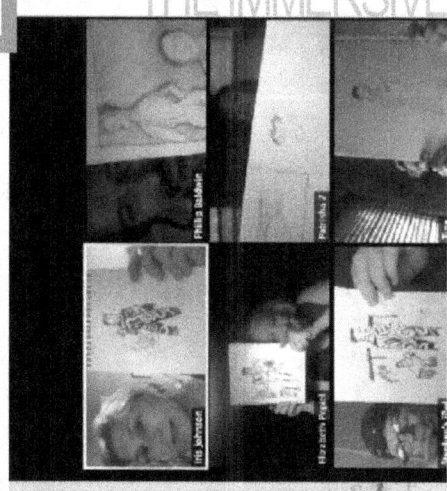

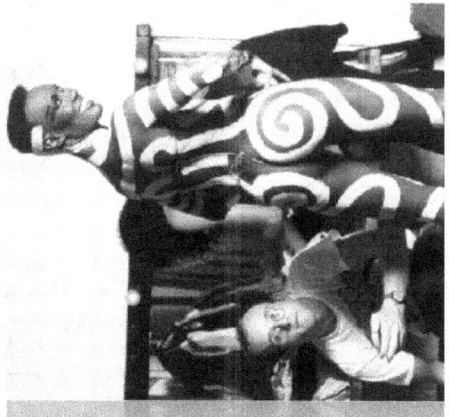

CHELSEA CRAWL CREW

DRAWERS AND CRAWLERS PLAGUE BOOK

PHILLIP.BALDWIN@GMAIL.COM

SELF THE IMMERSIVE

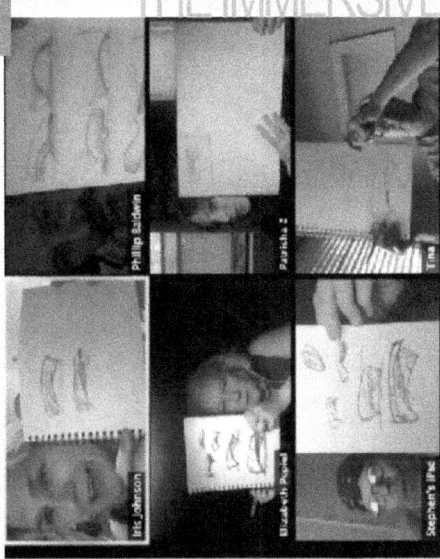

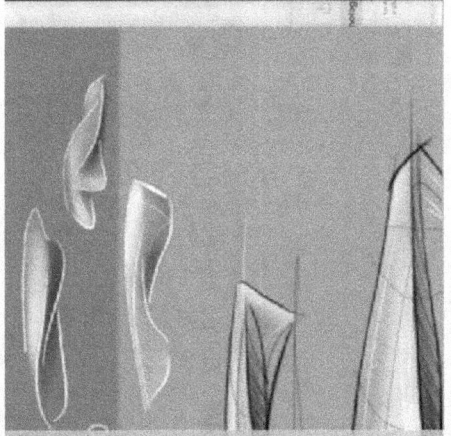

CHELSEA CRAWL CREW

DRAWERS AND CRAWLERS PLAGUE BOOK

PHILLIPBALDWIN@GMAIL.COM

SELF
THE IMMERSIVE

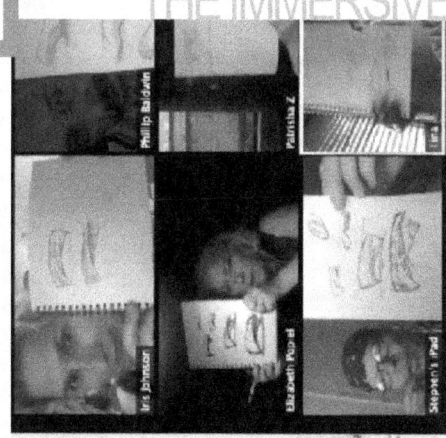

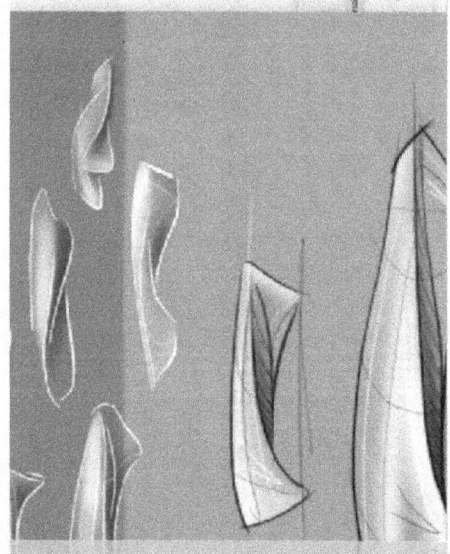

CHELSEA CRAWL CREW

SELF THE IMMERSIVE

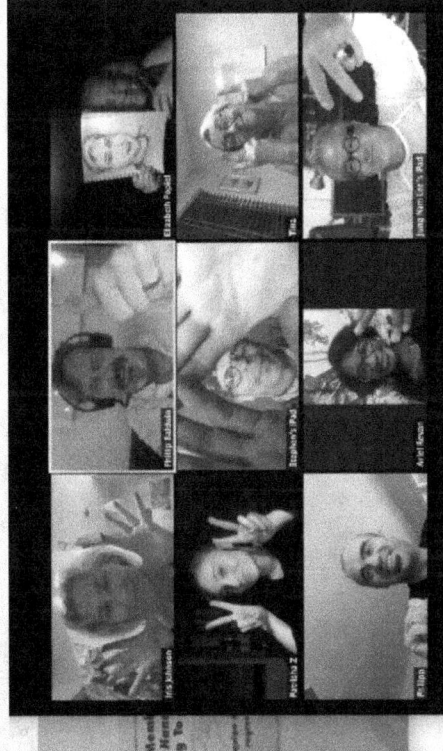

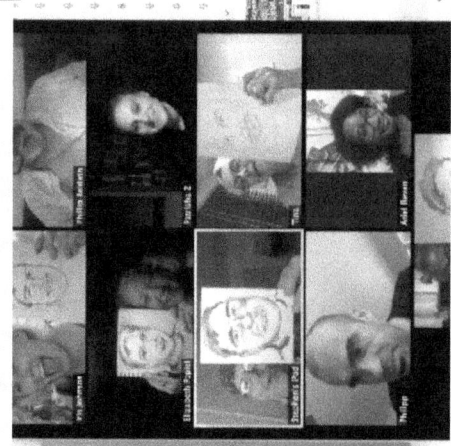

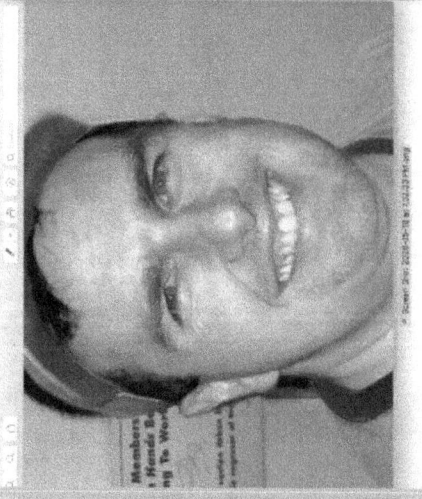

CHELSEA CRAWL CREW

DRAWERS AND CRAWLERS PLAGUE BOOK

PHILLIPBALDWIN@GMAIL.COM

SELF THE IMMERSIVE

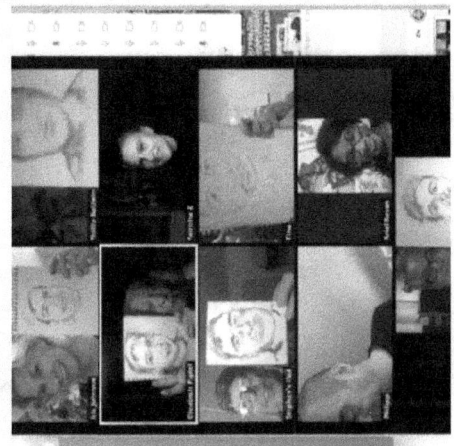

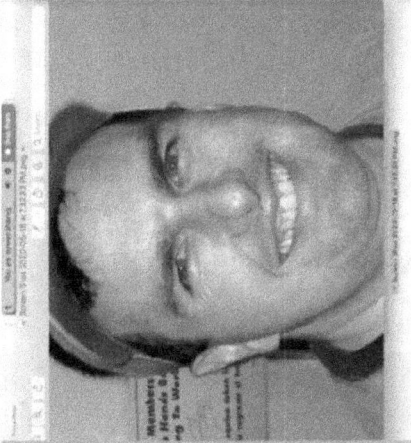

CHELSEA CRAWL CREW

DRAWERS AND CRAWLERS PLAGUE BOOK

PHILLIP.BALDWIN@GMAIL.COM

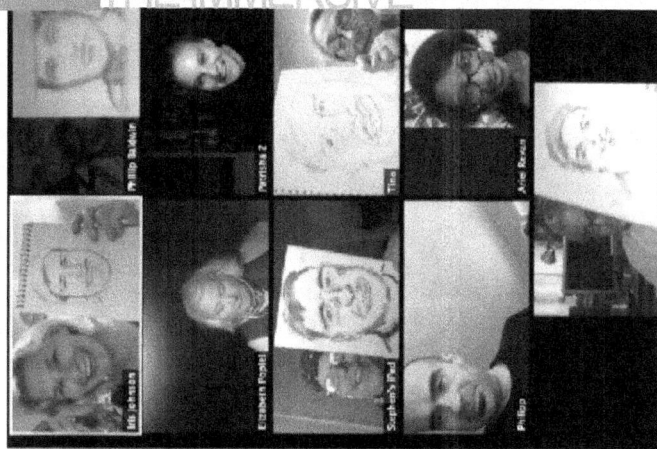

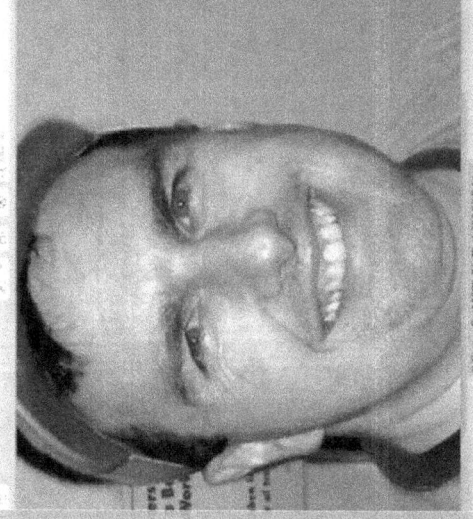

DRAWERS AND CRAWLERS PLAGUE BOOK
PHILLIP.BALDWIN@GMAIL.COM

CHELSEA CRAWL CREW

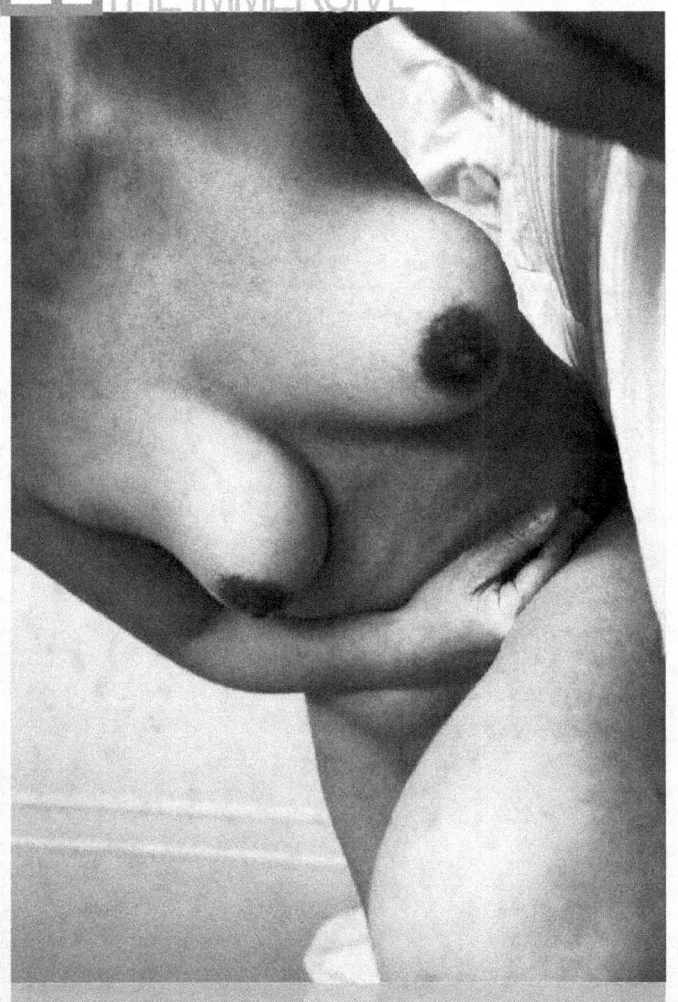

DRAWERS AND CRAWLERS PLAGUE BOOK

PHILLIP.BALDWIN@GMAIL.COM

CHELSEA CRAWL CREW

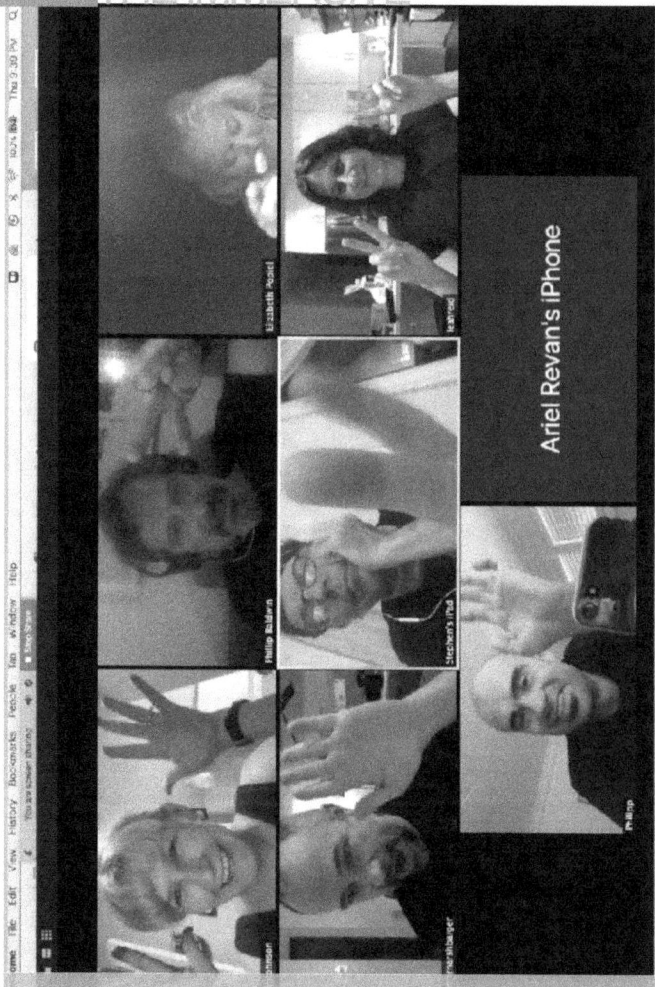

CHELSEA CRAWL CREW

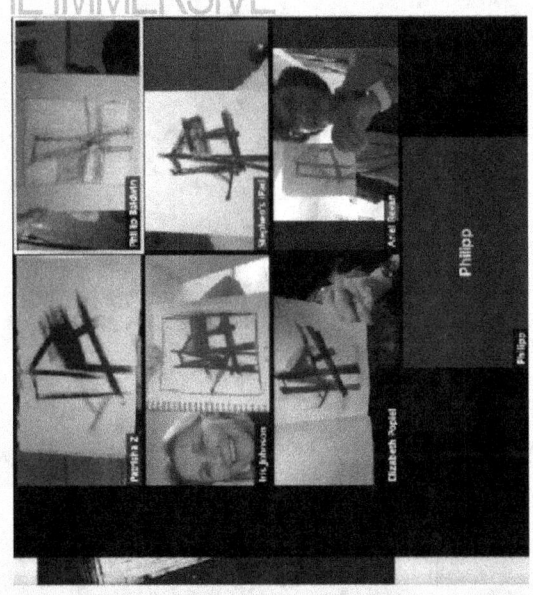

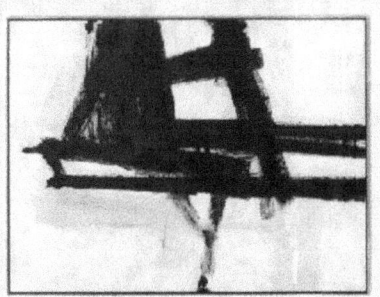

DRAWERS AND CRAWLERS PLAGUE BOOK
PHILLIP.BALDWIN@GMAIL.COM

CHELSEA CRAWL CREW

DRAWERS AND CRAWLERS PLAGUE BOOK
PHILLIPBALDWIN@GMAIL.COM

CHELSEA CRAWL CREW

Ariel Revan's iPh

CHELSEA CRAWL CREW

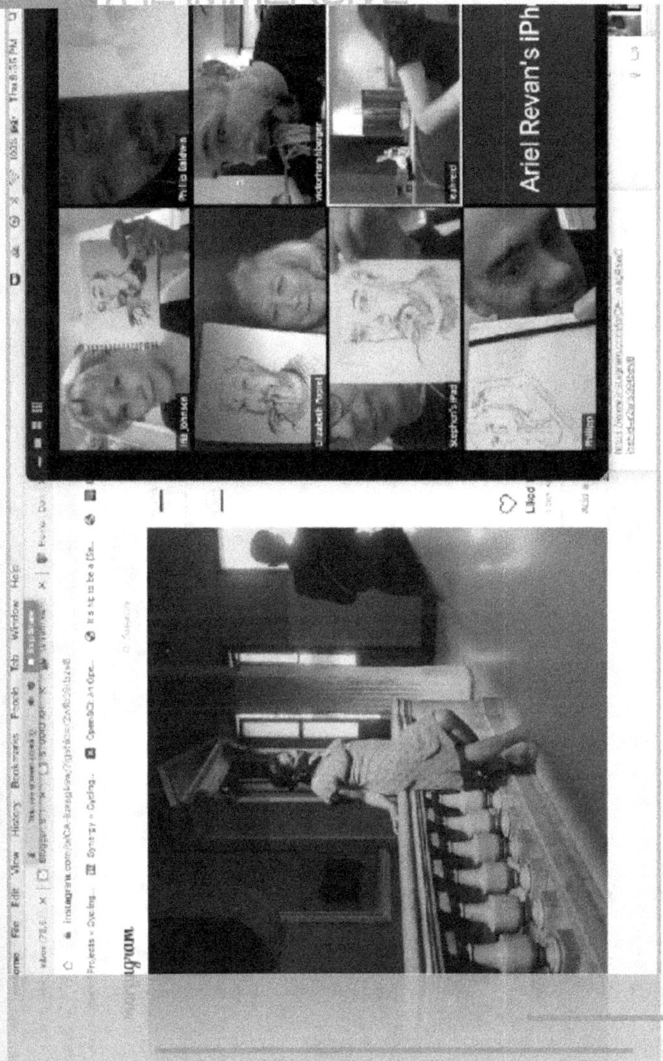

DRAWERS AND CRAWLERS PLAGUE BOOK
PHILLIPBALDWIN@GMAIL.COM CHELSEA CRAWL CREW

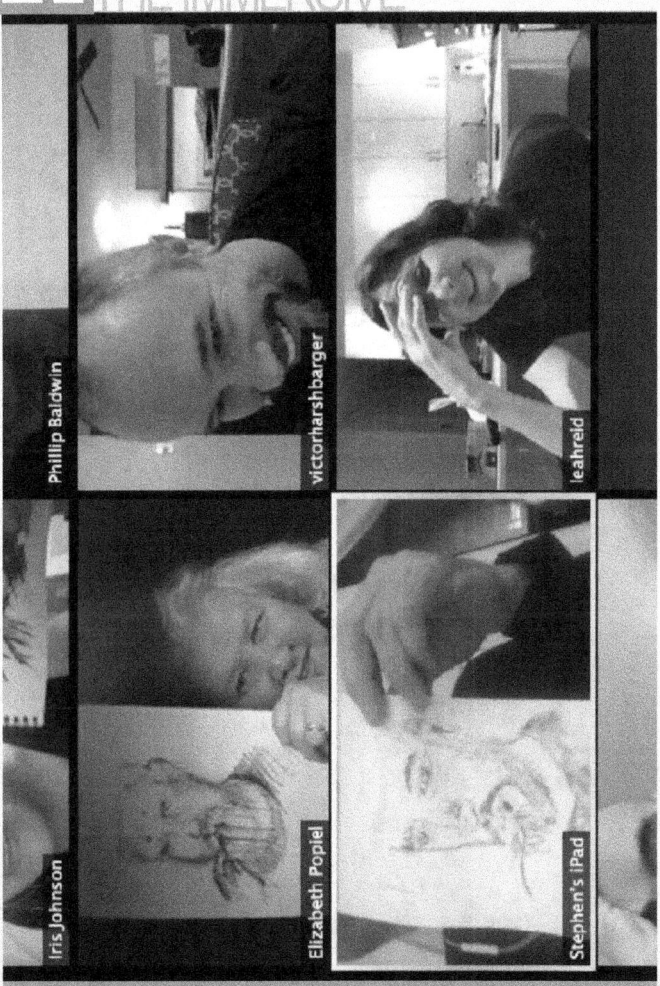

Phillip Baldwin

victorharshbarger

leahreid

Iris Johnson

Elizabeth Popiel

Stephen's iPad

DRAWERS AND CRAWLERS PLAGUE BOOK
PHILLIPBALDWIN@GMAIL.COM

CHELSEA CRAWL CREW

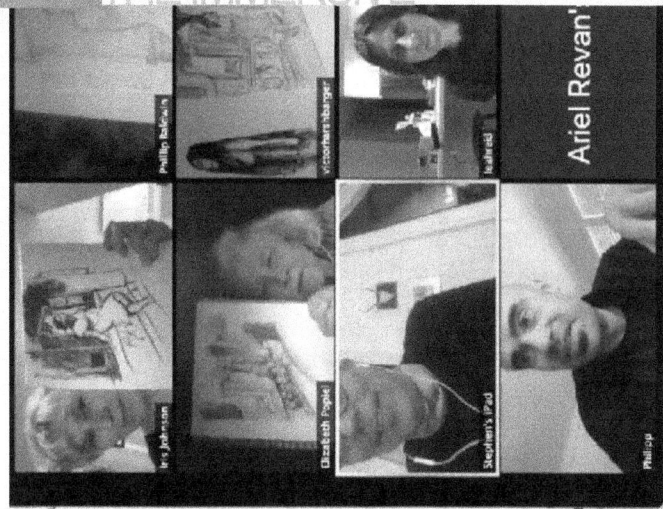

Ariel Revan

Phillip Baldwin

Iris Johnson

Elizabeth Popel

Stephen's iPad

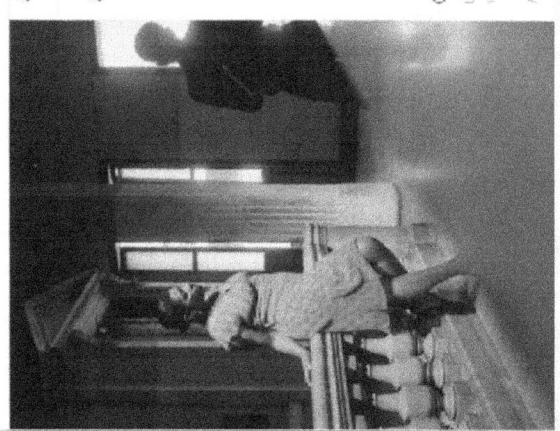

DRAWERS AND CRAWLERS PLAGUE BOOK

PHILLIP.BALDWIN@GMAIL.COM

CHELSEA CRAWL CREW

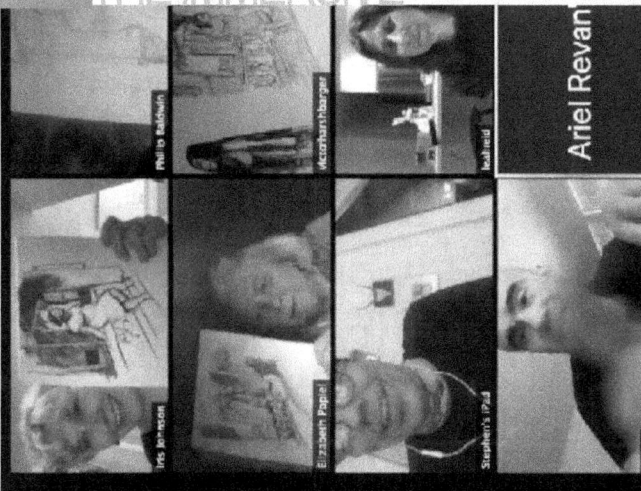

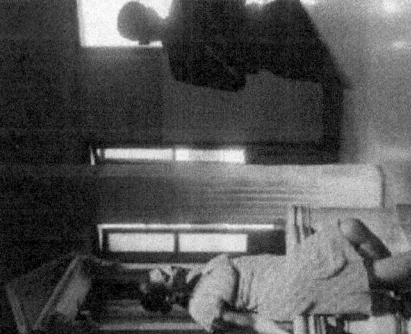

DRAWERS AND CRAWLERS PLAGUE BOOK

PHILLIPBALDWIN@GMAIL.COM

CHELSEA CRAWL CREW

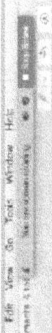

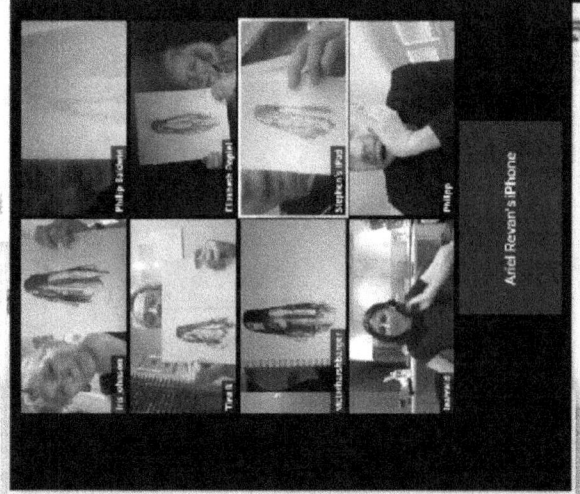

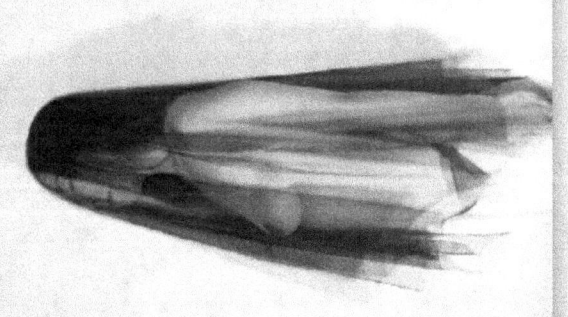

ELF THE IMMERSIVE

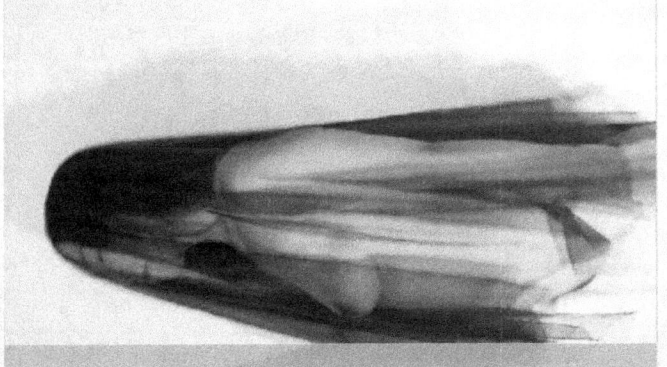

DRAWERS AND CRAWLERS PLAGUE BOOK
PHILLIP.BALDWIN@GMAIL.COM

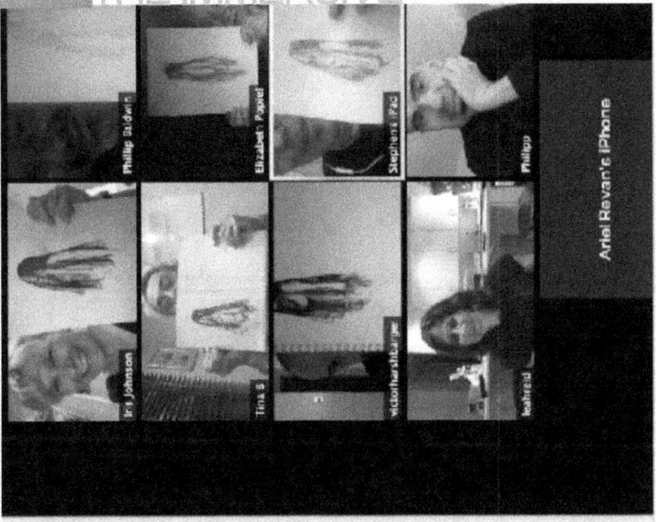

CHELSEA CRAWL CREW

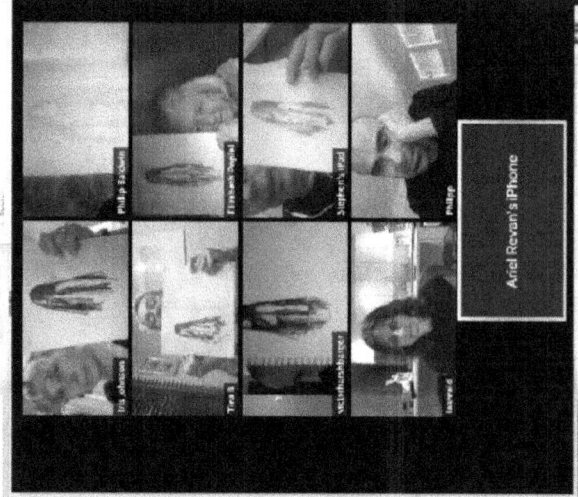

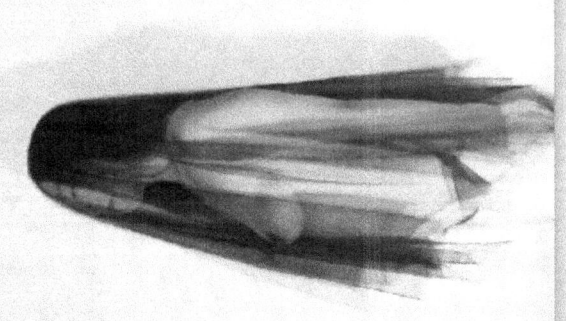

DRAWERS AND CRAWLERS PLAGUE BOOK
PHILLIPBALDWIN@GMAIL.COM CHELSEA CRAWL CREW

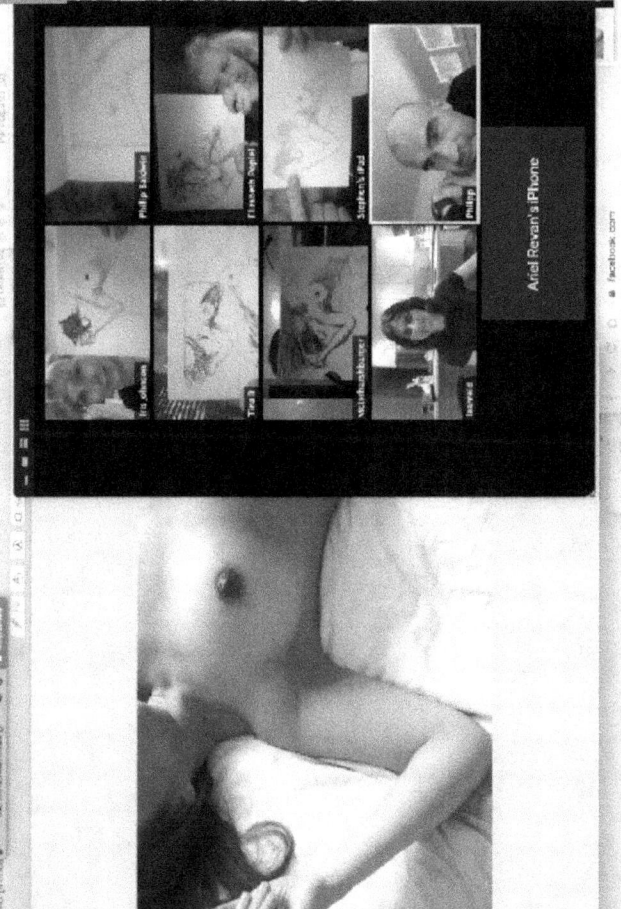

DRAWERS AND CRAWLERS PLAGUE BOOK
PHILLIPBALDWIN@GMAIL.COM

CHELSEA CRAWL CREW

SELF
THE IMMERSIVE

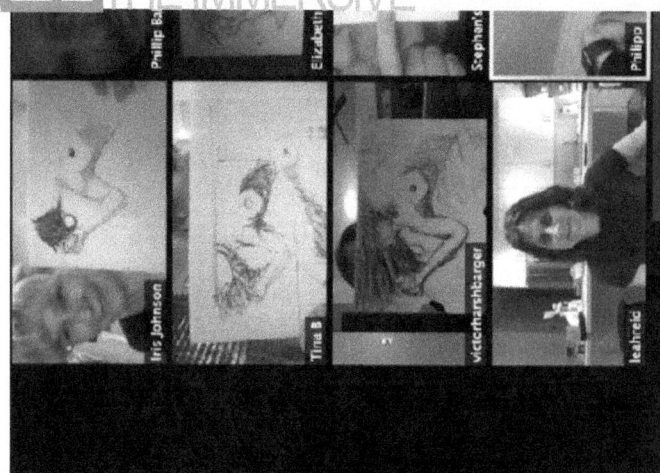

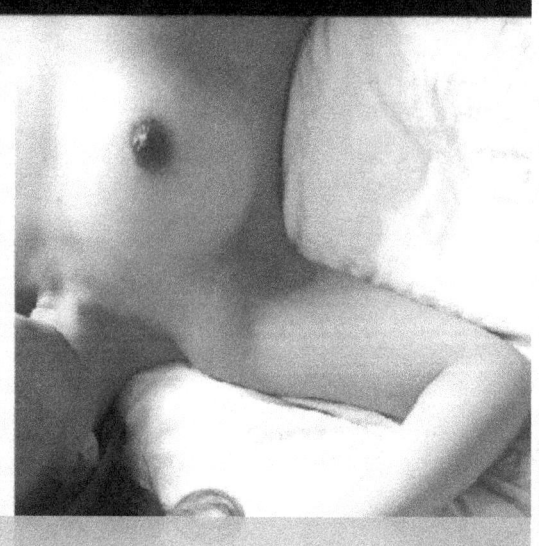

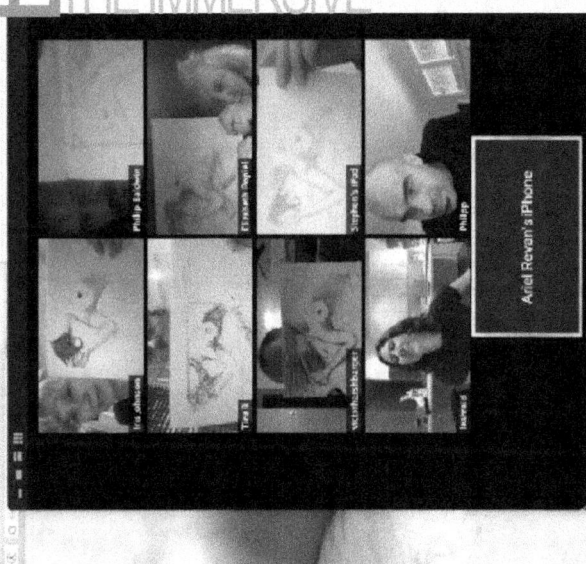

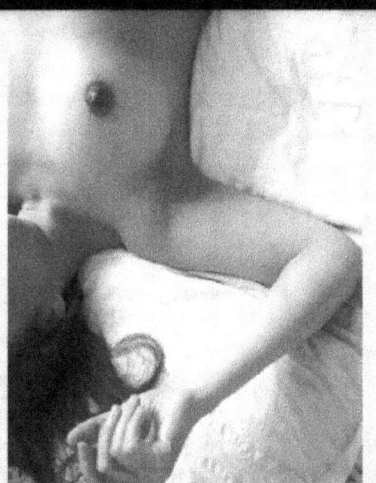

DRAWERS AND CRAWLERS PLAGUE BOOK
PHILLIP.BALDWIN@GMAIL.COM

CHELSEA CRAWL CREW

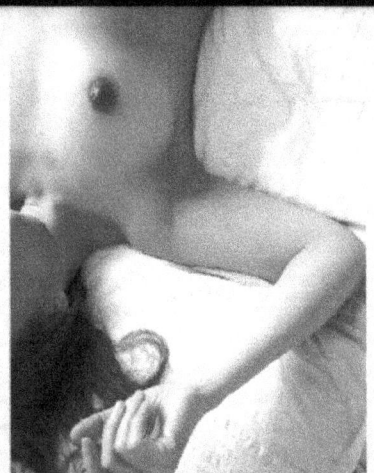

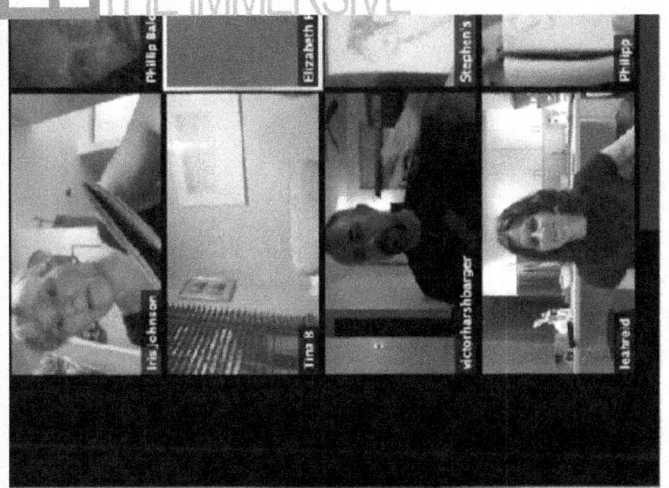

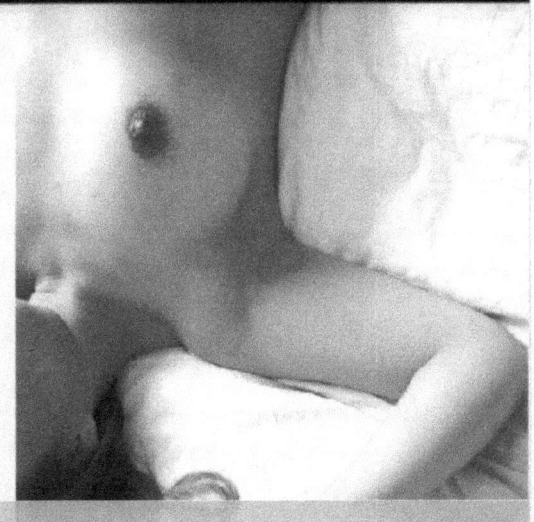

DRAWERS AND CRAWLERS PLAGUE BOOK
PHILLIP.BALDWIN@GMAIL.COM CHELSEA CRAWL CREW

DRAWERS AND CRAWLERS PLAGUE BOOK
PHILLIP.BALDWIN@GMAIL.COM CHELSEA CRAWL CREW

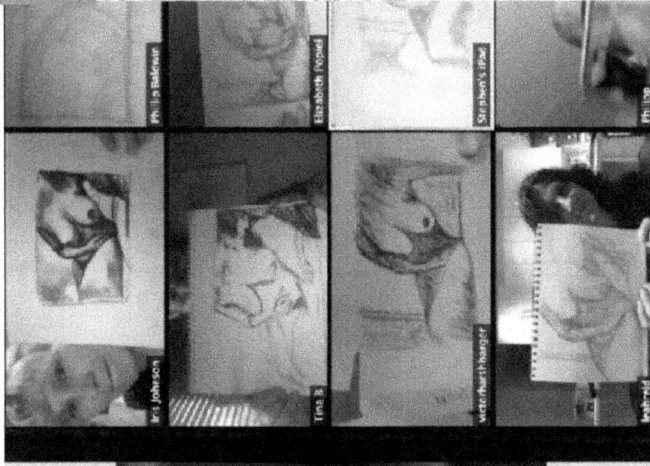

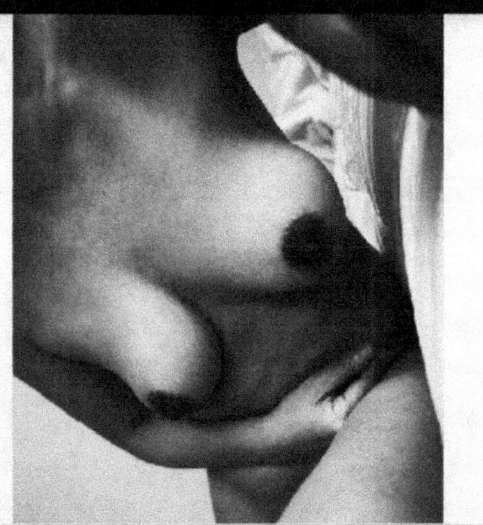

DRAWERS AND CRAWLERS PLAGUE BOOK
PHILLIP.BALDWIN@GMAIL.COM

CHELSEA CRAWL CREW

SELF
THE IMMERSIVE

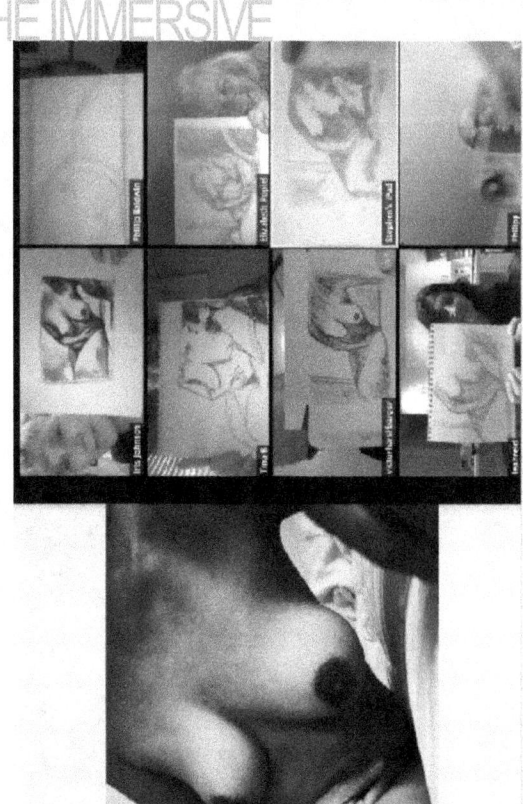

DRAWERS AND CRAWLERS PLAGUE BOOK
PHILLIP.BALDWIN@GMAIL.COM

CHELSEA CRAWL CREW

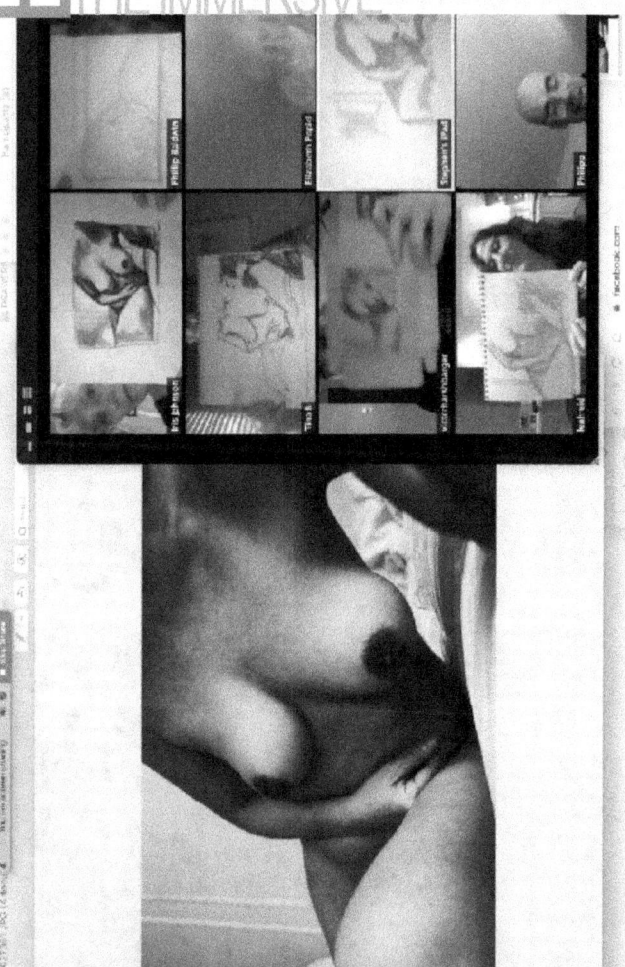

DRAWERS AND CRAWLERS PLAGUE BOOK
PHILLIP.BALDWIN@GMAIL.COM

CHELSEA CRAWL CREW

SELF
THE IMMERSIVE

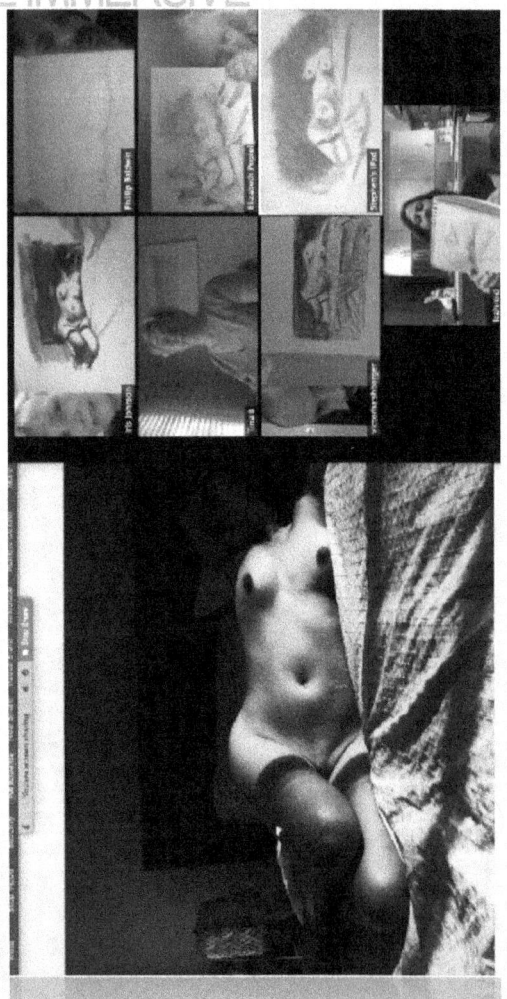

DRAWERS AND CRAWLERS PLAGUE BOOK

PHILLIP.BALDWIN@GMAIL.COM

CHELSEA CRAWL CREW

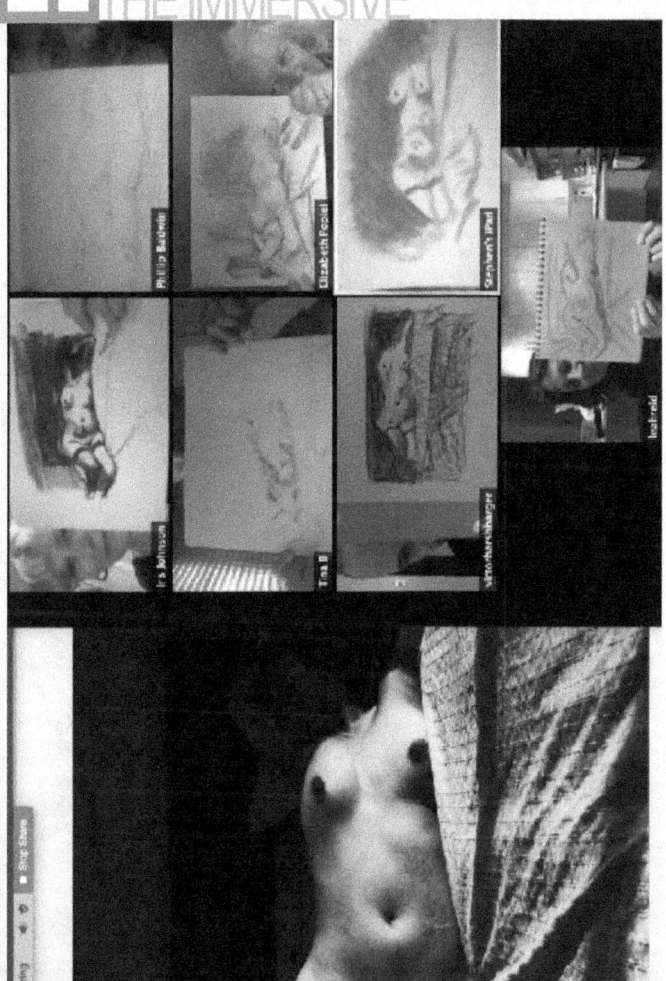

DRAWERS AND CRAWLERS PLAGUE BOOK
PHILLIP.BALDWIN@GMAIL.COM

CHELSEA CRAWL CREW

SELF
THE IMMERSIVE

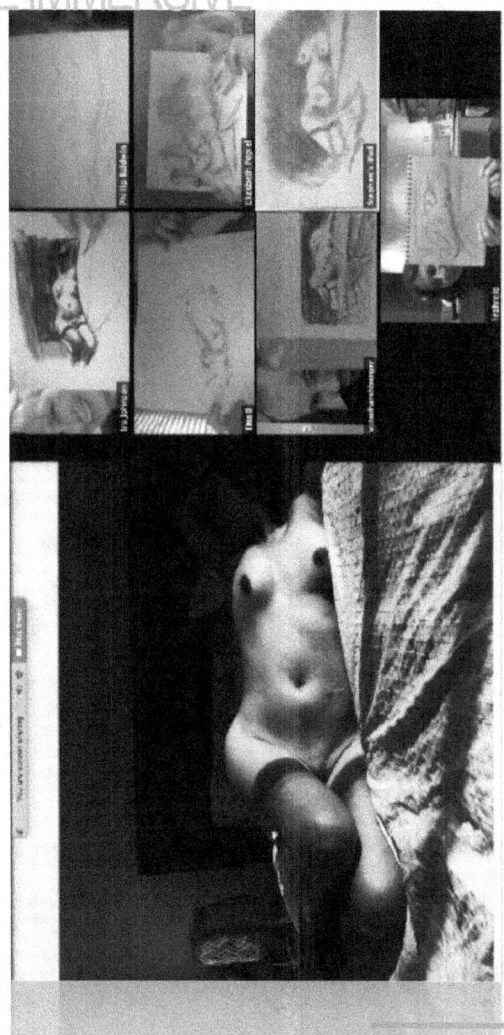

DRAWERS AND CRAWLERS PLAGUE BOOK
PHILLIPBALDWIN@GMAIL.COM

CHELSEA CRAWL CREW

111

DRAWERS AND CRAWLERS PLAGUE BOOK
PHILLIPBALDWIN@GMAIL.COM CHELSEA CRAWL CREW

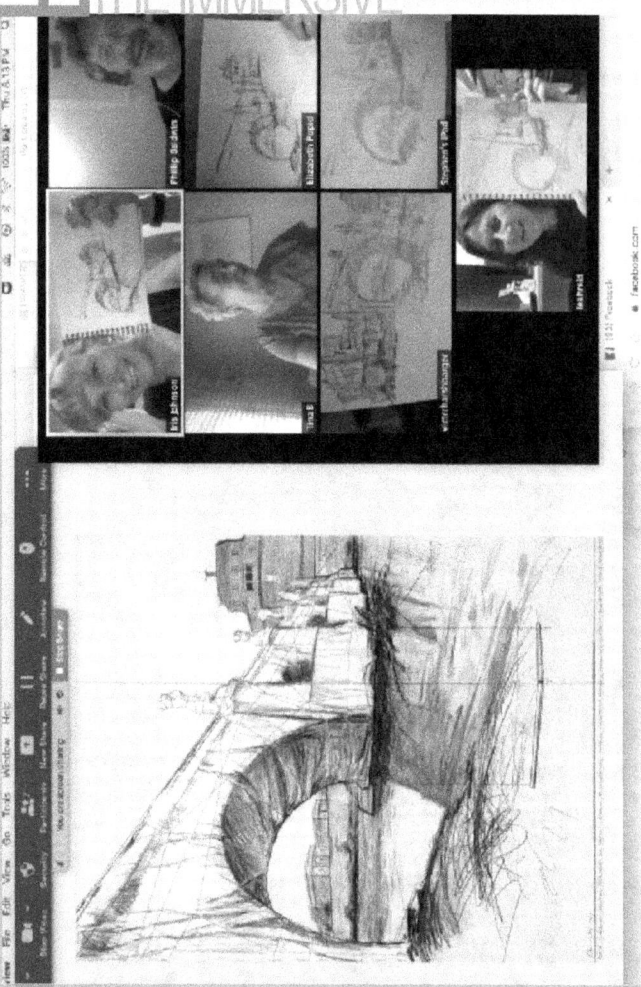

113

SELF
THE IMMERSIVE

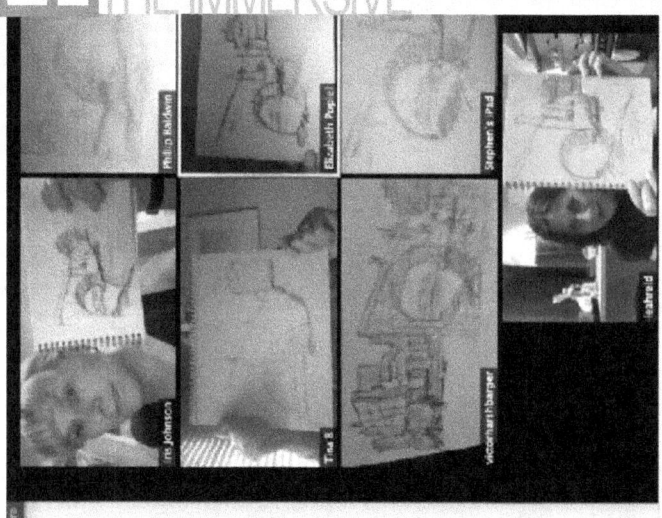

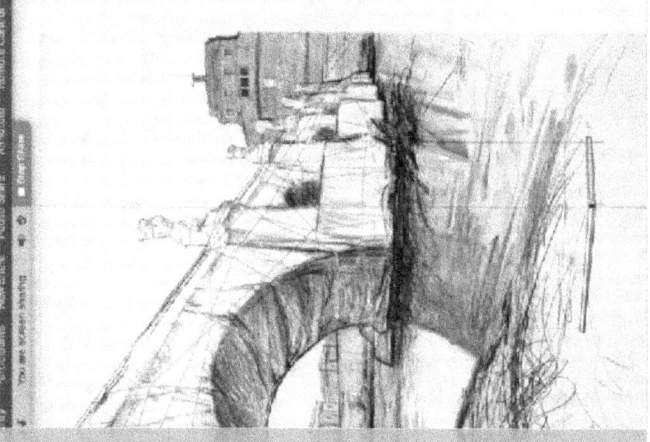

DRAWERS AND CRAWLERS PLAGUE BOOK

PHILLIP.BALDWIN@GMAIL.COM

CHELSEA CRAWL CREW

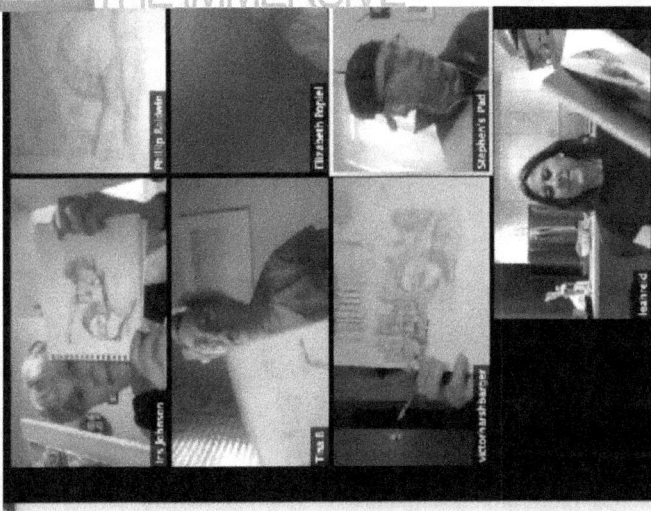

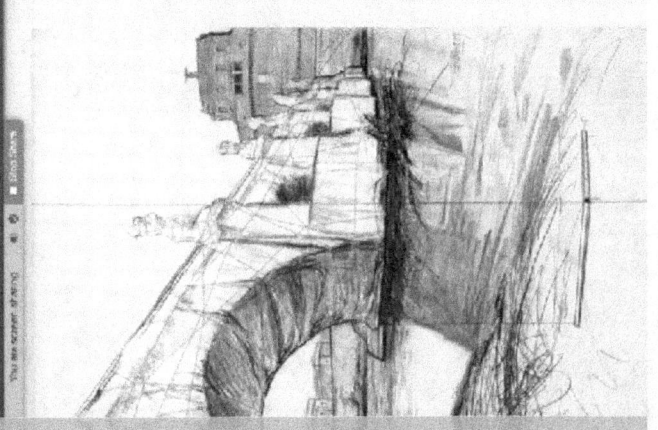

DRAWERS AND CRAWLERS PLAGUE BOOK
PHILLIP.BALDWIN@GMAIL.COM

CHELSEA CRAWL CREW

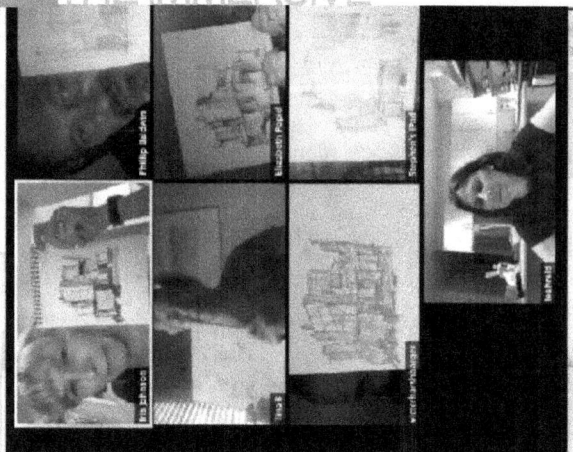

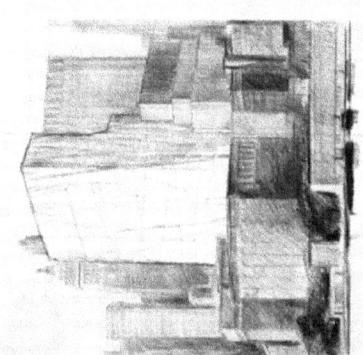

DRAWERS AND CRAWLERS PLAGUE BOOK
PHILLIP.BALDWIN@GMAIL.COM
CHELSEA CRAWL CREW

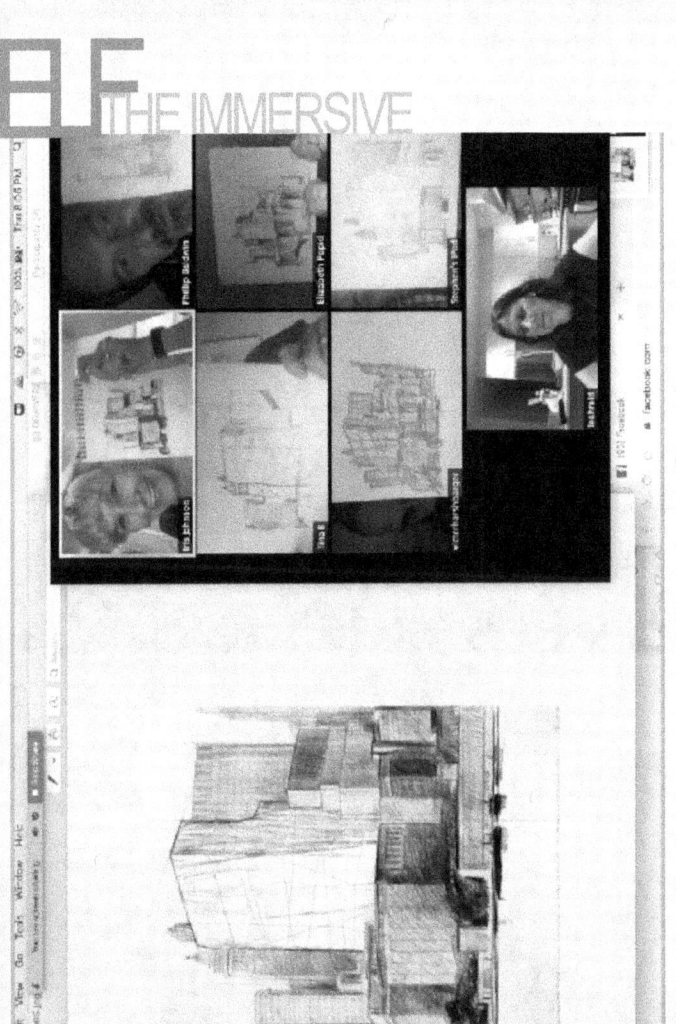

DRAWERS AND CRAWLERS PLAGUE BOOK
PHILLIPBALDWIN@GMAIL.COM

CHELSEA CRAWL CREW

SELF THE IMMERSIVE

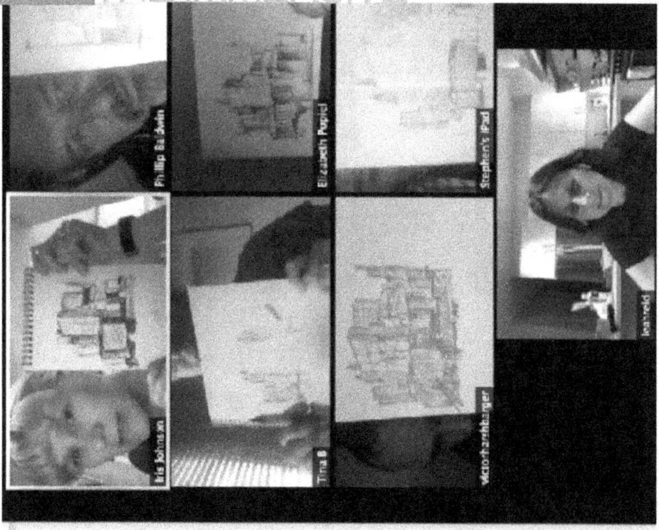

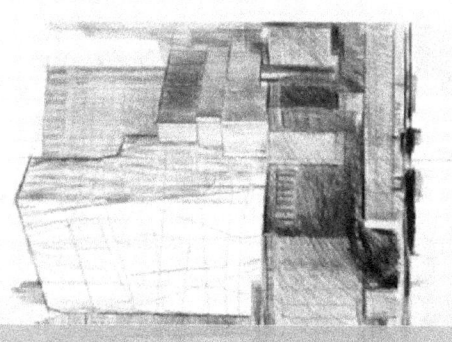

Phillip Baldwin

Elizabeth Puopol

Stephen's iPad

leonold

Iris Johnson

Tina B

victoria-zellinger

CHELSEA CRAWL CREW

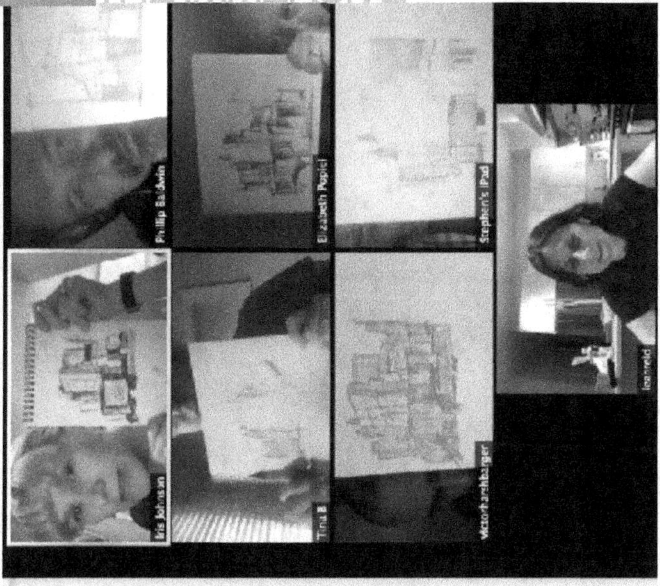

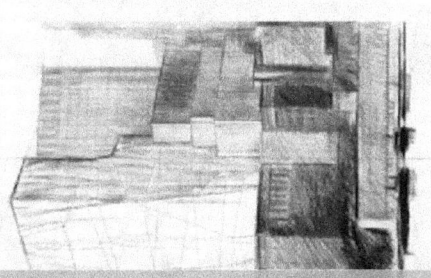

Phillip Baldwin

Elizabeth Pogid

Stephen's iPad

Iris Johnson

Tina

Victor Kirchhinger

Icarvold

DRAWERS AND CRAWLERS PLAGUE BOOK
PHILLIP.BALDWIN@GMAIL.COM

CHELSEA CRAWL CREW

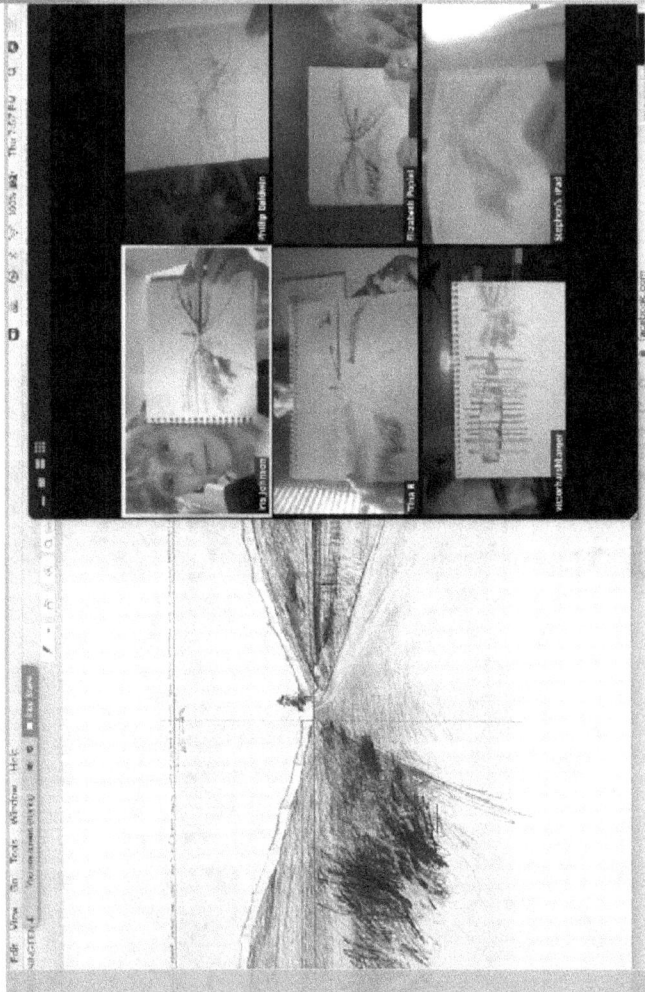

ELF THE IMMERSIVE

Phillip Baldwin

Elizabeth Pool

Stephen's iPad

Iris Johnson

Tina B

victor.hashberger

DRAWERS AND CRAWLERS PLAGUE BOOK
PHILLIP.BALDWIN@GMAIL.COM

CHELSEA CRAWL CREW

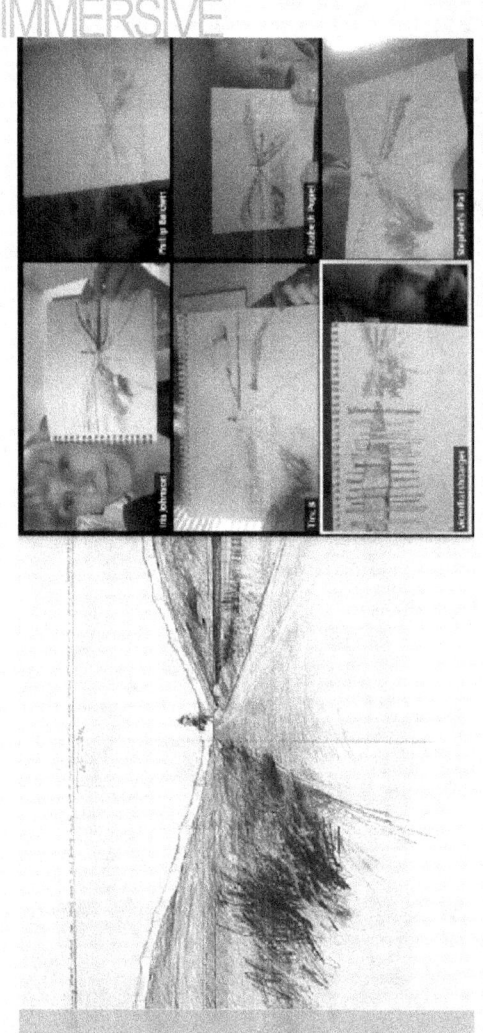

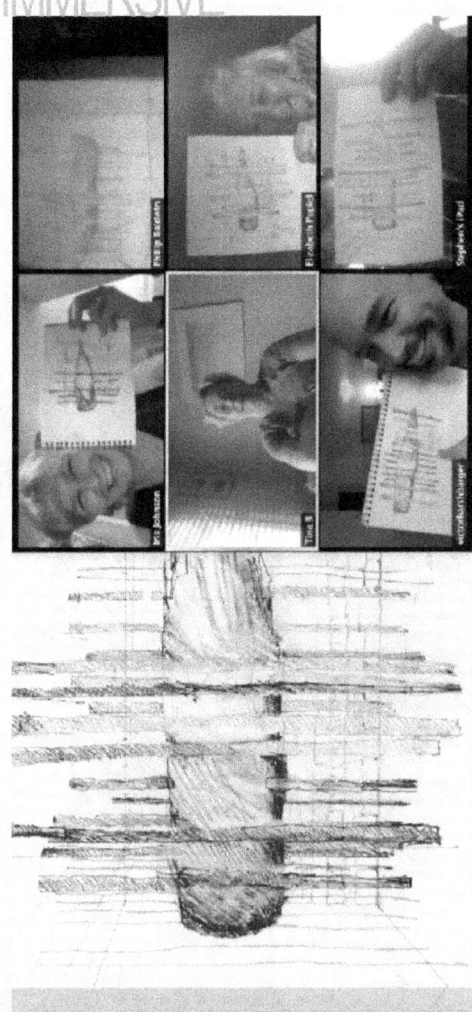

DRAWERS AND CRAWLERS PLAGUE BOOK
PHILLIP.BALDWIN@GMAIL.COM

CHELSEA CRAWL CREW

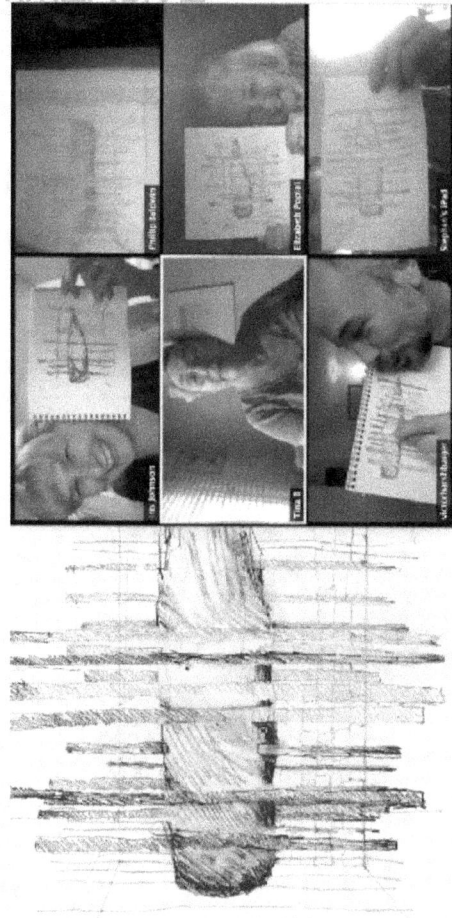

DRAWERS AND CRAWLERS PLAGUE BOOK
PHILLIP.BALDWIN@GMAIL.COM

CHELSEA CRAWL CREW

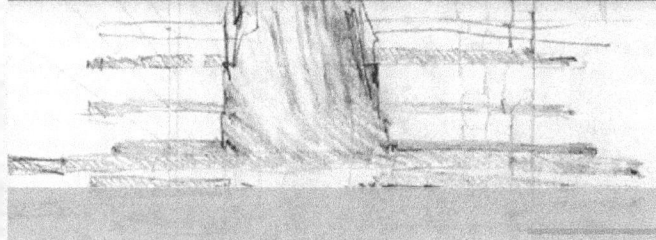

Phillip Baldwin

Elizabeth Peplau

Stephen's iPad

Iris Johnson

Lina B

victor.harshbarger

DRAWERS AND CRAWLERS PLAGUE BOOK
PHILLIP.BALDWIN@GMAIL.COM

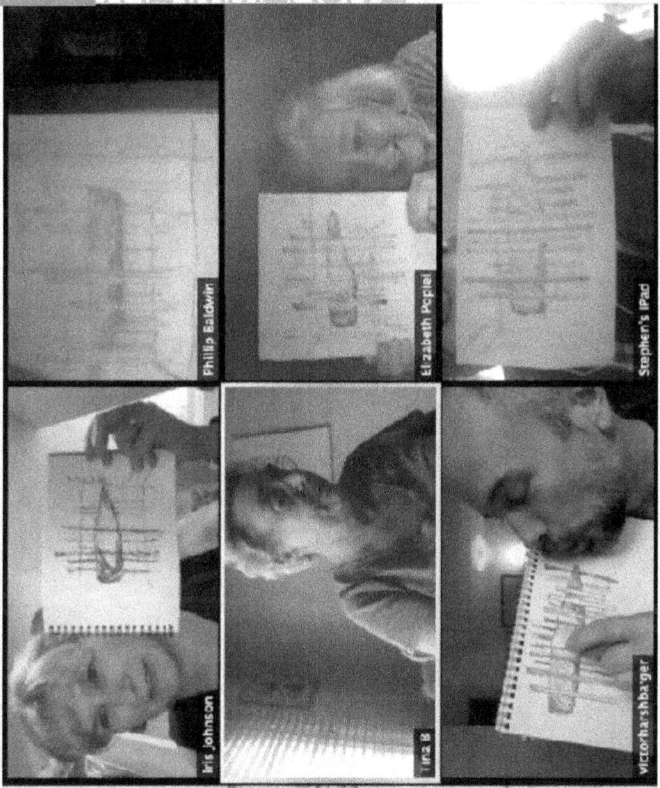

CHELSEA CRAWL CREW

SELF
THE IMMERSIVE

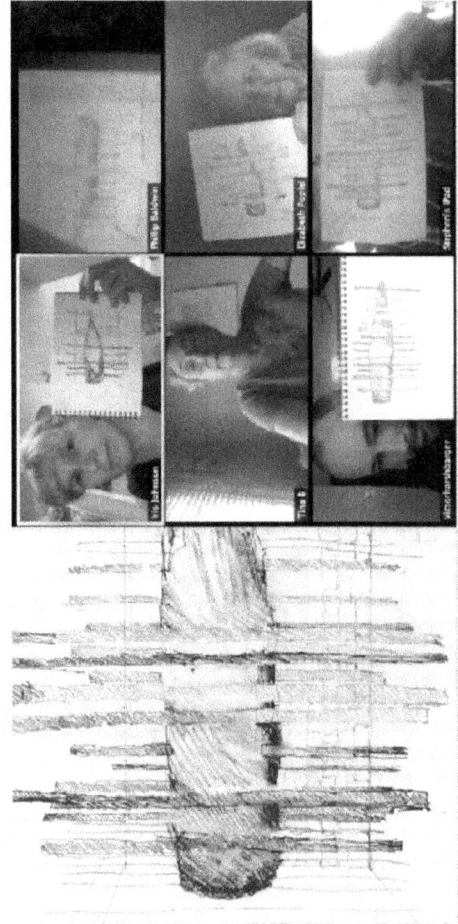

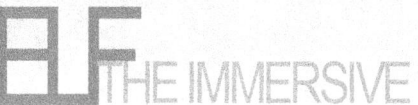

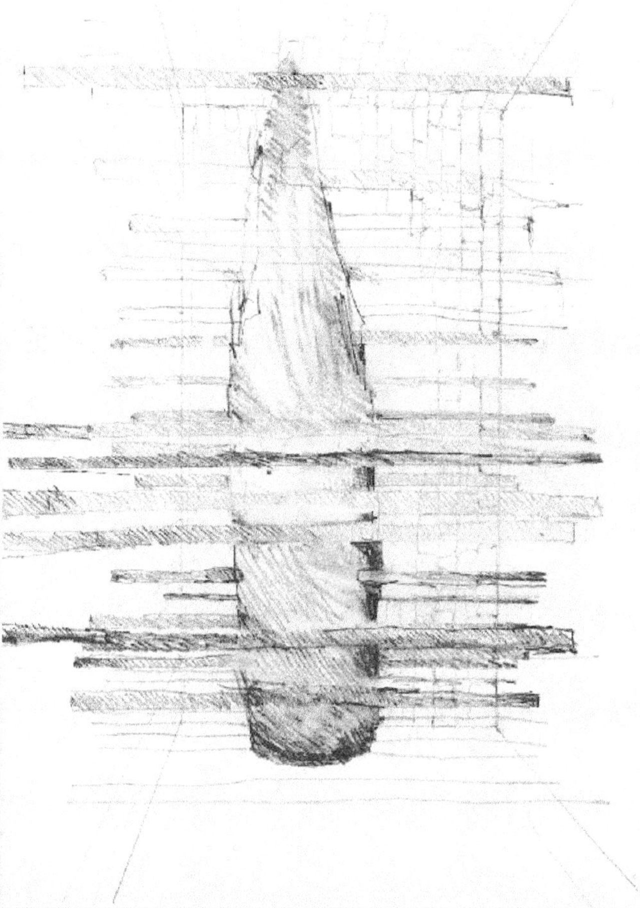

DRAWERS AND CRAWLERS PLAGUE BOOK

PHILLIPBALDWIN@GMAIL.COM

CHELSEA CRAWL CREW

SELF THE IMMERSIVE

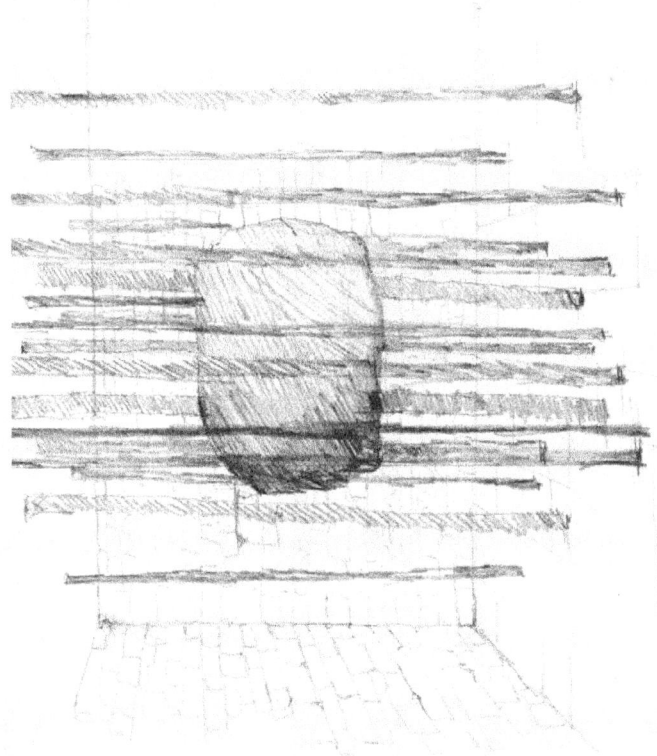

DRAWERS AND CRAWLERS PLAGUE BOOK
PHILLIP.BALDWIN@GMAIL.COM

CHELSEA CRAWL CREW

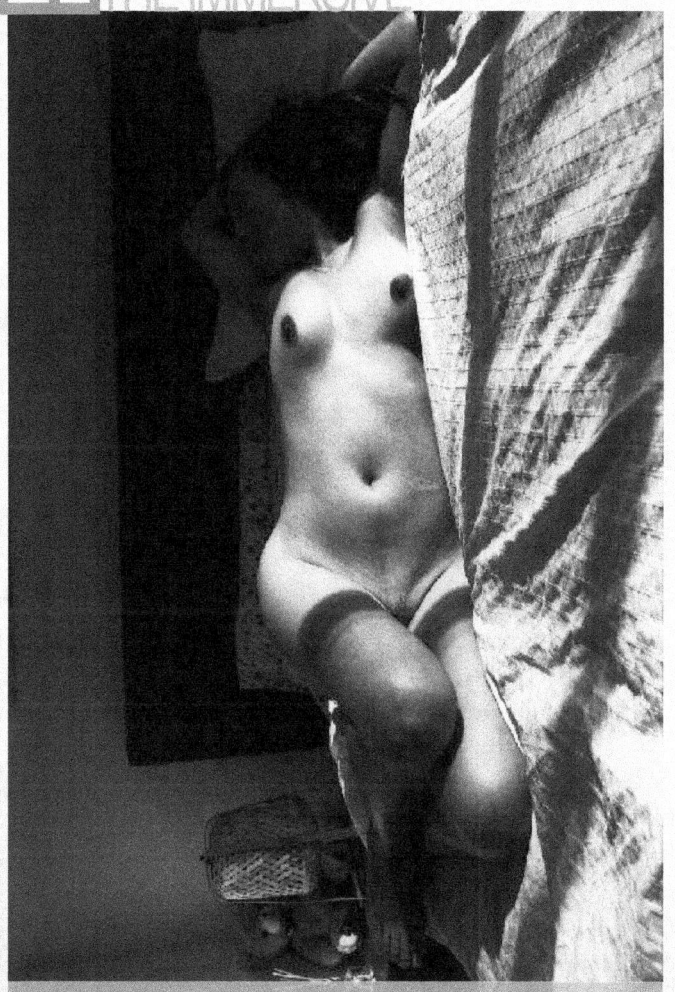

DRAWERS AND CRAWLERS PLAGUE BOOK
PHILLIP.BALDWIN@GMAIL.COM CHELSEA CRAWL CREW

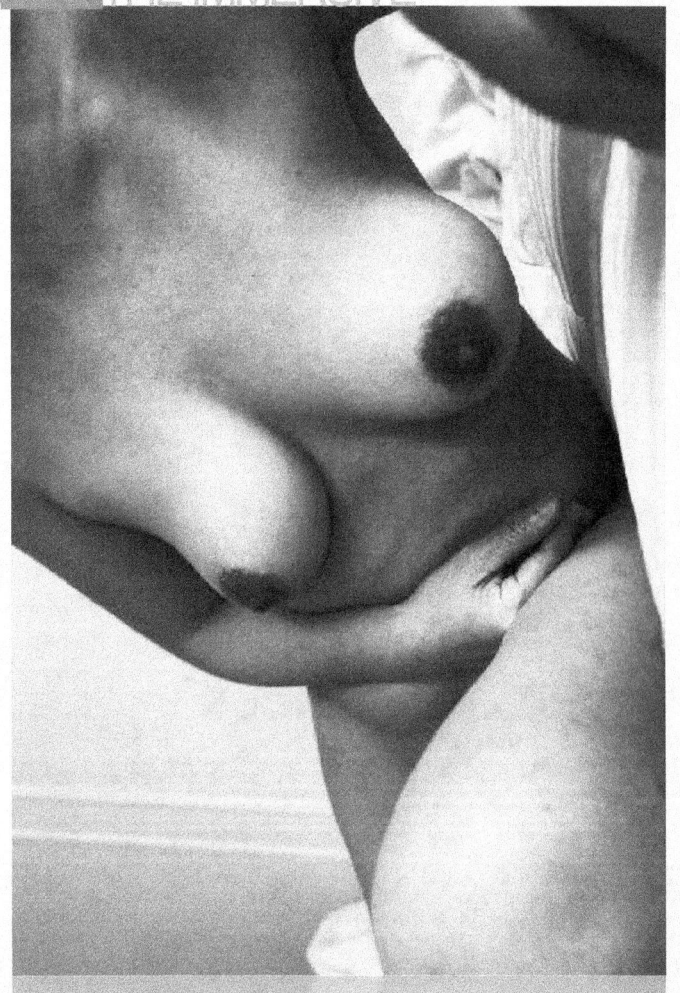

DRAWERS AND CRAWLERS PLAGUE BOOK

PHILLIP.BALDWIN@GMAIL.COM

CHELSEA CRAWL CREW

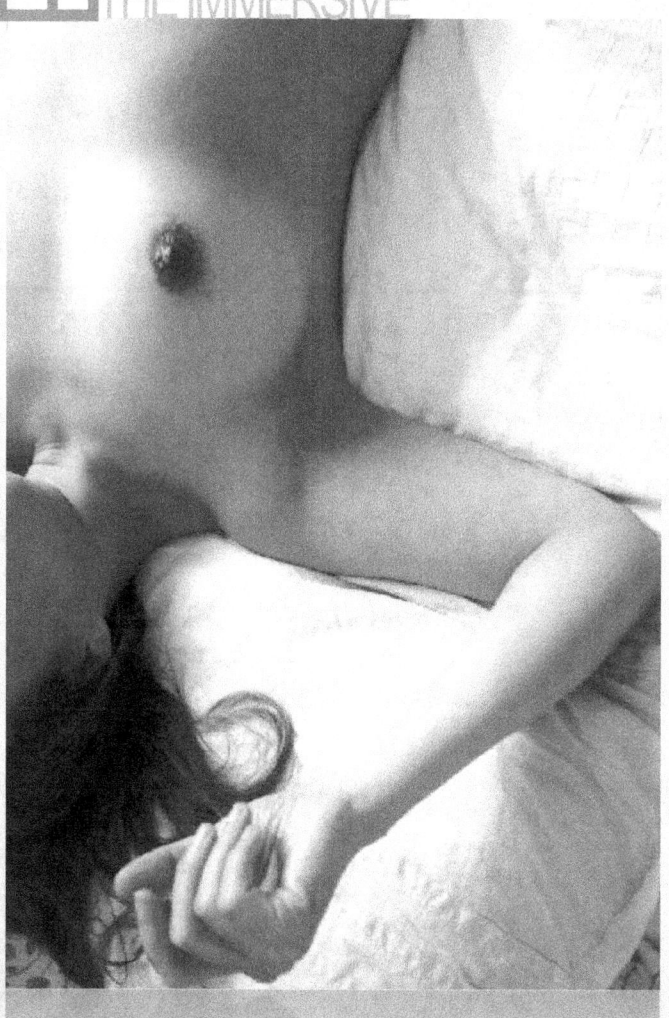

DRAWERS AND CRAWLERS PLAGUE BOOK
PHILLIP.BALDWIN@GMAIL.COM
CHELSEA CRAWL CREW

SELF
THE IMMERSIVE

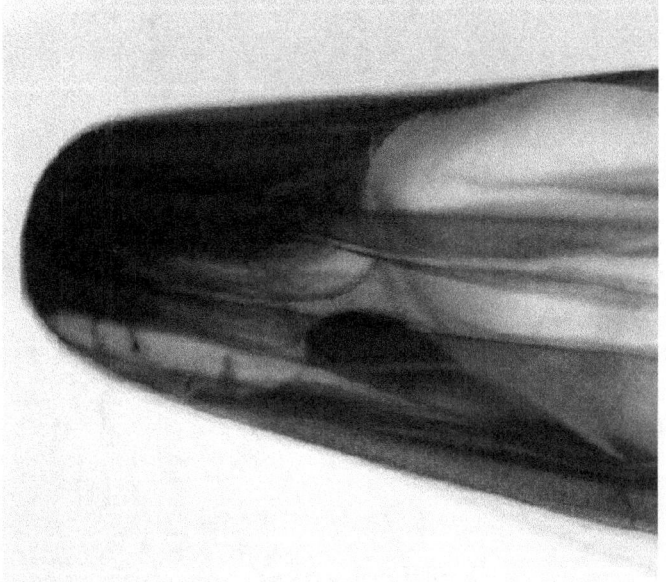

DRAWERS AND CRAWLERS PLAGUE BOOK
PHILLIP.BALDWIN@GMAIL.COM

CHELSEA CRAWL CREW

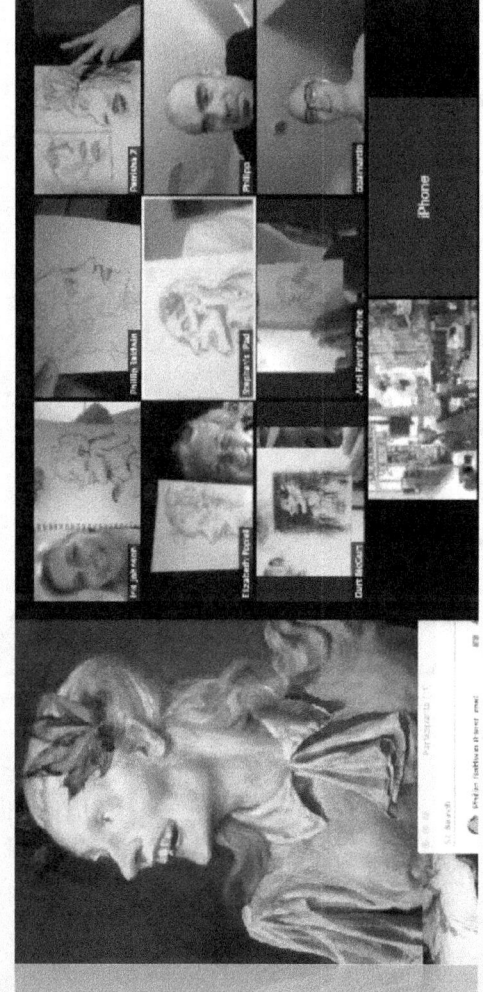

DRAWERS AND CRAWLERS PLAGUE BOOK
PHILLIPBALDWIN@GMAIL.COM

CHELSEA CRAWL CREW

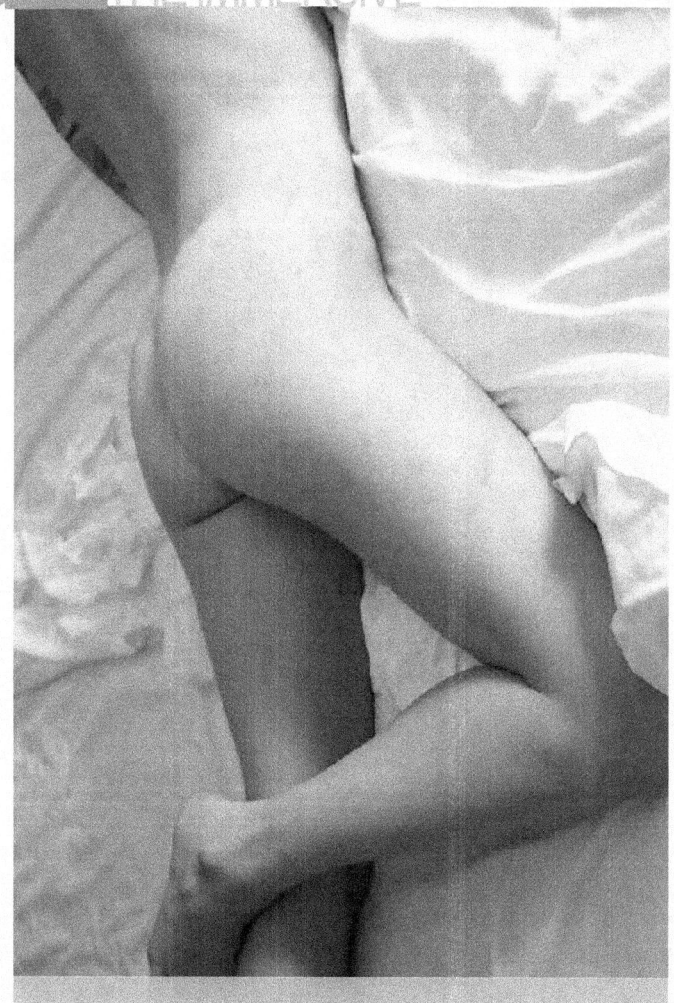

DRAWERS AND CRAWLERS PLAGUE BOOK
PHILLIP.BALDWIN@GMAIL.COM

CHELSEA CRAWL CREW

ELF THE IMMERSIVE

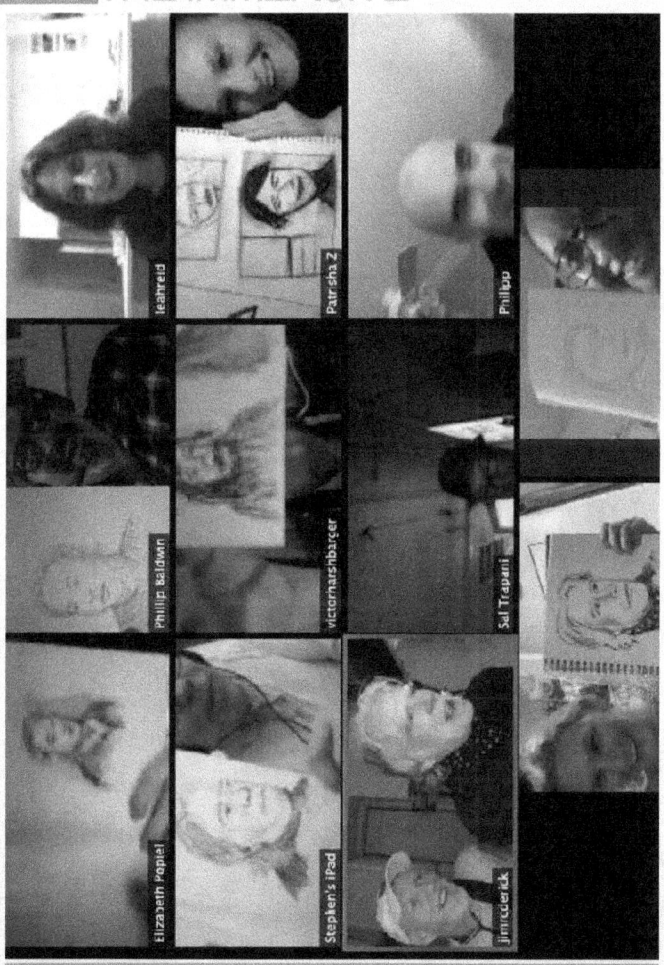

DRAWERS AND CRAWLERS PLAGUE BOOK
PHILIP.BALDWIN@GMAIL.COM

CHELSEA CRAWL CREW

SELF
THE IMMERSIVE

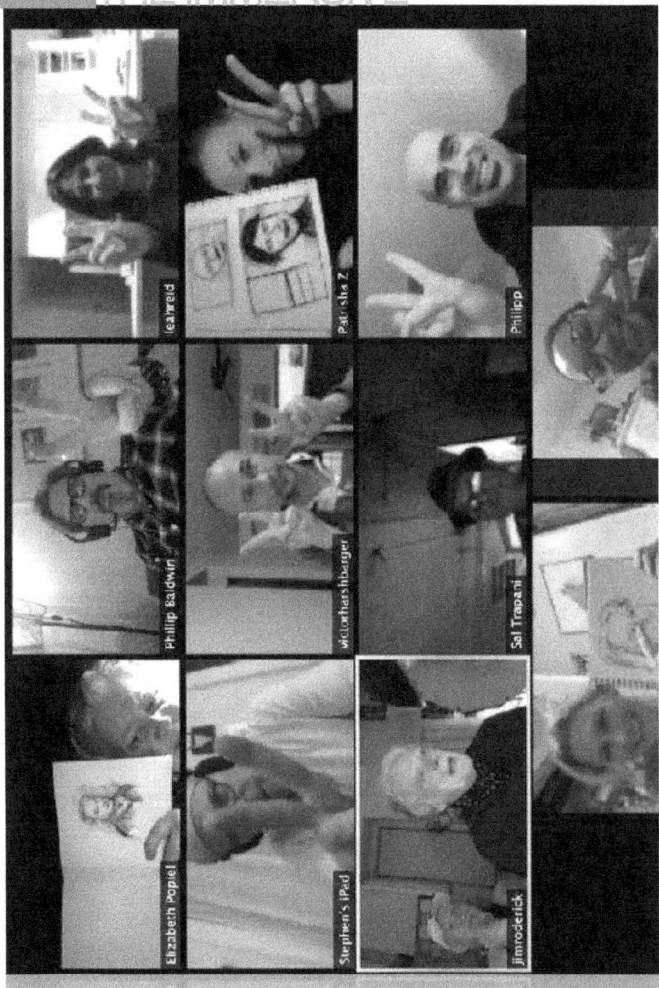

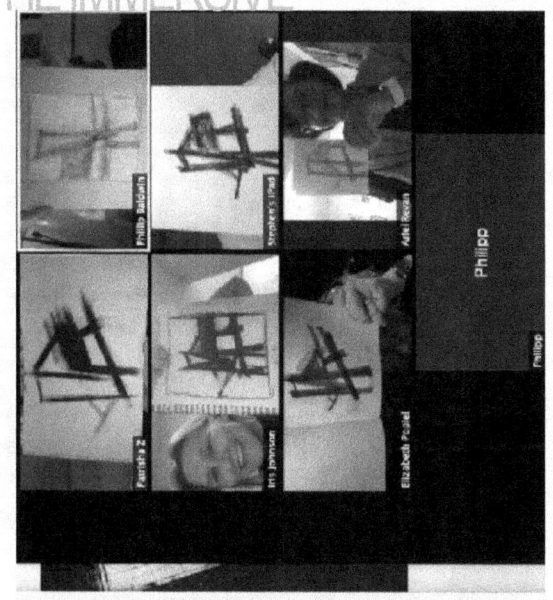

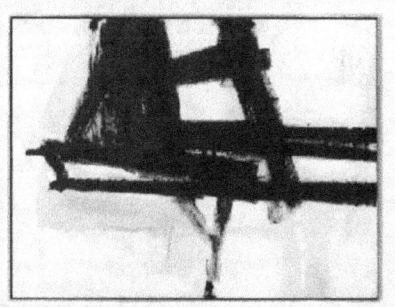

DRAWERS AND CRAWLERS PLAGUE BOOK

PHILLIP.BALDWIN@GMAIL.COM

CHELSEA CRAWL CREW

SELF THE IMMERSIVE

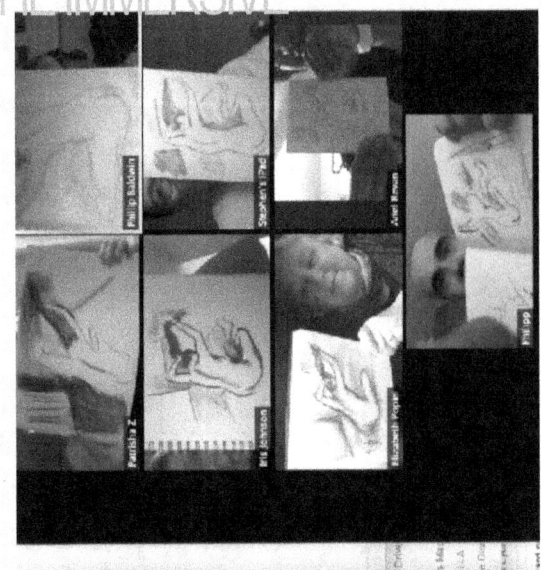

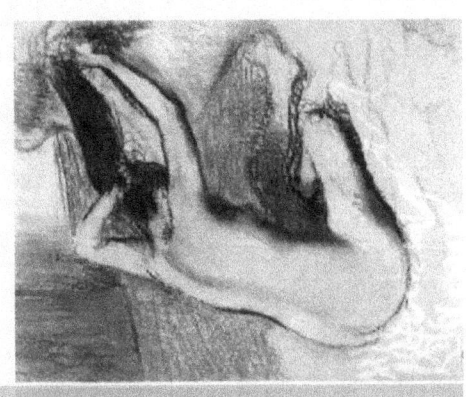

DRAWERS AND CRAWLERS PLAGUE BOOK
PHILLIPBALDWIN@GMAIL.COM

CHELSEA CRAWL CREW

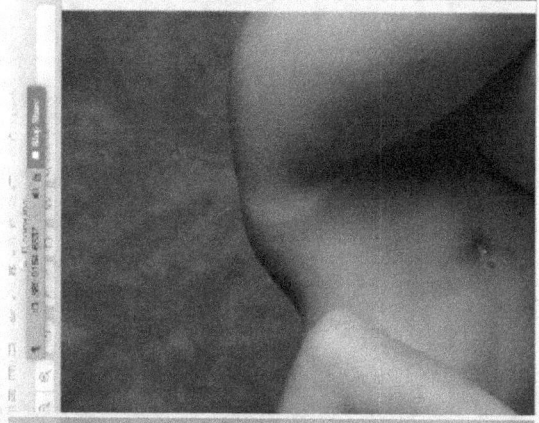

CHELSEA CRAWL CREW

SELF THE IMMERSIVE

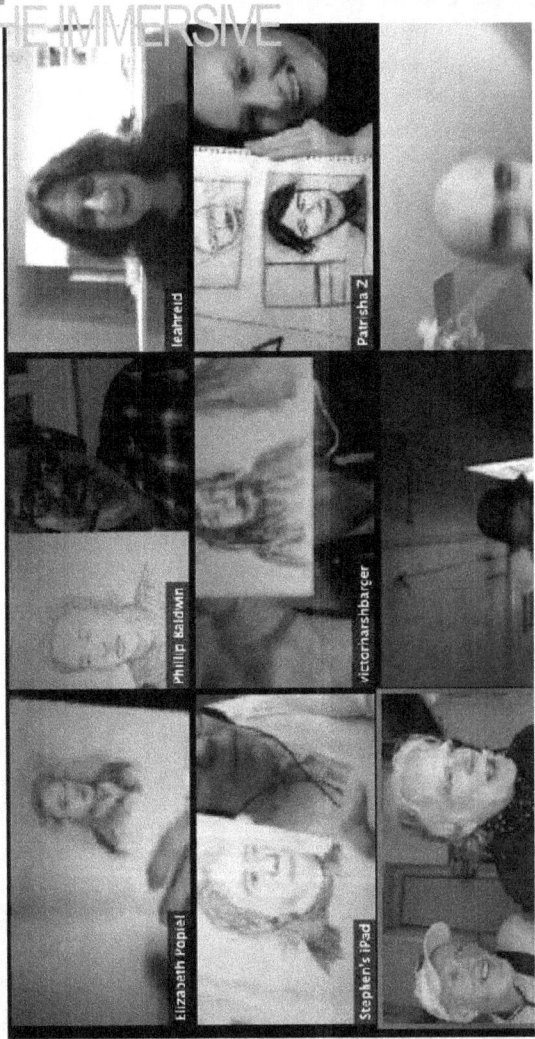

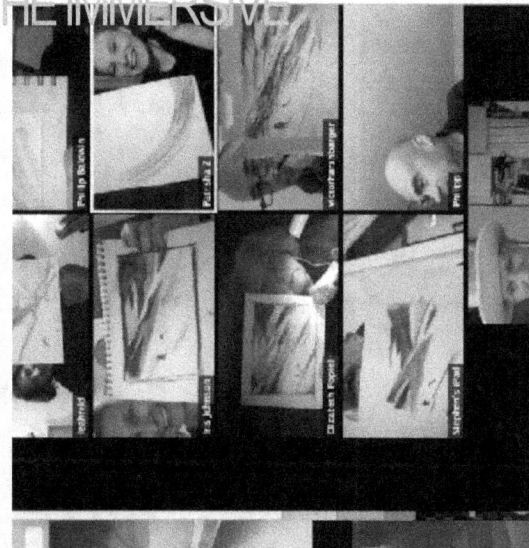

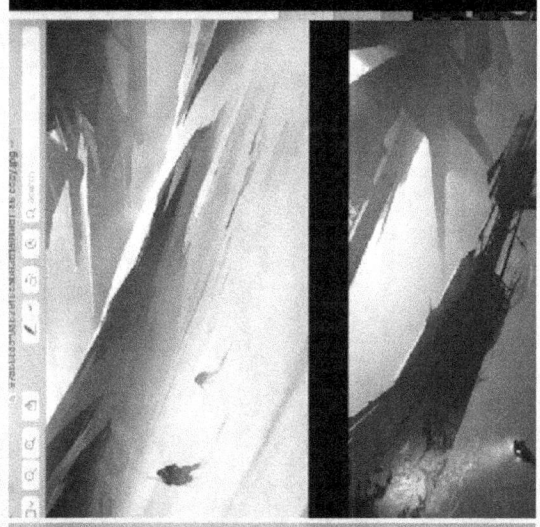

DRAWERS AND CRAWLERS PLAGUE BOOK
PHILLIPBALDWIN@GMAIL.COM
CHELSEA CRAWL CREW

SELF
THE IMMERSIVE

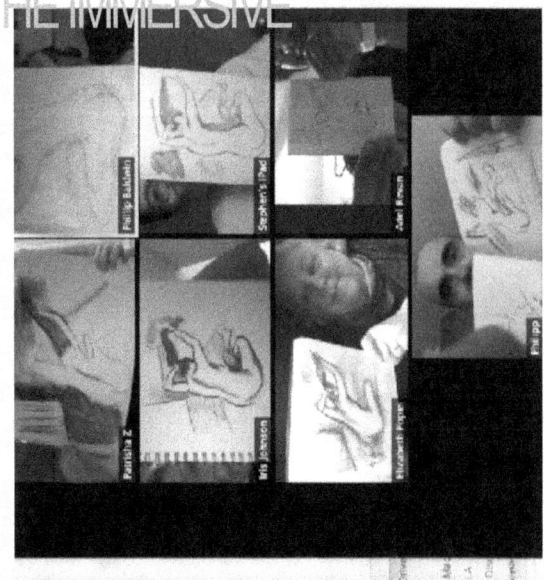

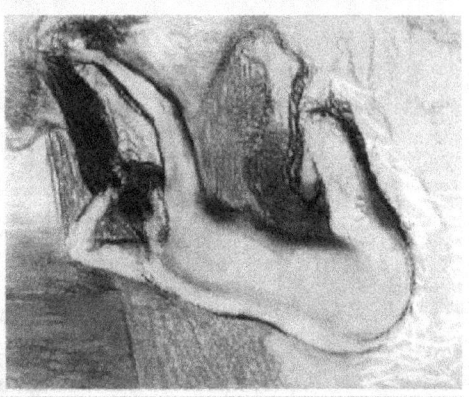

DRAWERS AND CRAWLERS PLAGUE BOOK
PHILLIP.BALDWIN@GMAIL.COM

CHELSEA CRAWL CREW

DRAWERS AND CRAWLERS PLAGUE BOOK
PHILLIPBALDWIN@GMAIL.COM

CHELSEA CRAWL CREW

SELF
THE IMMERSIVE

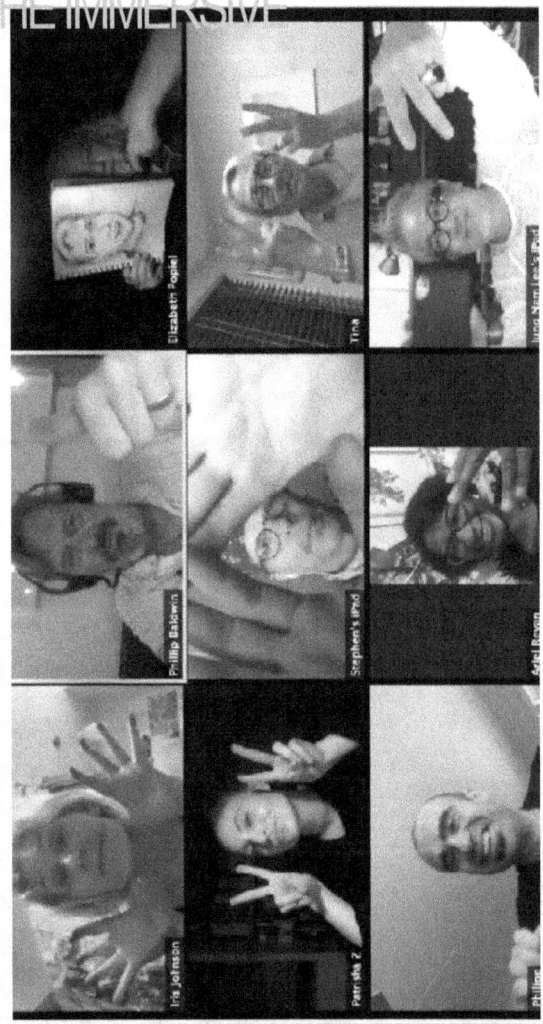

CHELSEA CRAWL CREW

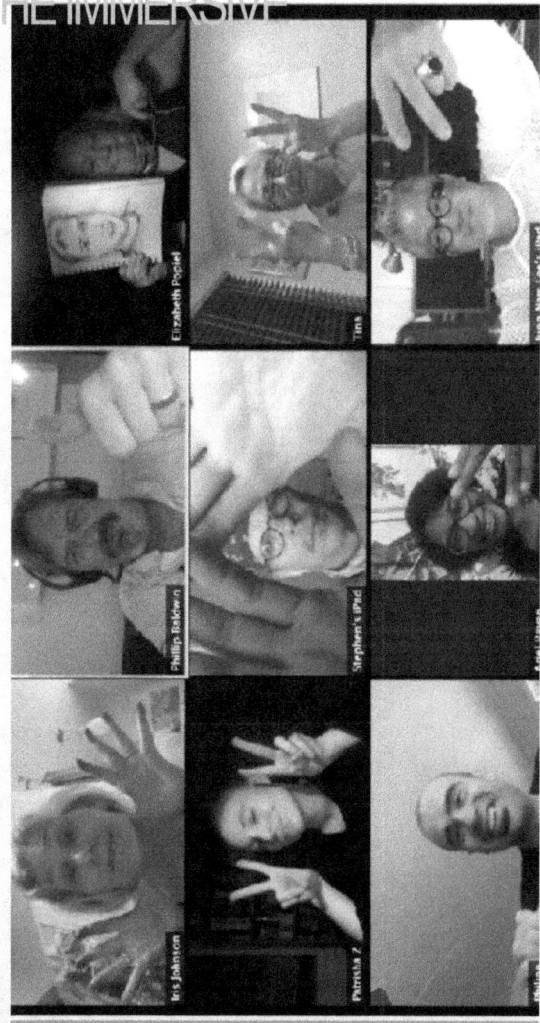

DRAWERS AND CRAWLERS PLAGUE BOOK
PHILLIPBALDWIN@GMAIL.COM

CHELSEA CRAWL CREW

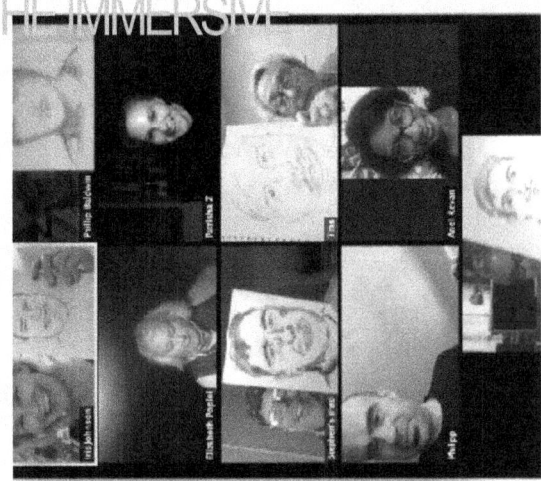

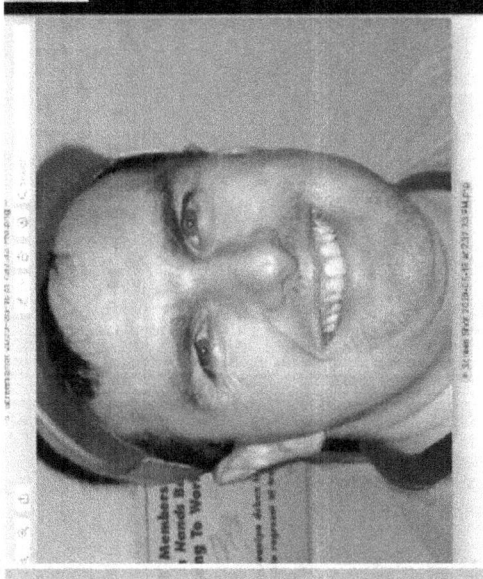

DRAWERS AND CRAWLERS PLAGUE BOOK
PHILLIP.BALDWIN@GMAIL.COM

CHELSEA CRAWL CREW

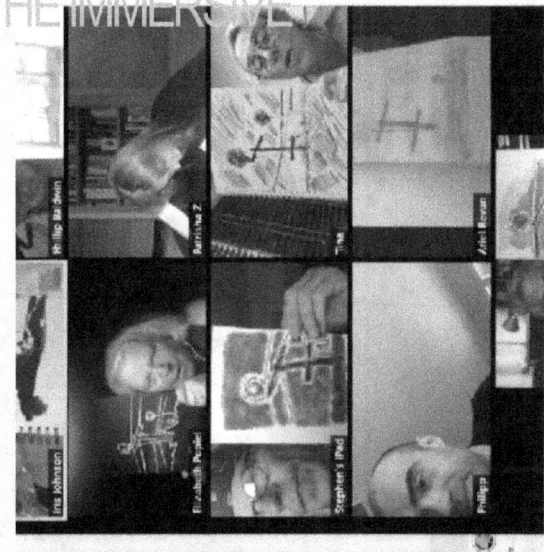

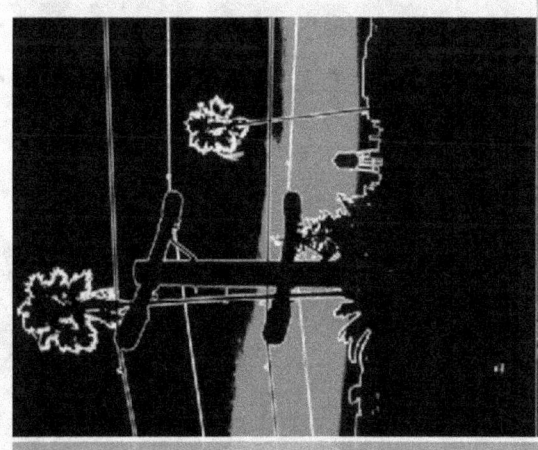

DRAWERS AND CRAWLERS PLAGUE BOOK
PHILLIP.BALDWIN@GMAIL.COM CHELSEA CRAWL CREW

SELF THE IMMERSIVE

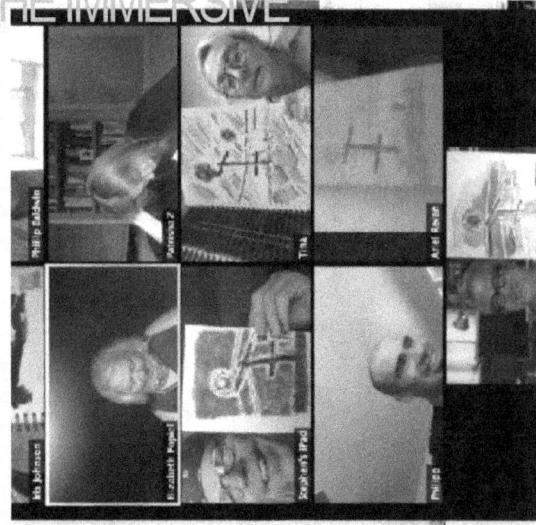

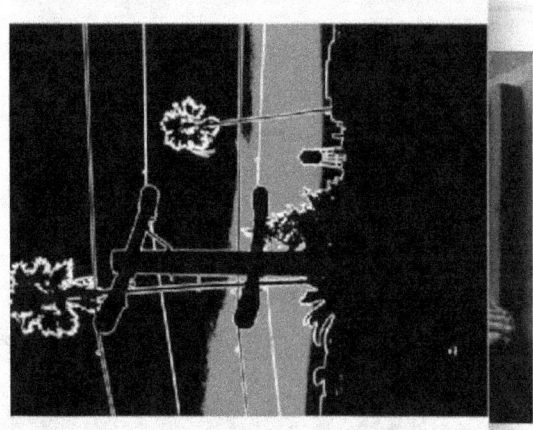

PHILLIP.BALDWIN@GMAIL.COM

CHELSEA CRAWL CREW

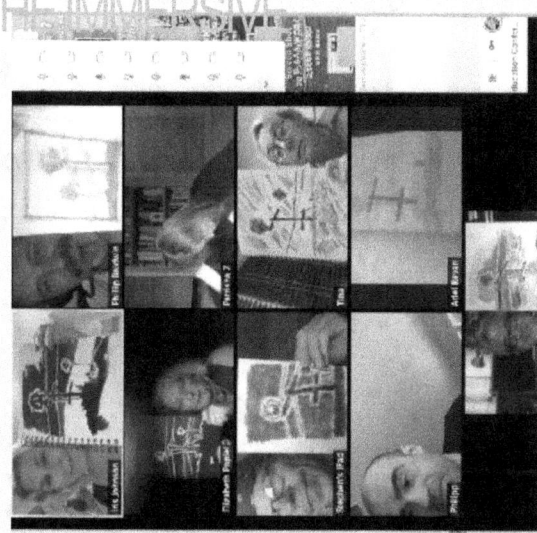

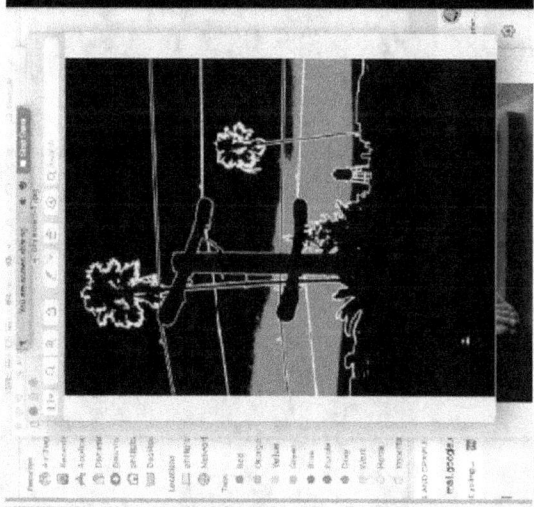

DRAWERS AND CRAWLERS PLAGUE BOOK

CHELSEA CRAWL CREW

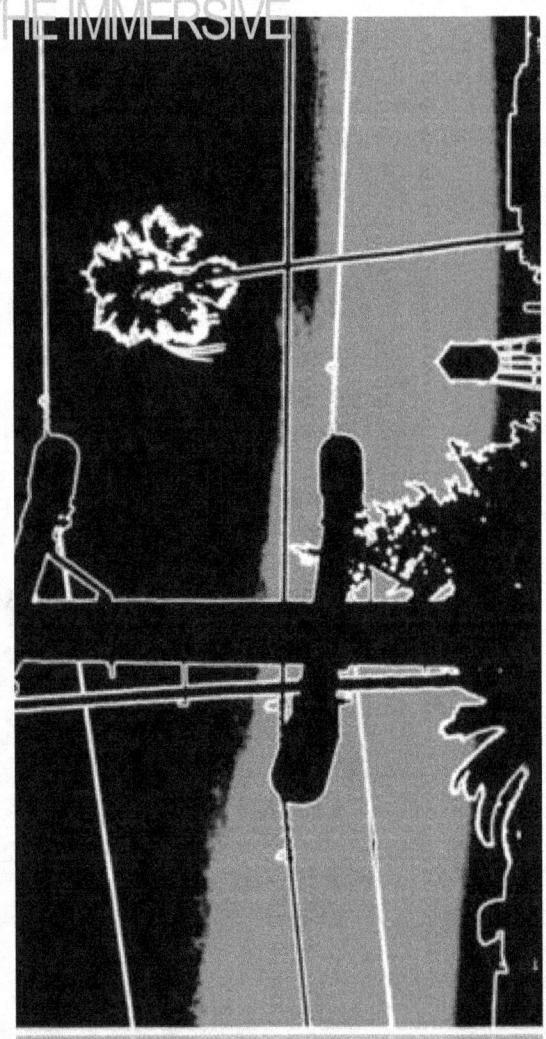

CHELSEA CRAWL CREW

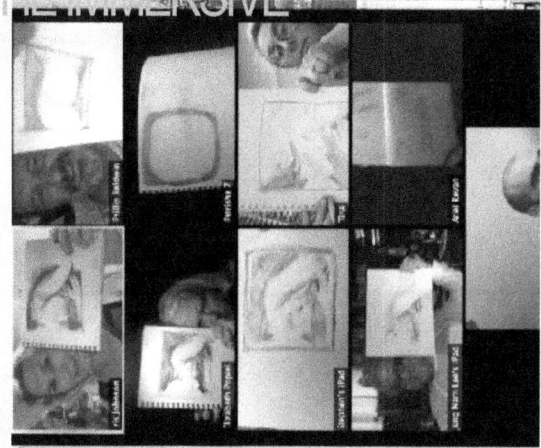

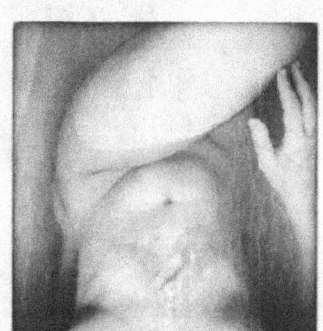

DRAWERS AND CRAWLERS PLAGUE BOOK

CHELSEA CRAWL CREW

SELF
THE IMMERSIVE

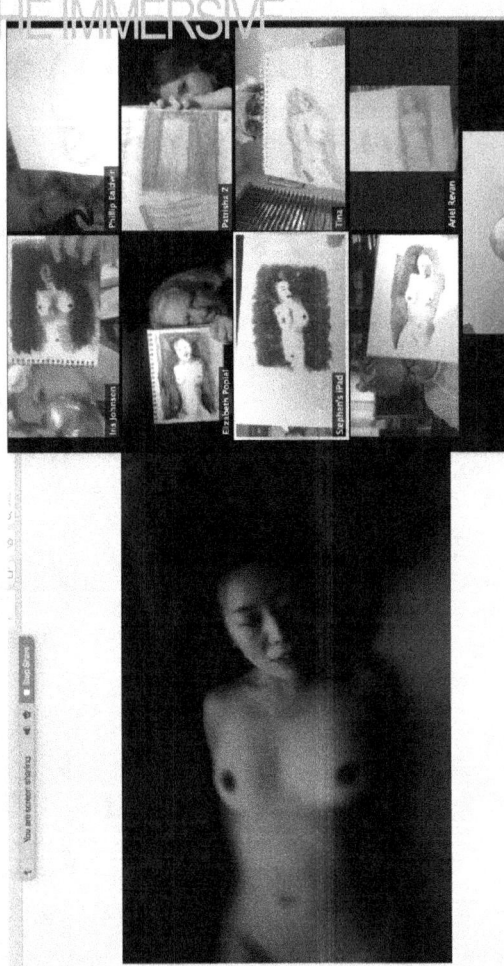

DRAWERS AND CRAWLERS PLAGUE BOOK
PHILLIP.BALDWIN@GMAIL.COM

CHELSEA CRAWL CREW

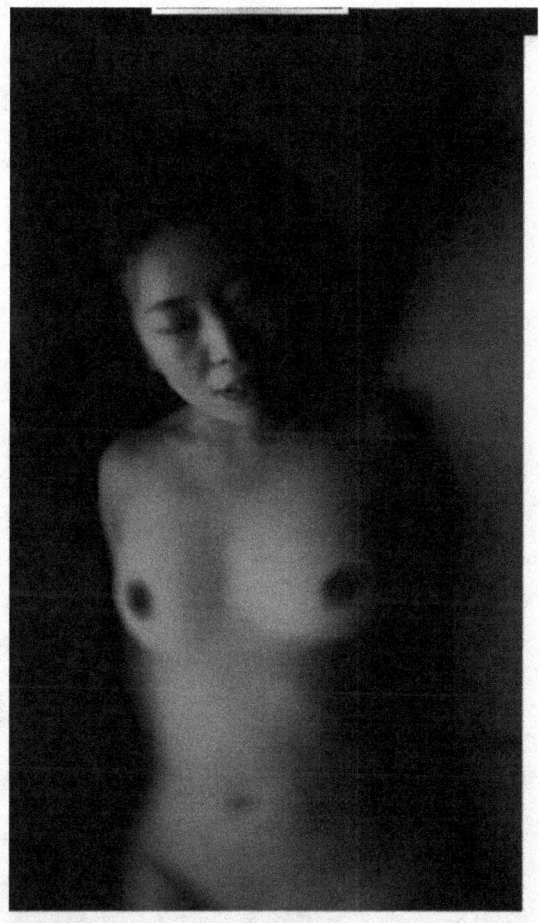

DRAWERS AND CRAWLERS PLAGUE BOOK
PHILLIP.BALDWIN@GMAIL.COM

CHELSEA CRAWL CREW

SELF THE IMMERSIVE

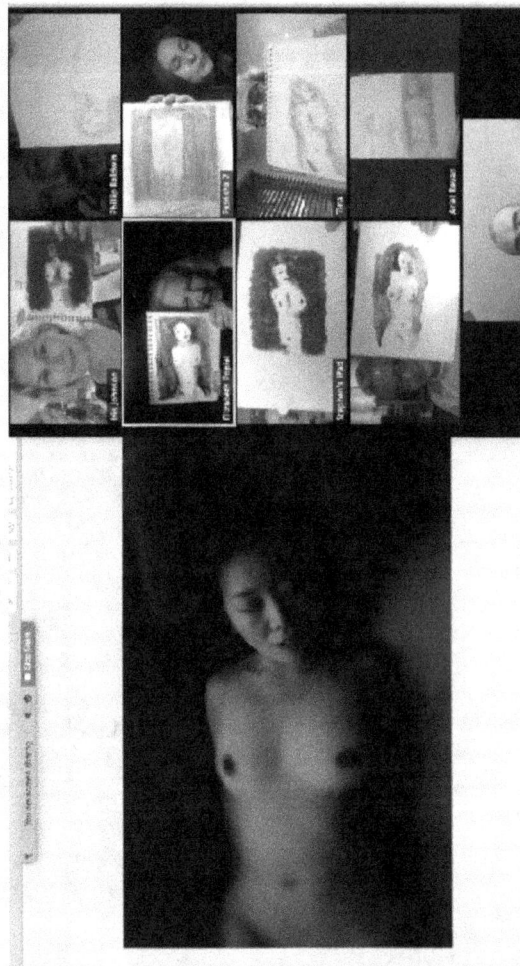

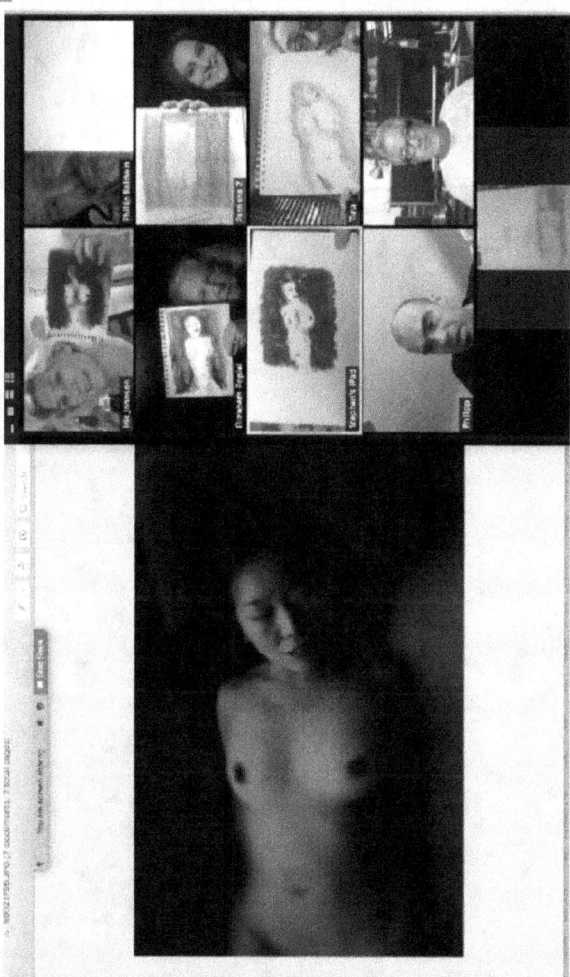

DRAWERS AND CRAWLERS PLAGUE BOOK
PHILLIP.BALDWIN@GMAIL.COM CHELSEA CRAWL CREW

SELF
THE IMMERSIVE

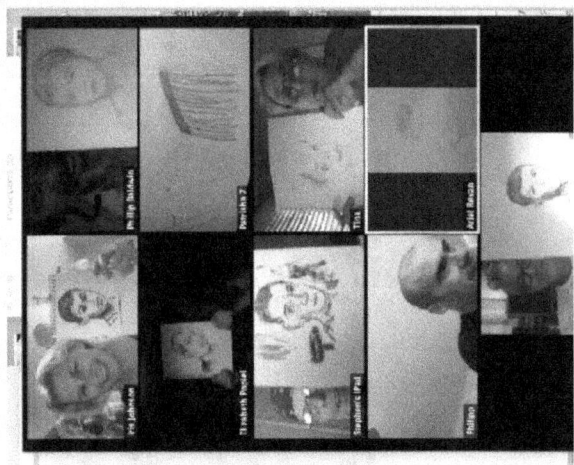

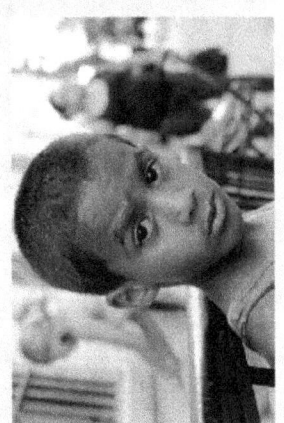

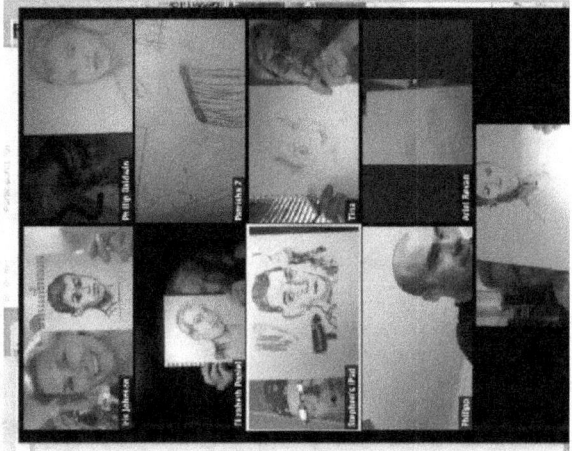

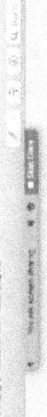

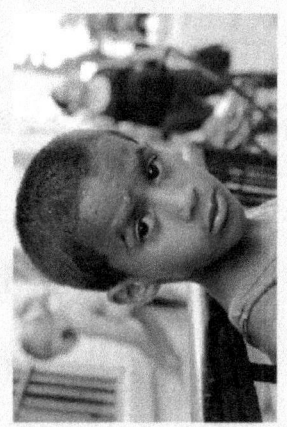

DRAWERS AND CRAWLERS PLAGUE BOOK
PHILLIPBALDWIN@GMAIL.COM

CHELSEA CRAWL CREW

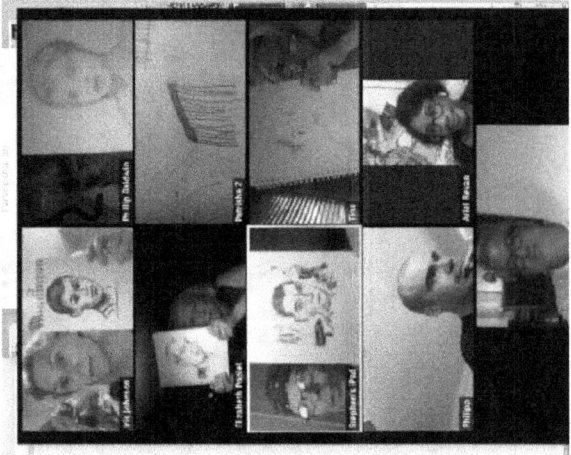

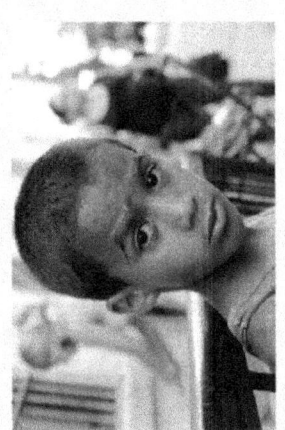

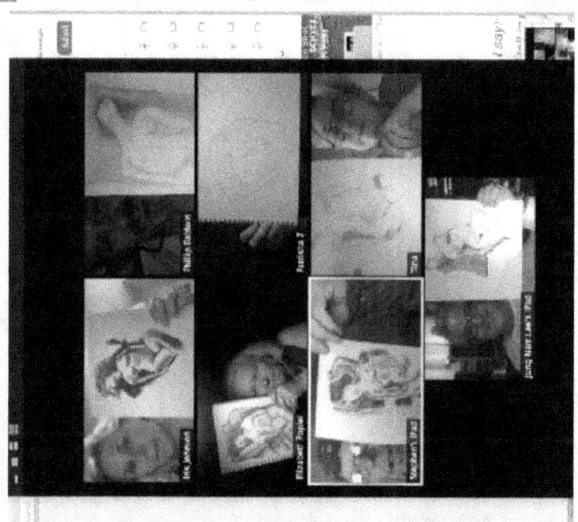

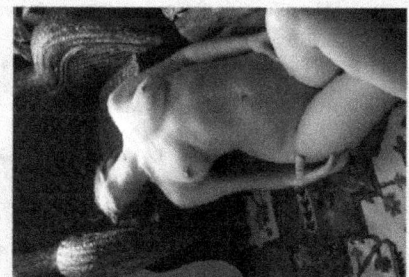

DRAWERS AND CRAWLERS PLAGUE BOOK
PHILLIP.BALDWIN@GMAIL.COM

CHELSEA CRAWL CREW

SELF
THE IMMERSIVE

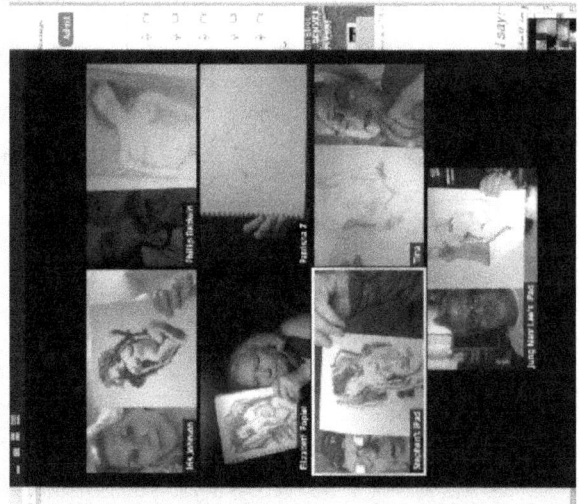

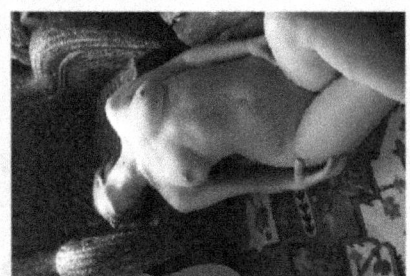

DRAWERS AND CRAWLERS PLAGUE BOOK
PHILLIP.BALDWIN@GMAIL.COM

CHELSEA CRAWL CREW

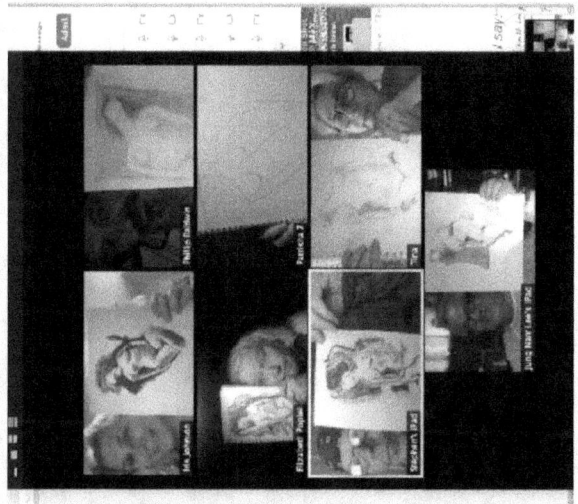

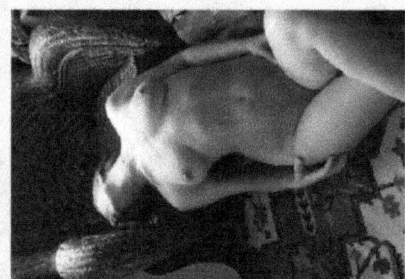

DRAWERS AND CRAWLERS PLAGUE BOOK
PHILLIPBALDWIN@GMAIL.COM

CHELSEA CRAWL CREW

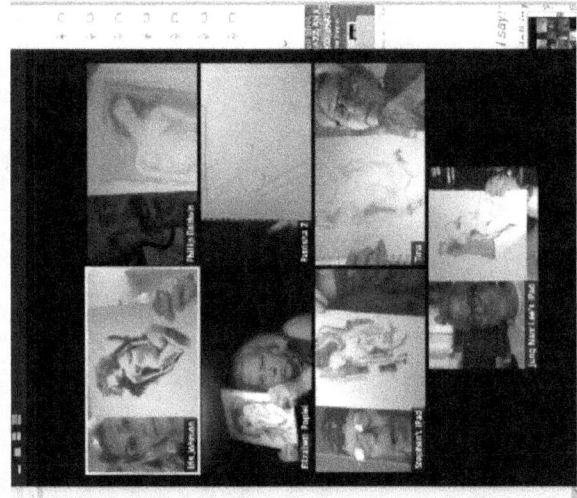

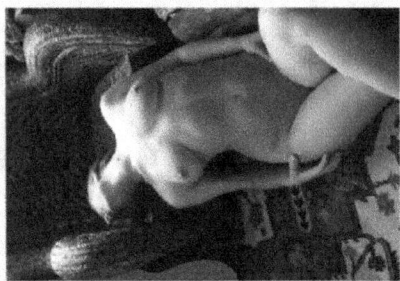

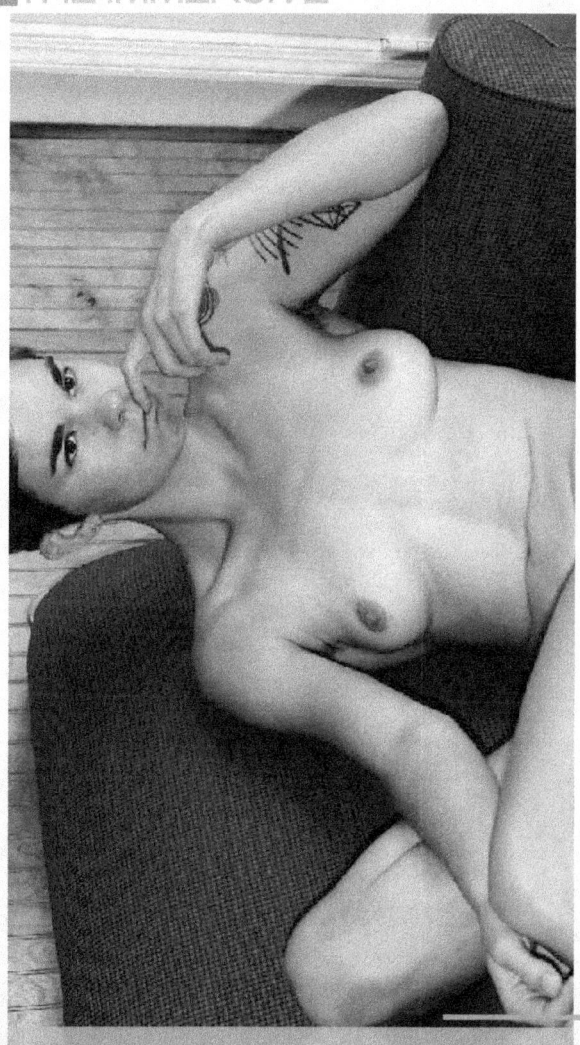

DRAWERS AND CRAWLERS PLAGUE BOOK
PHILLIPBALDWIN@GMAIL.COM CHELSEA CRAWL CREW

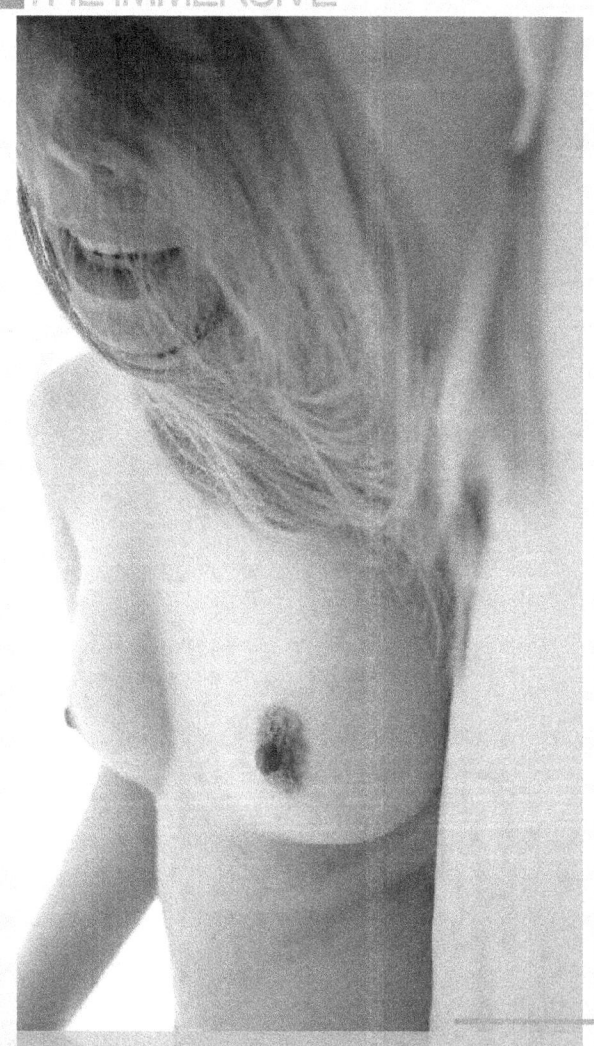

DRAWERS AND CRAWLERS PLAGUE BOOK

PHILLIPBALDWIN@GMAIL.COM CHELSEA CRAWL CREW

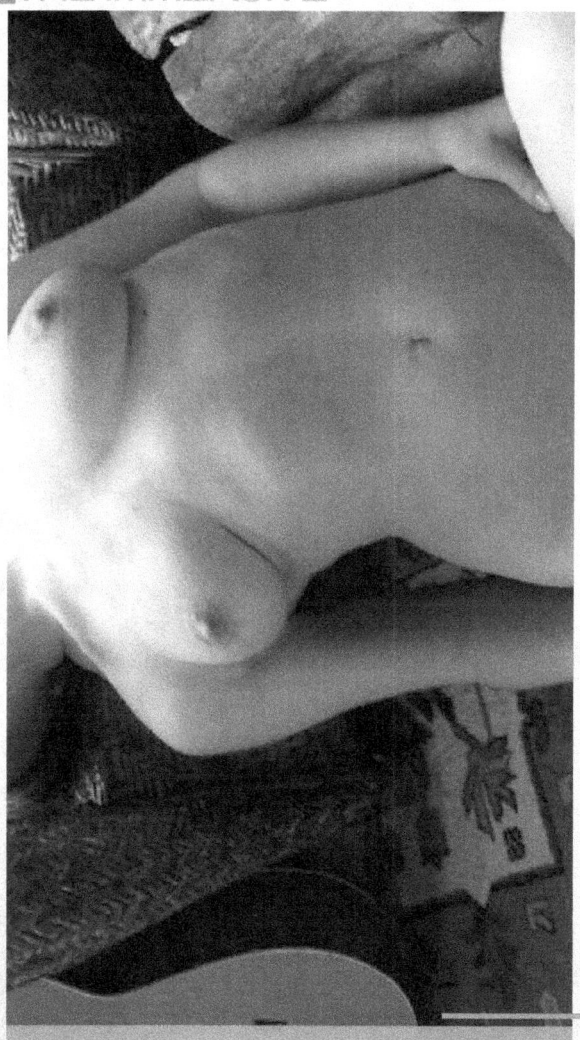

DRAWERS AND CRAWLERS PLAGUE BOOK
PHILLIP.BALDWIN@GMAIL.COM

CHELSEA CRAWL CREW

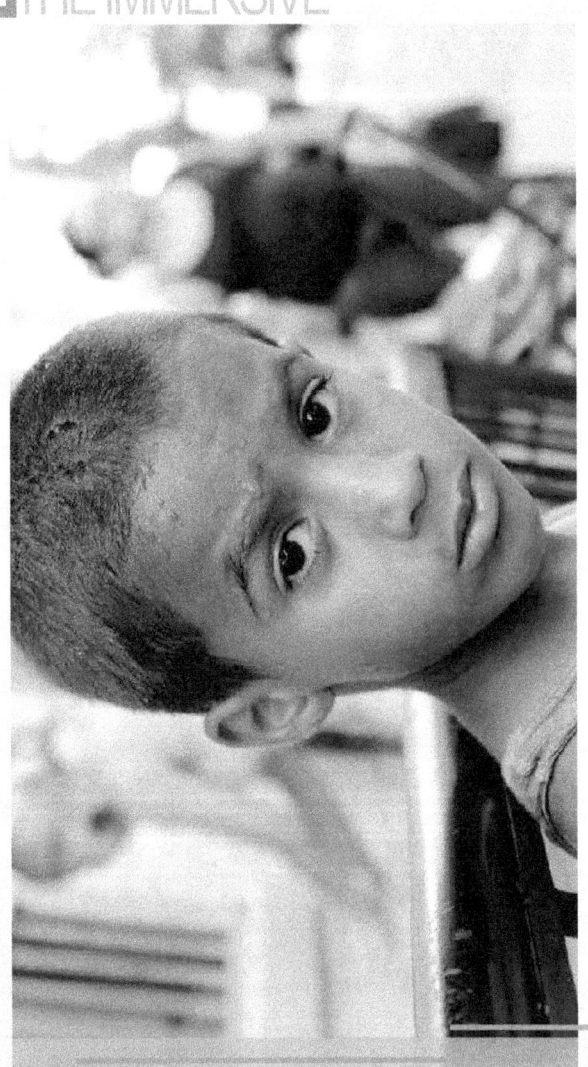

DRAWERS AND CRAWLERS PLAGUE BOOK
PHILLIPBALDWIN@GMAIL.COM

CHELSEA CRAWL CREW

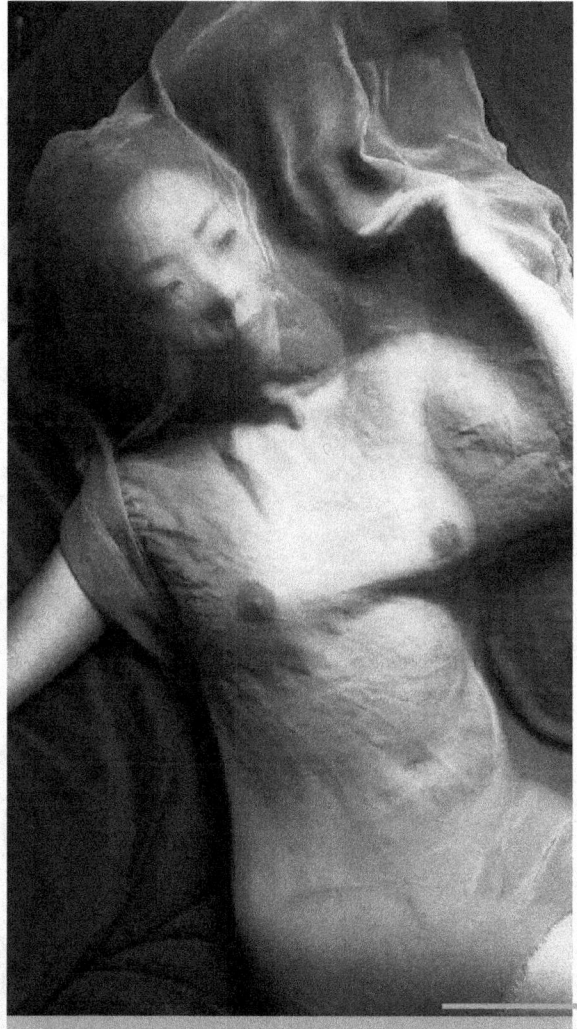

DRAWERS AND CRAWLERS PLAGUE BOOK
PHILLIP.BALDWIN@GMAIL.COM
CHELSEA CRAWL CREW

SELF
THE IMMERSIVE

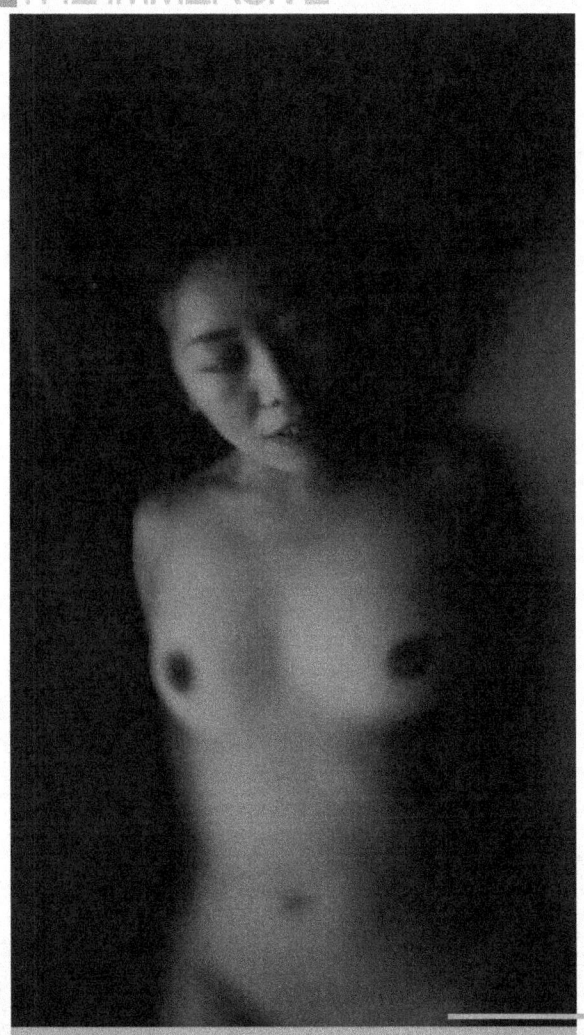

DRAWERS AND CRAWLERS PLAGUE BOOK

CHELSEA CRAWL CREW

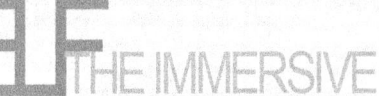
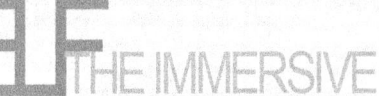

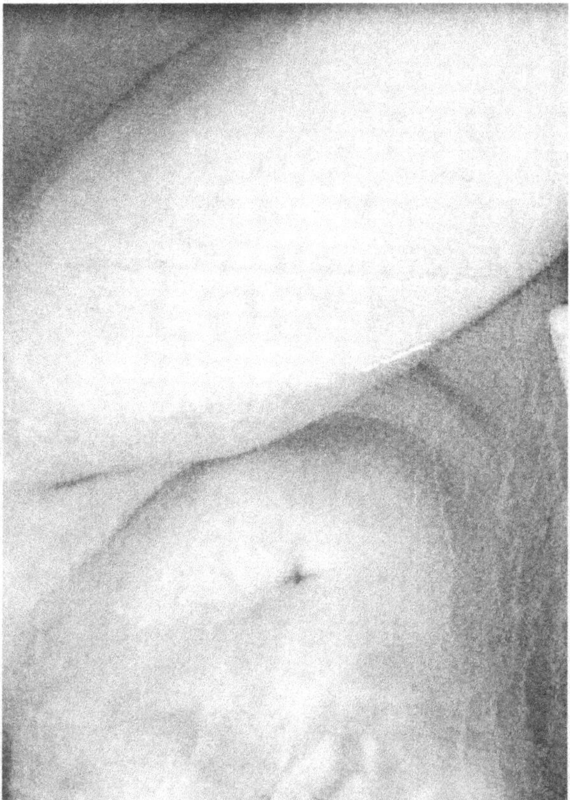

DRAWERS AND CRAWLERS PLAGUE BOOK

PHILLIPBALDWIN@GMAIL.COM

CHELSEA CRAWL CREW

SELF
THE IMMERSIVE

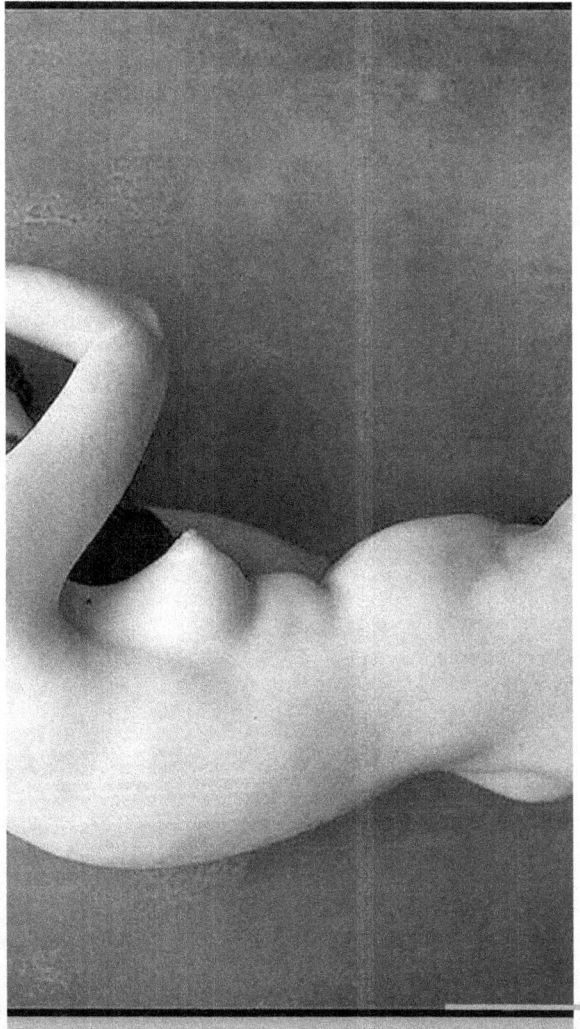

DRAWERS AND CRAWLERS PLAGUE BOOK
PHILLIP.BALDWIN@GMAIL.COM
CHELSEA CRAWL CREW

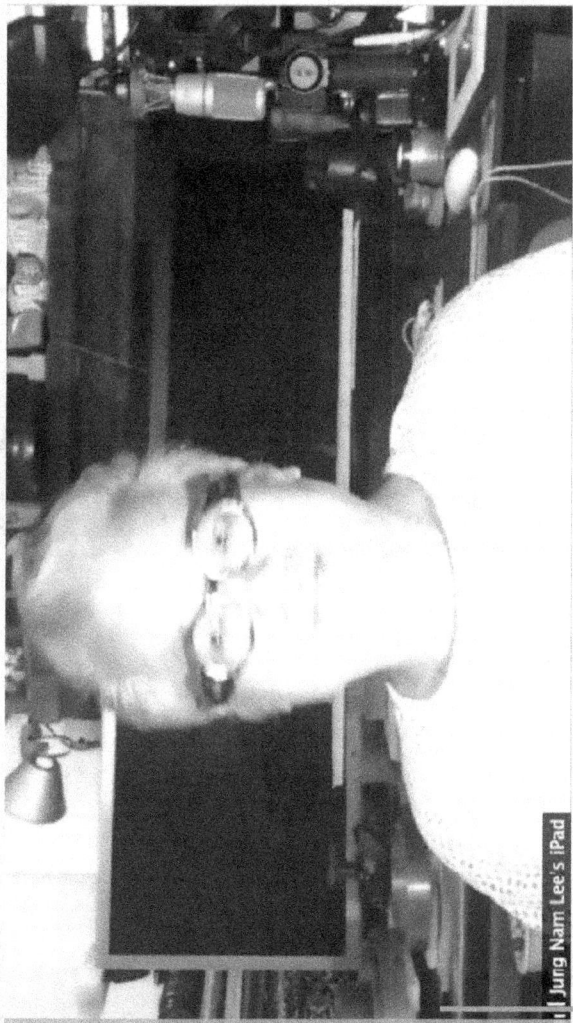

Jung Nam Lee's iPad

DRAWERS AND CRAWLERS PLAGUE BOOK

CHELSEA CRAWL CREW

SELF
THE IMMERSIVE

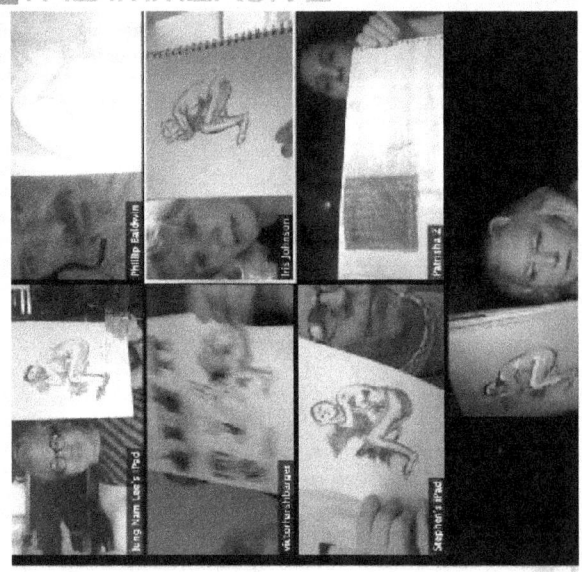

Phillip Baldwin | Iris Johnson | Patrisha Z

Jung Nam Lee's iPad | viktoriia rahbouset | Serge Mrikira iPad

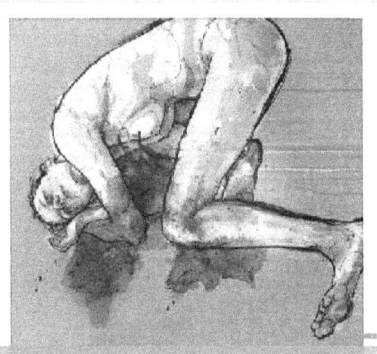

Screen Shot 2020-05-19 at 7.36.10 PM.png

Screen Shot 2020-05-12 at 12.60.08 PM.png

DRAWERS AND CRAWLERS PLAGUE BOOK
PHILLIP.BALDWIN@GMAIL.COM CHELSEA CRAWL CREW

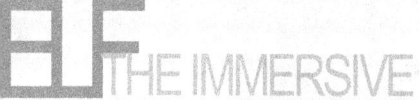

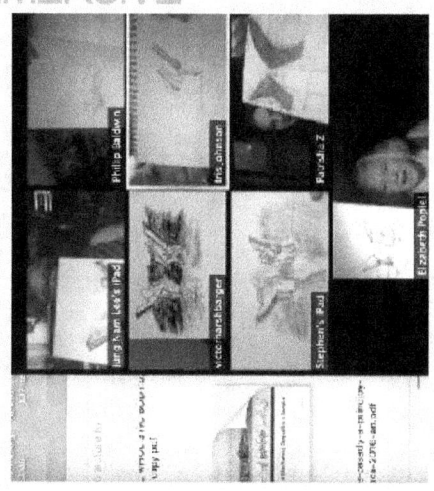

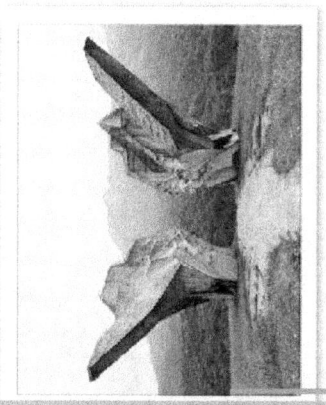

DRAWERS AND CRAWLERS PLAGUE BOOK
PHILLIP.BALDWIN@GMAIL.COM

CHELSEA CRAWL CREW

SELF
THE IMMERSIVE

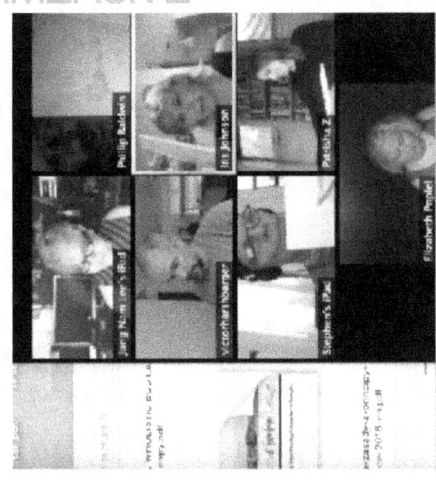

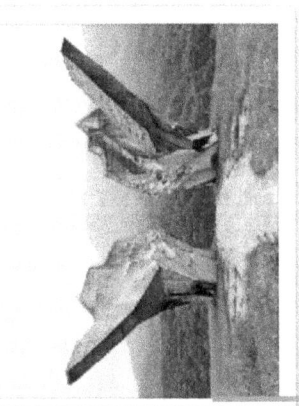

DRAWERS AND CRAWLERS PLAGUE BOOK
PHILLIP.BALDWIN@GMAIL.COM

CHELSEA CRAWL CREW

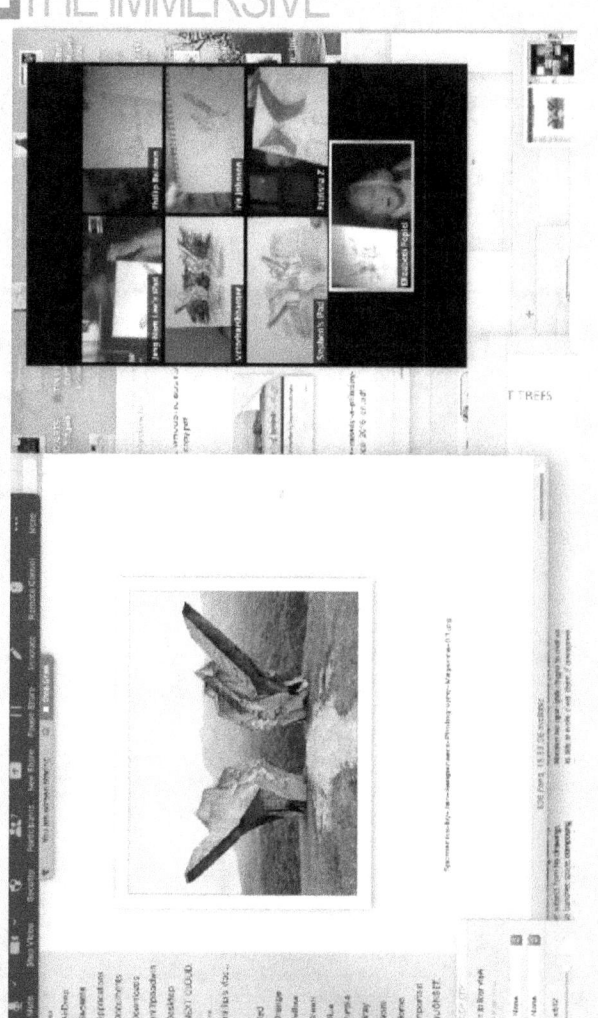

DRAWERS AND CRAWLERS PLAGUE BOOK
PHILLIPBALDWIN@GMAIL.COM
CHELSEA CRAWL CREW

SELF
THE IMMERSIVE

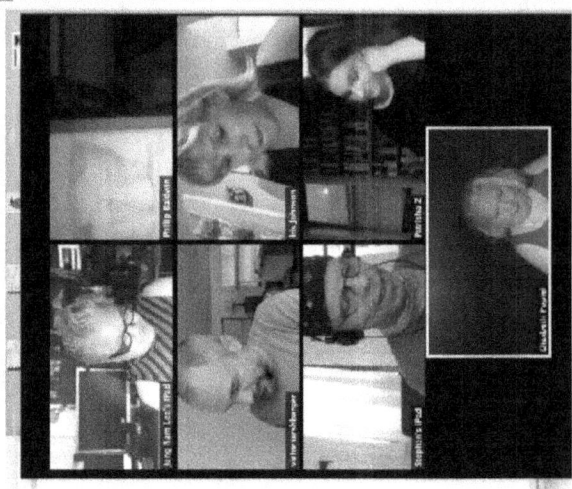

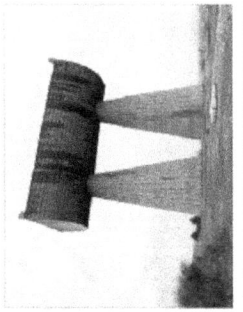

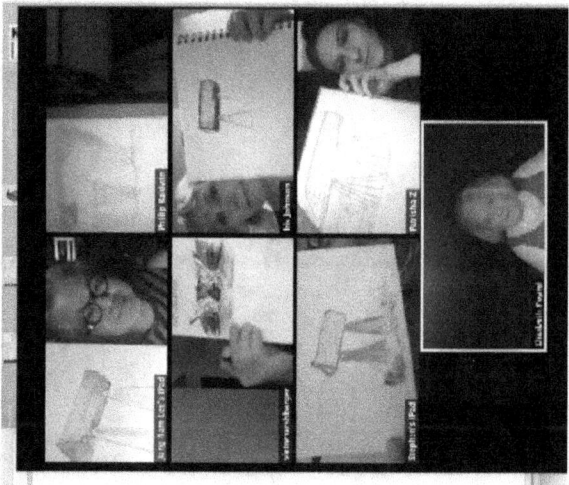

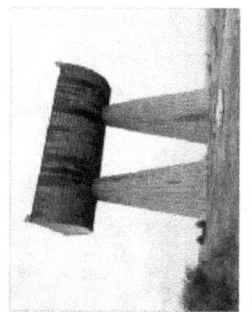

CHELSEA CRAWL CREW

SELF
THE IMMERSIVE

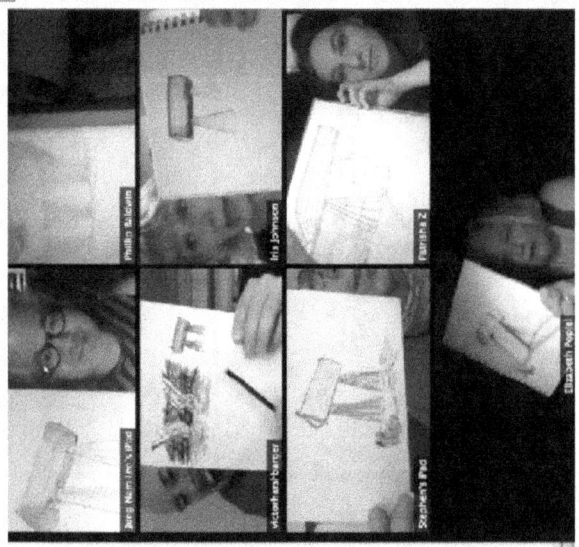

Phillip Baldwin
Iris Johnson
Tanisha Z.
Jane Meurline Lind
Victoria Hardbarber
Stephen's Pad
Elizabeth Pepsi

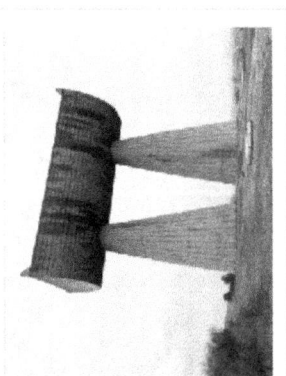

CHELSEA CRAWL CREW

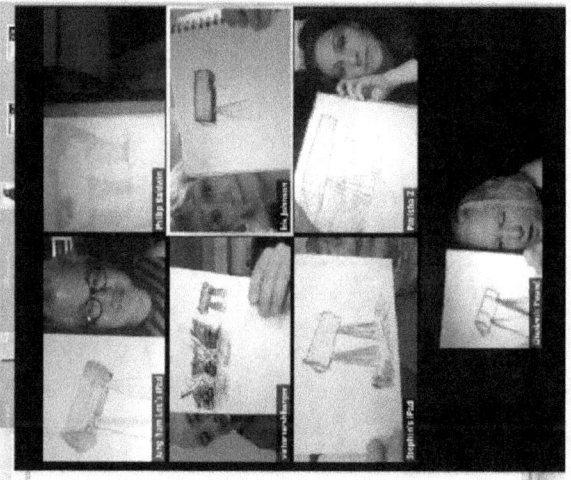

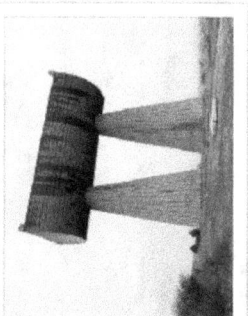

CHELSEA CRAWL CREW

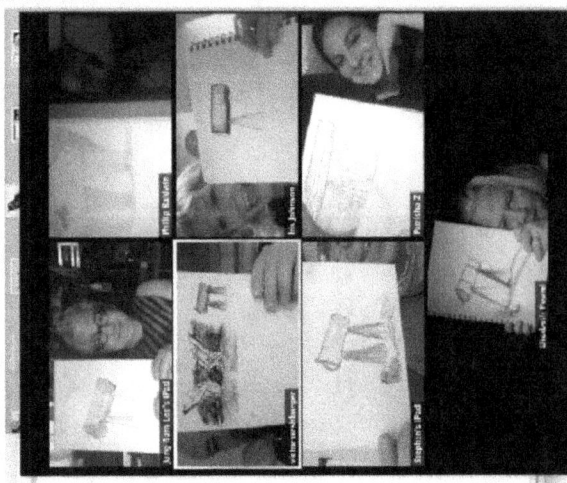

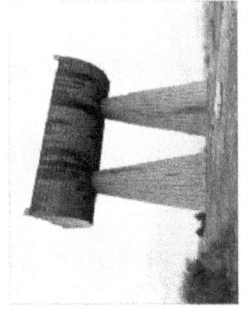

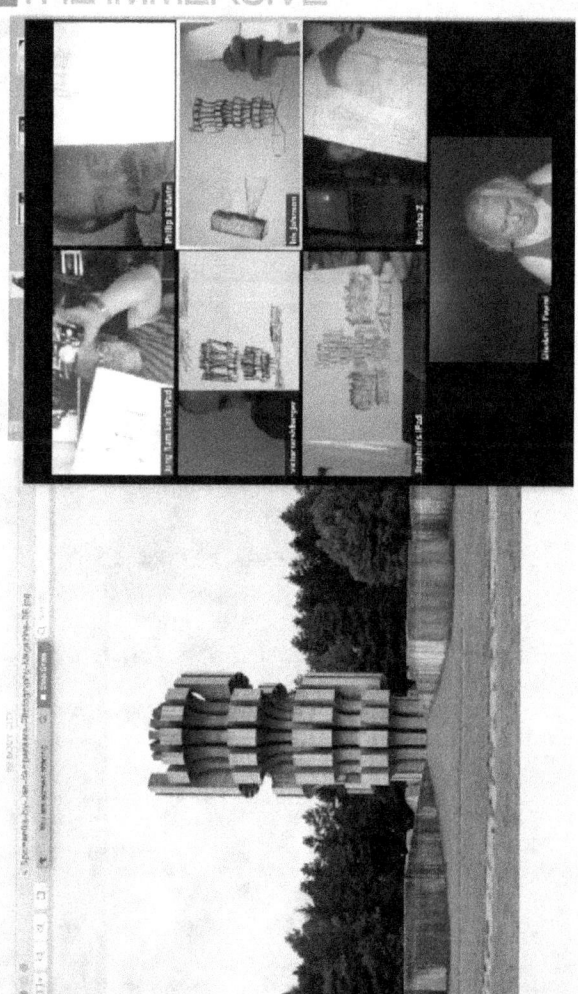

DRAWERS AND CRAWLERS PLAGUE BOOK
PHILLIPBALDWIN@GMAIL.COM

CHELSEA CRAWL CREW

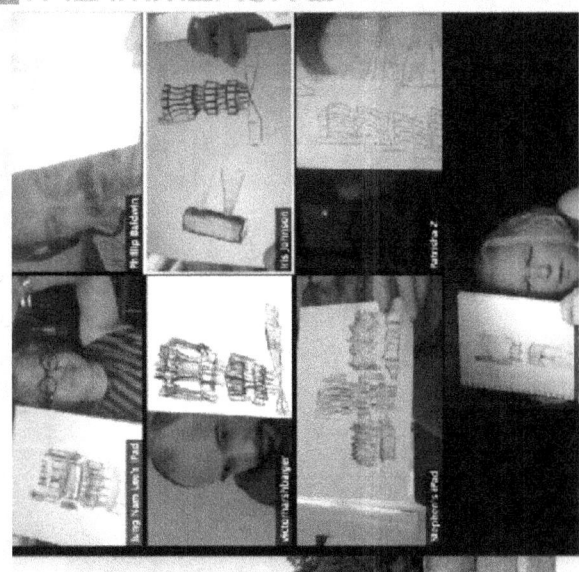

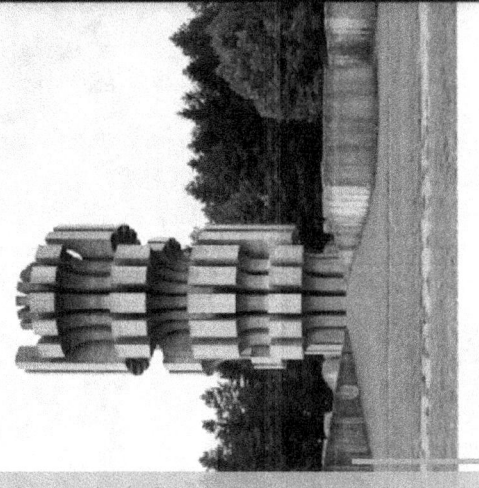

DRAWERS AND CRAWLERS PLAGUE BOOK
PHILLIPBALDWIN@GMAIL.COM

CHELSEA CRAWL CREW

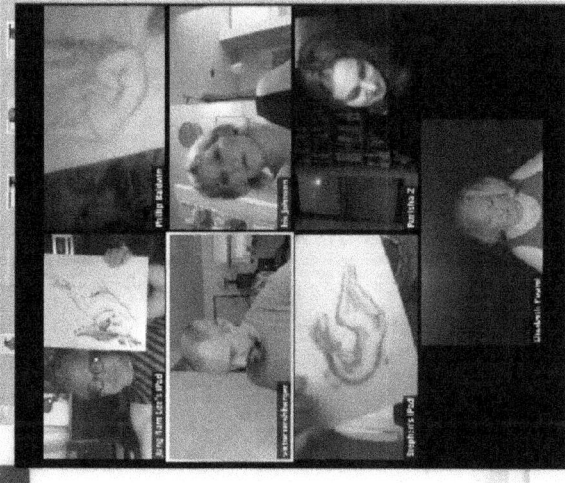

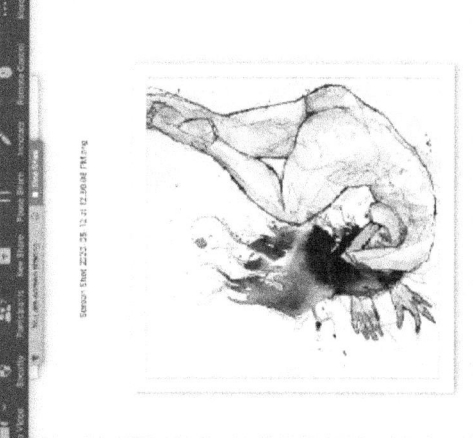

DRAWERS AND CRAWLERS PLAGUE BOOK
PHILLIP.BALDWIN@GMAIL.COM
CHELSEA CRAWL CREW

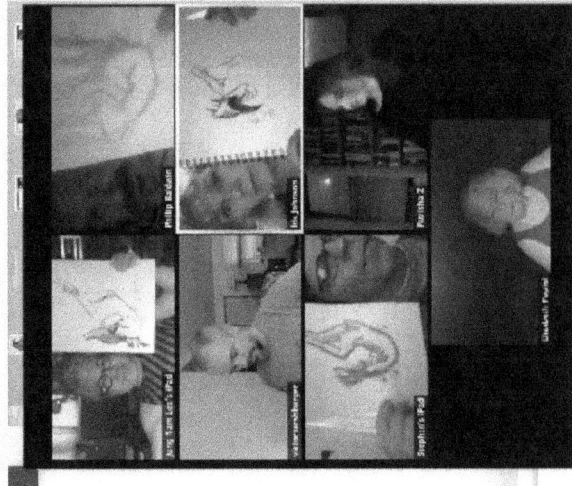

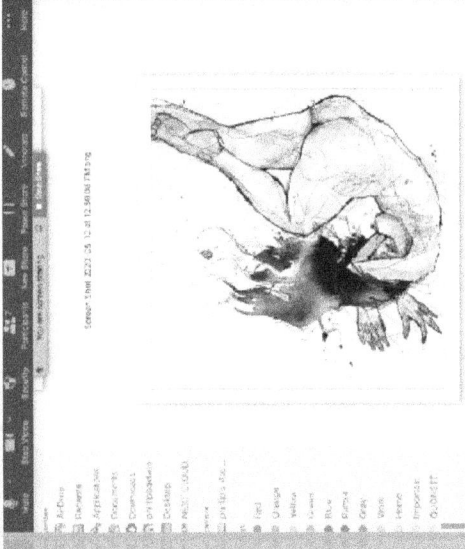

DRAWERS AND CRAWLERS PLAGUE BOOK
PHILLIPBALDWIN@GMAIL.COM

CHELSEA CRAWL CREW

ELF THE IMMERSIVE

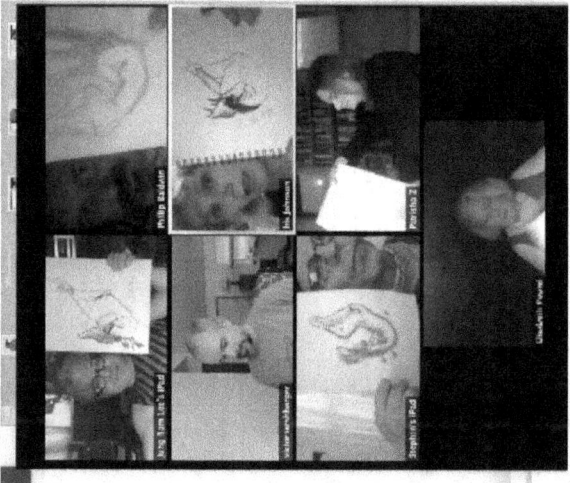

DRAWERS AND CRAWLERS PLAGUE BOOK
PHILLIPBALDWIN@GMAIL.COM

CHELSEA CRAWL CREW

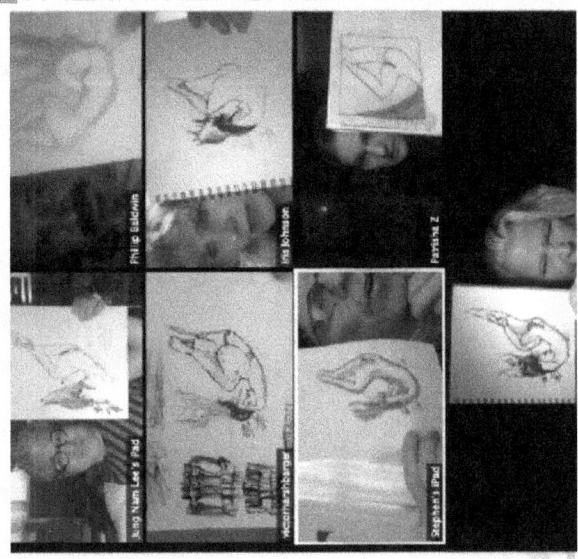

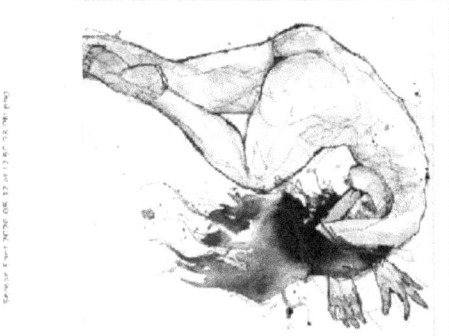

DRAWERS AND CRAWLERS PLAGUE BOOK
PHILLIPBALDWIN@GMAIL.COM
CHELSEA CRAWL CREW

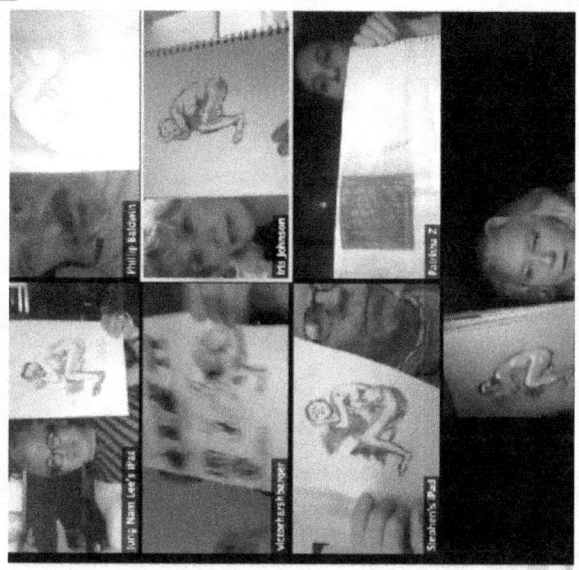

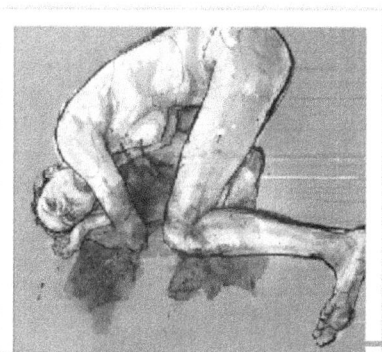

DRAWERS AND CRAWLERS PLAGUE BOOK

PHILLIPBALDWIN@GMAIL.COM

CHELSEA CRAWL CREW

SELF
THE IMMERSIVE

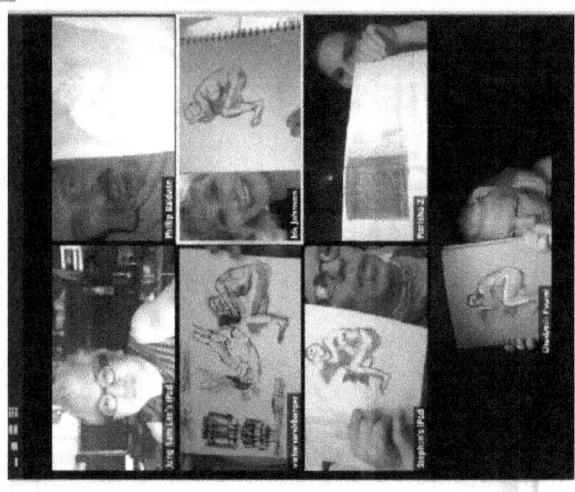

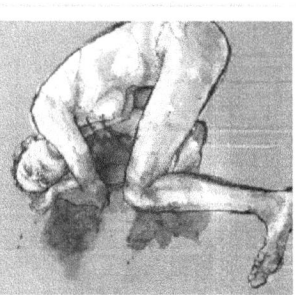

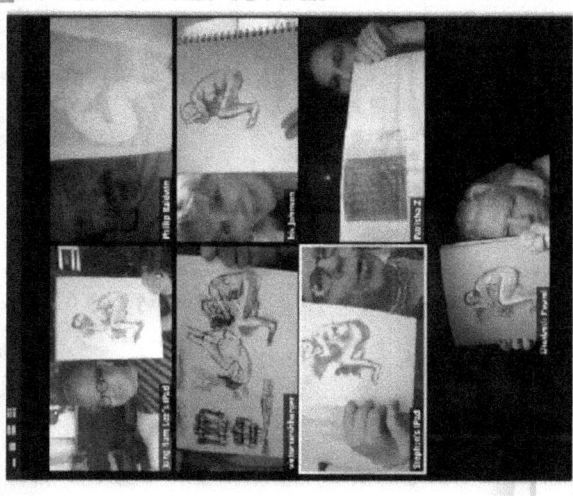

DRAWERS AND CRAWLERS PLAGUE BOOK
PHILLIP.BALDWIN@GMAIL.COM
CHELSEA CRAWL CREW

SELF
THE IMMERSIVE

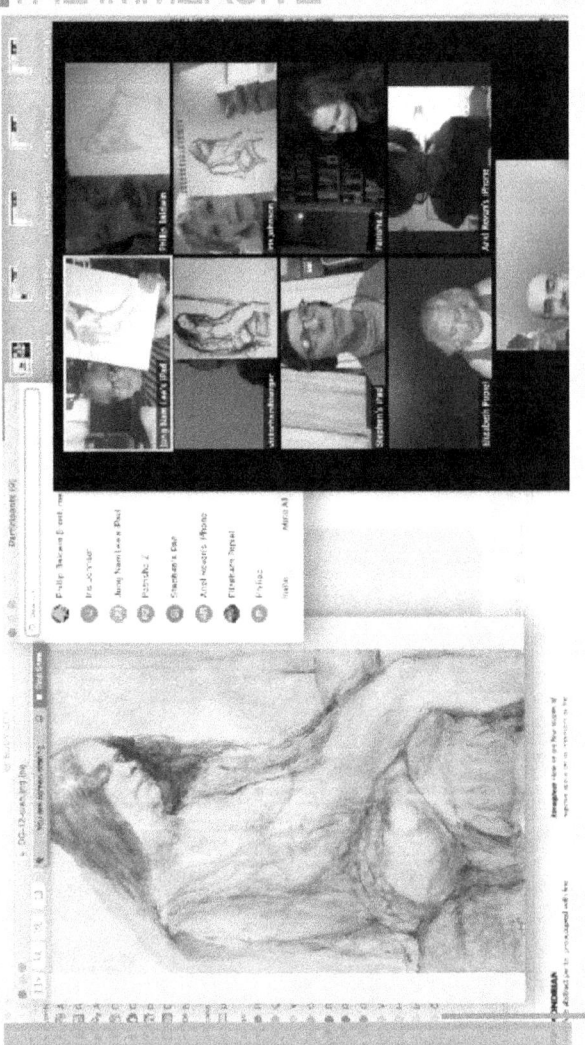

DRAWERS AND CRAWLERS PLAGUE BOOK
PHILLIP.BALDWIN@GMAIL.COM
CHELSEA CRAWL CREW

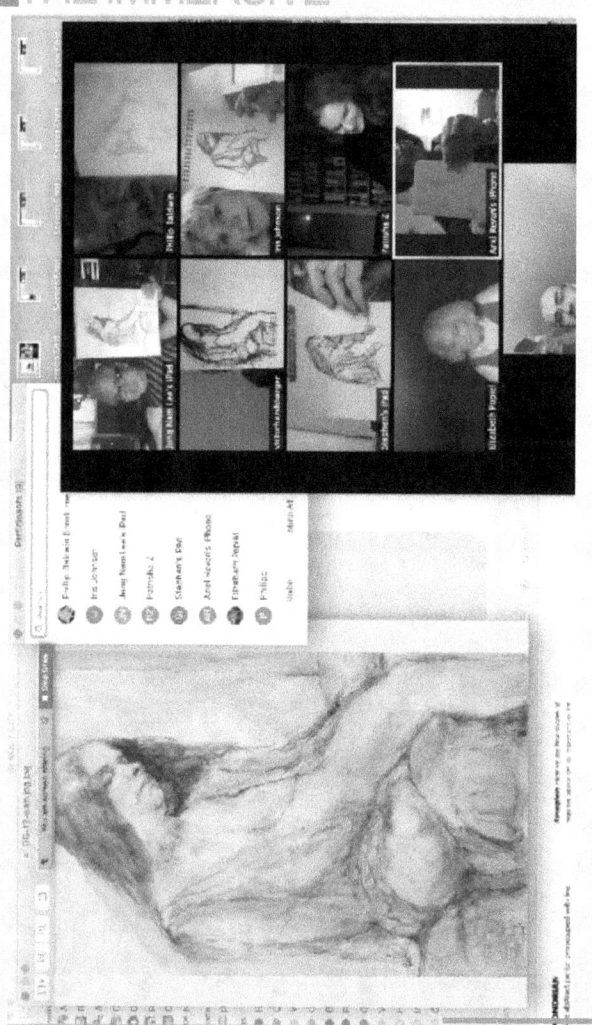

DRAWERS AND CRAWLERS PLAGUE BOOK
PHILLIPBALDWIN@GMAIL.COM

CHELSEA CRAWL CREW

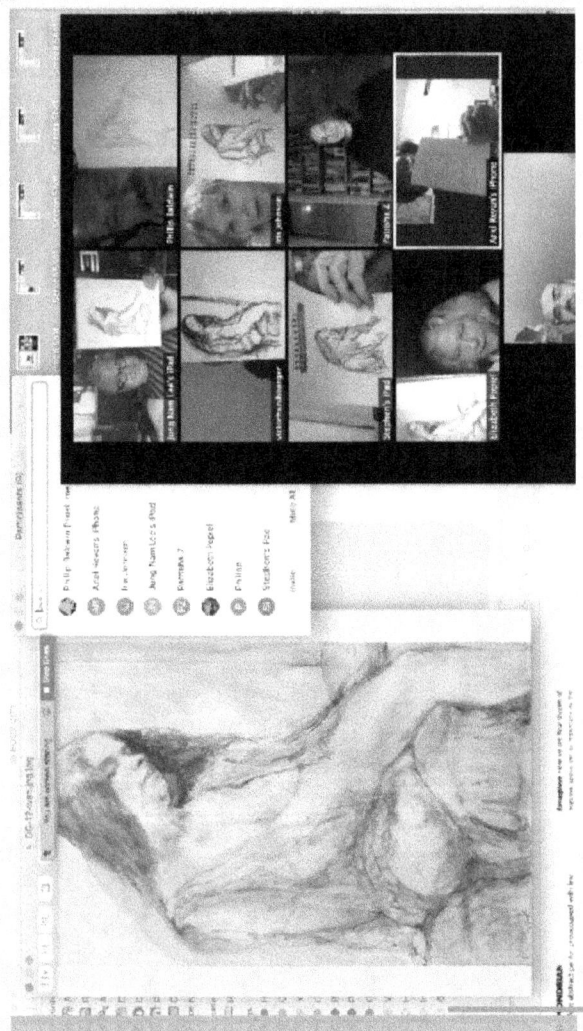

DRAWERS AND CRAWLERS PLAGUE BOOK
PHILLIPBALDWIN@GMAIL.COM

CHELSEA CRAWL CREW

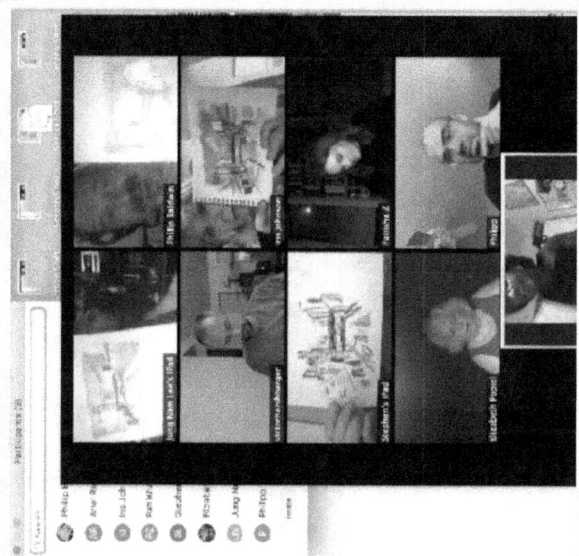

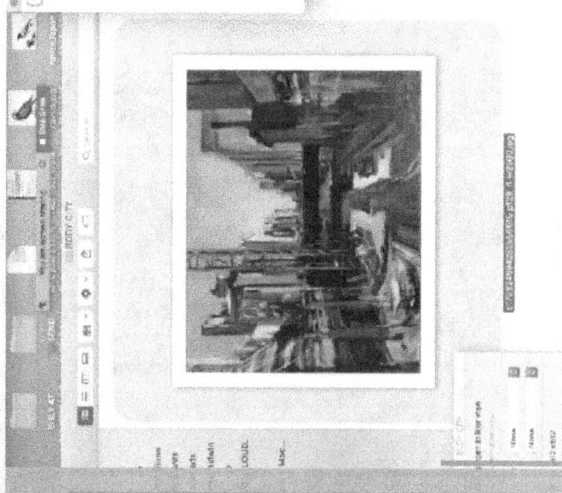

DRAWERS AND CRAWLERS PLAGUE BOOK

CHELSEA CRAWL CREW

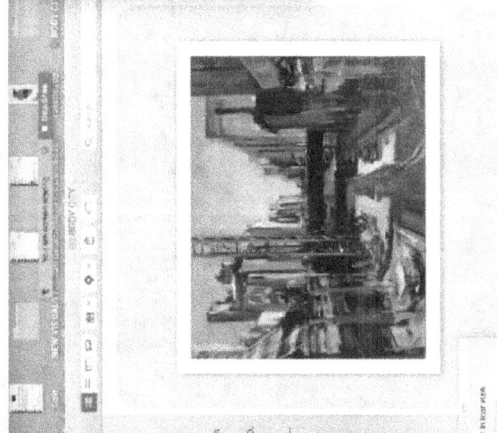

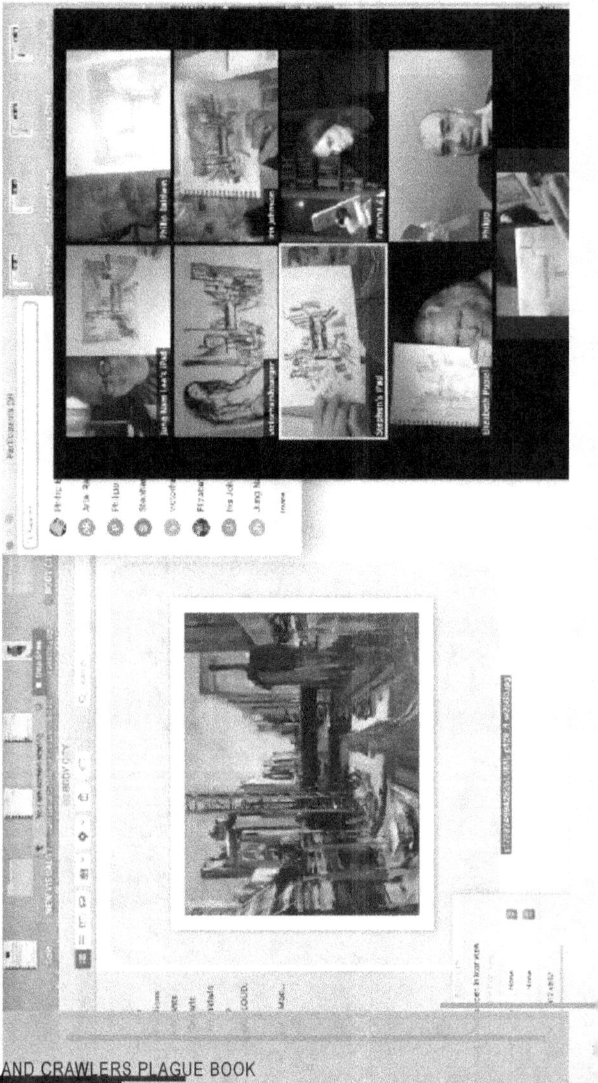

SELF
THE IMMERSIVE

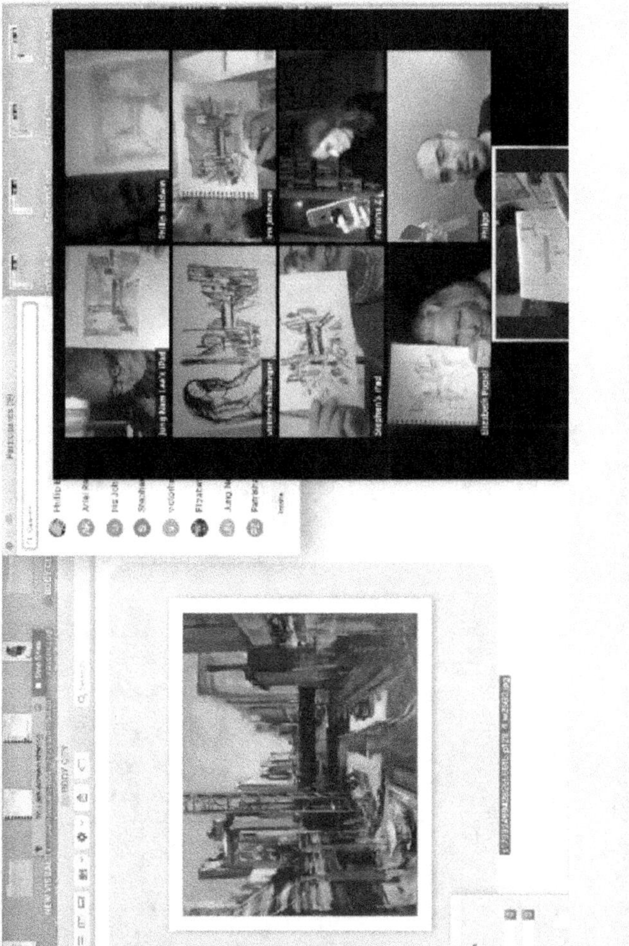

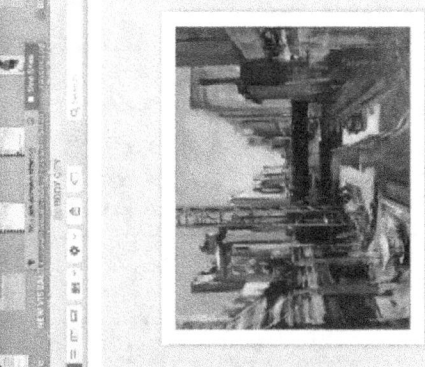

DRAWERS AND CRAWLERS PLAGUE BOOK
PHILLIP.BALDWIN@GMAIL.COM

CHELSEA CRAWL CREW

SELF
THE IMMERSIVE

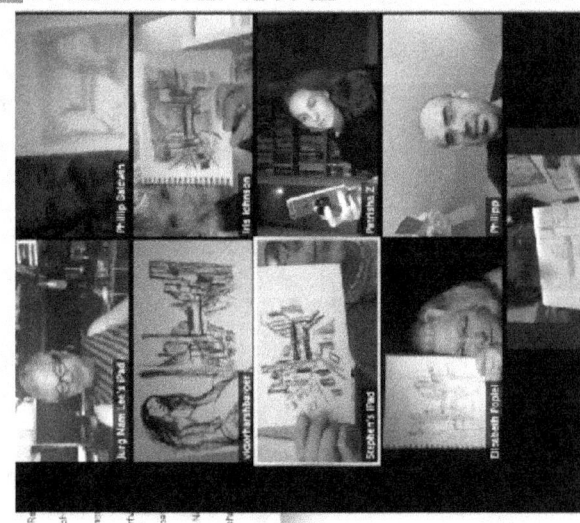

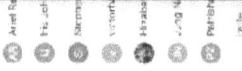

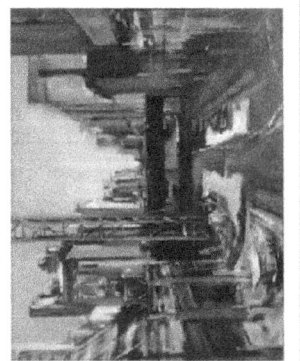

DRAWERS AND CRAWLERS PLAGUE BOOK
PHILLIP.BALDWIN@GMAIL.COM

CHELSEA CRAWL CREW

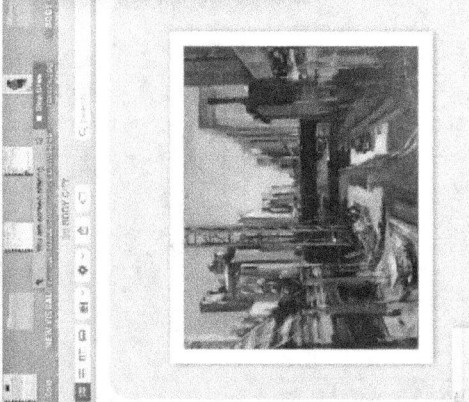

DRAWERS AND CRAWLERS PLAGUE BOOK
PHILLIPBALDWIN@GMAIL.COM

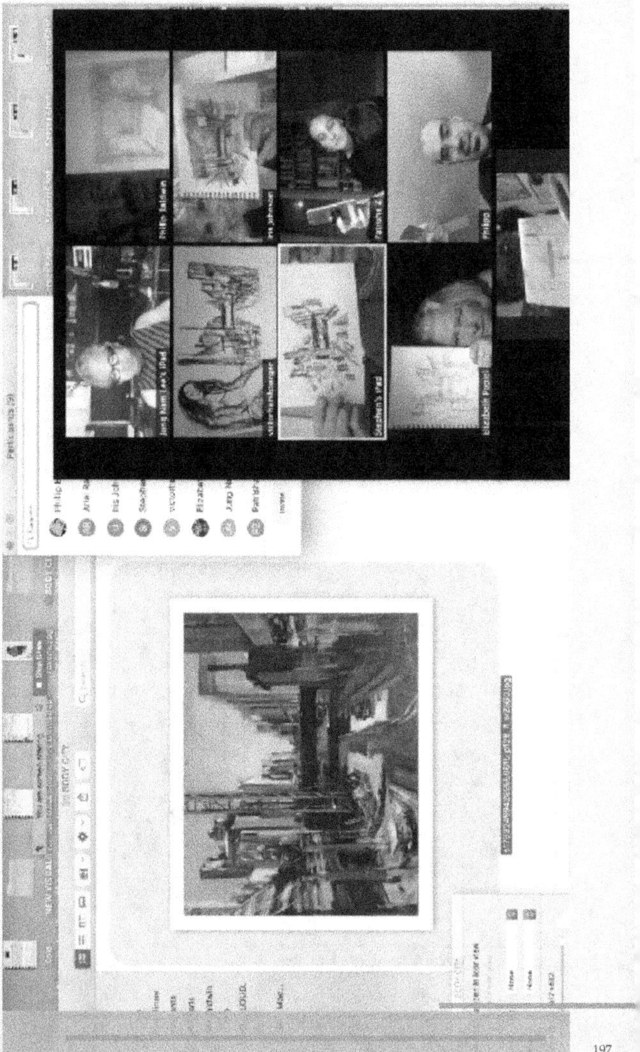

CHELSEA CRAWL CREW

SELF
THE IMMERSIVE

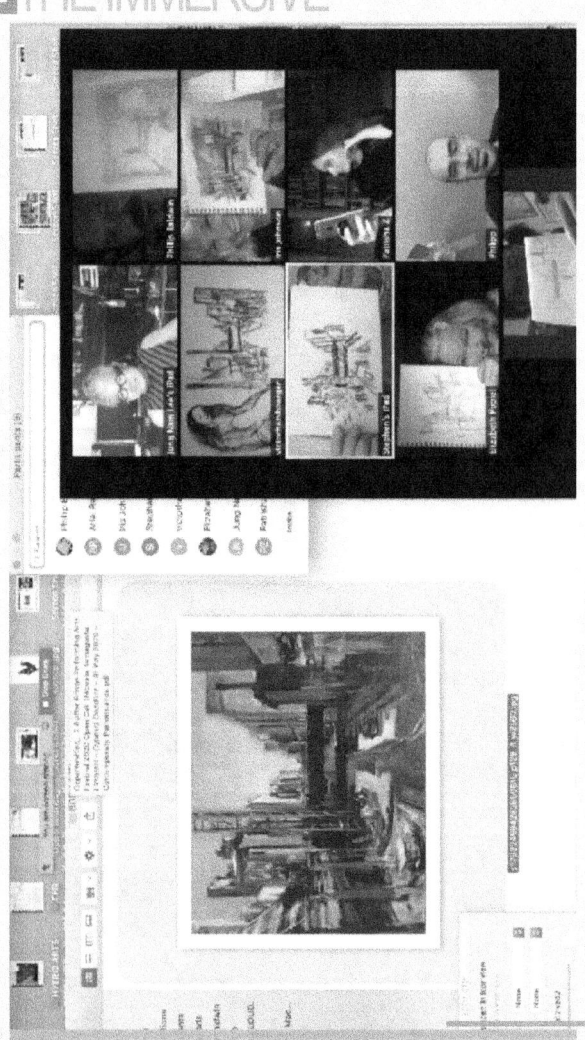

DRAWERS AND CRAWLERS PLAGUE BOOK
PHILLIP.BALDWIN@GMAIL.COM

CHELSEA CRAWL CREW

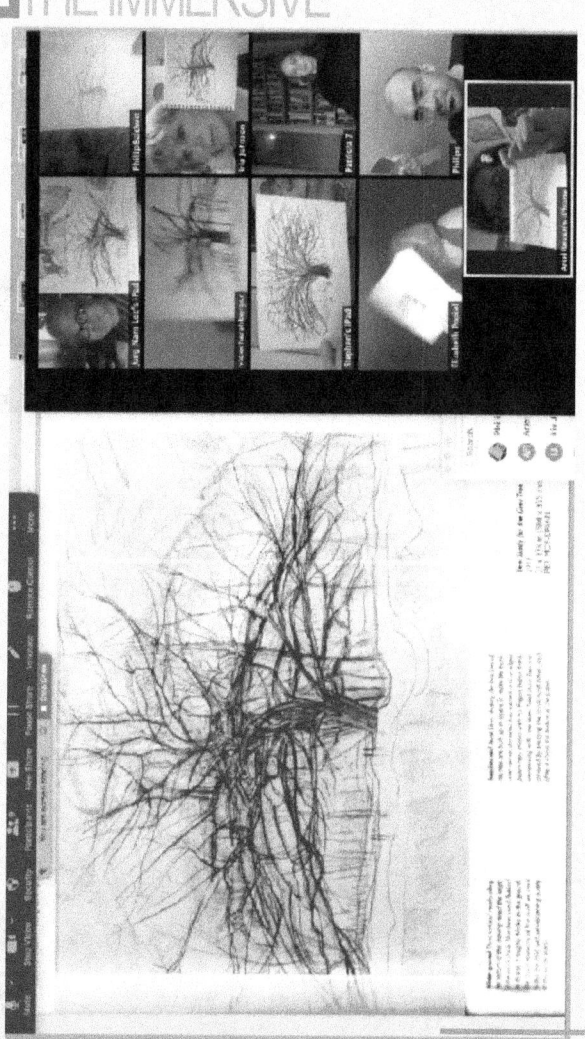

DRAWERS AND CRAWLERS PLAGUE BOOK
PHILLIPBALDWIN@GMAIL.COM

CHELSEA CRAWL CREW

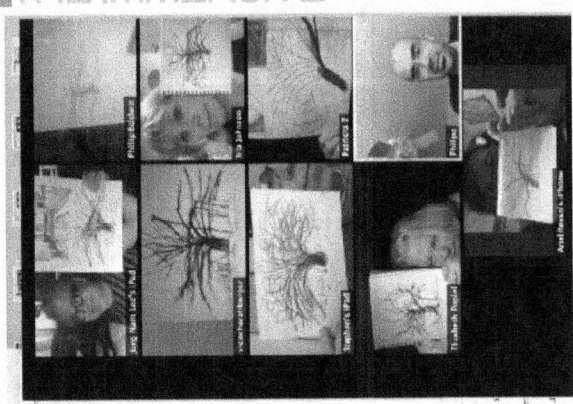

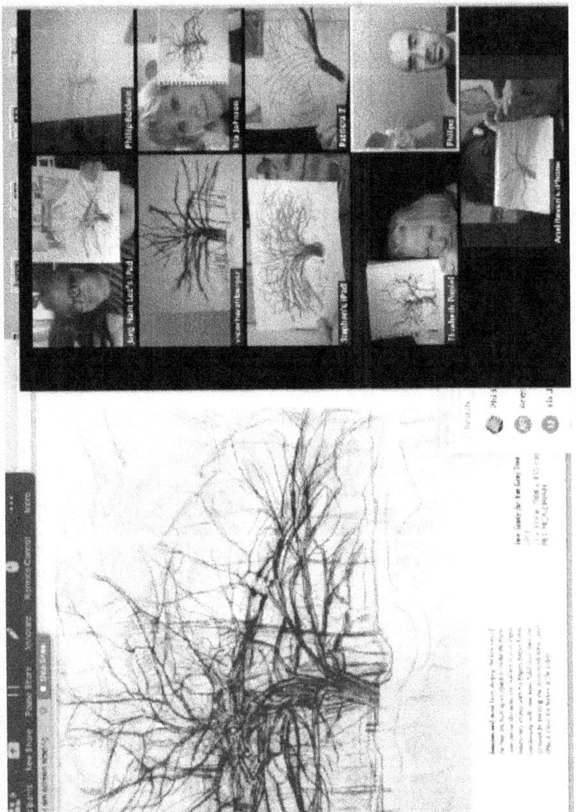

DRAWERS AND CRAWLERS PLAGUE BOOK
PHILLIP.BALDWIN@GMAIL.COM
CHELSEA CRAWL CREW

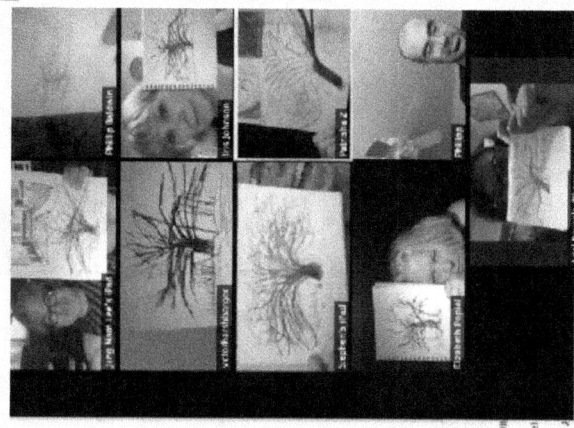

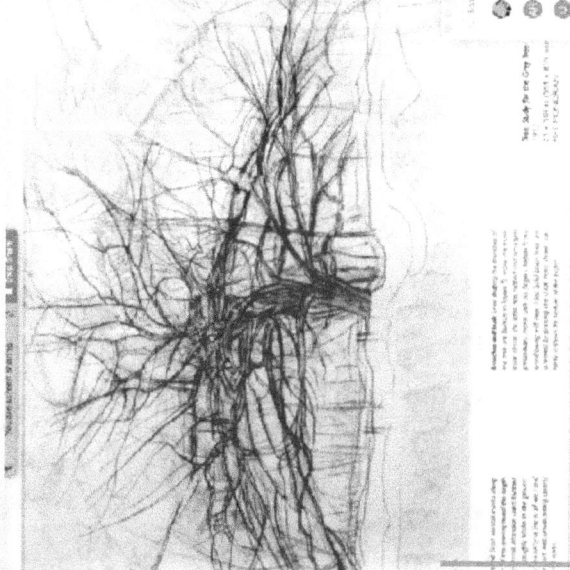

DRAWERS AND CRAWLERS PLAGUE BOOK

PHILLIPBALDWIN@GMAIL.COM

CHELSEA CRAWL CREW

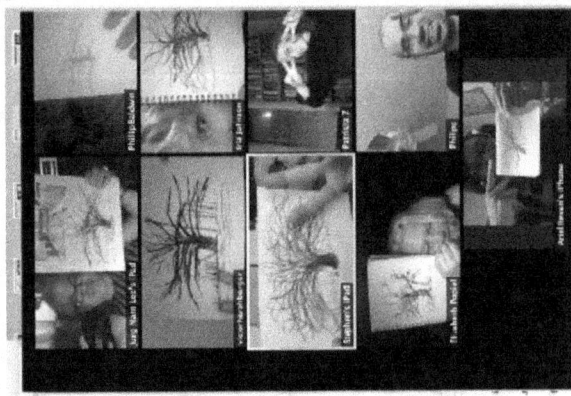

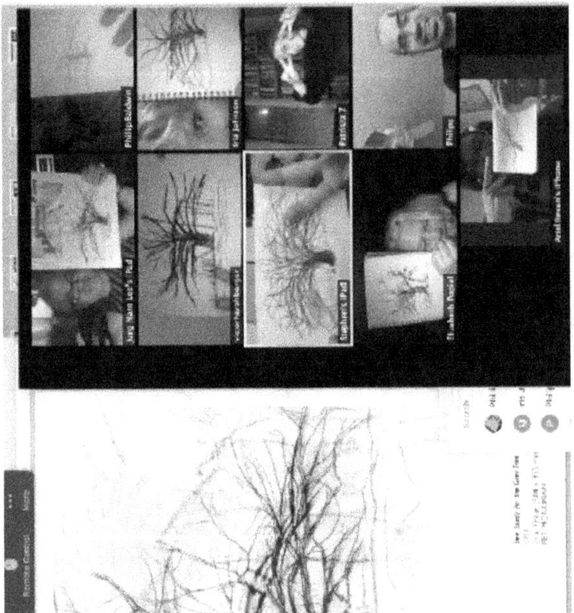

DRAWERS AND CRAWLERS PLAGUE BOOK
PHILLIPBALDWIN@GMAIL.COM

CHELSEA CRAWL CREW

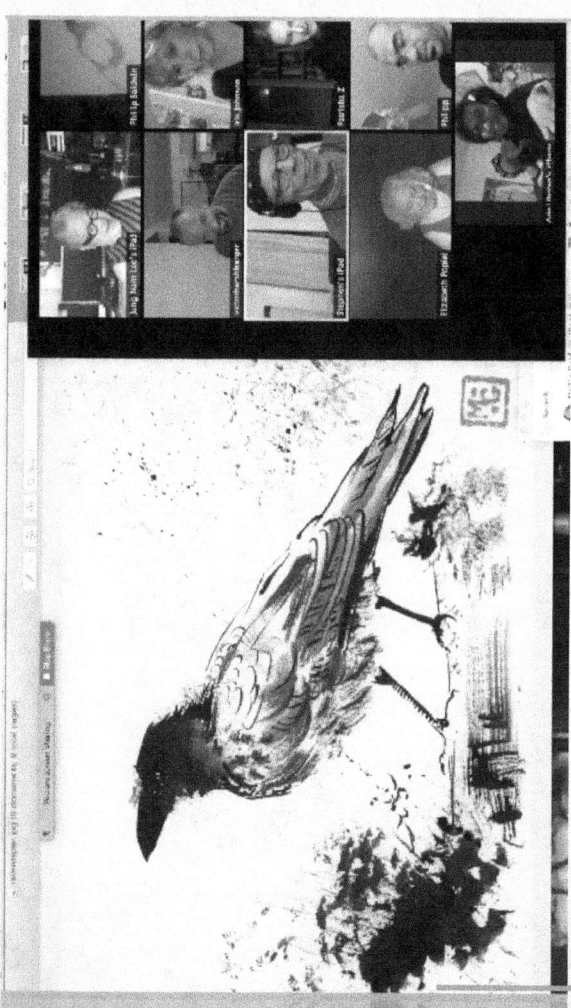

CHELSEA CRAWL CREW

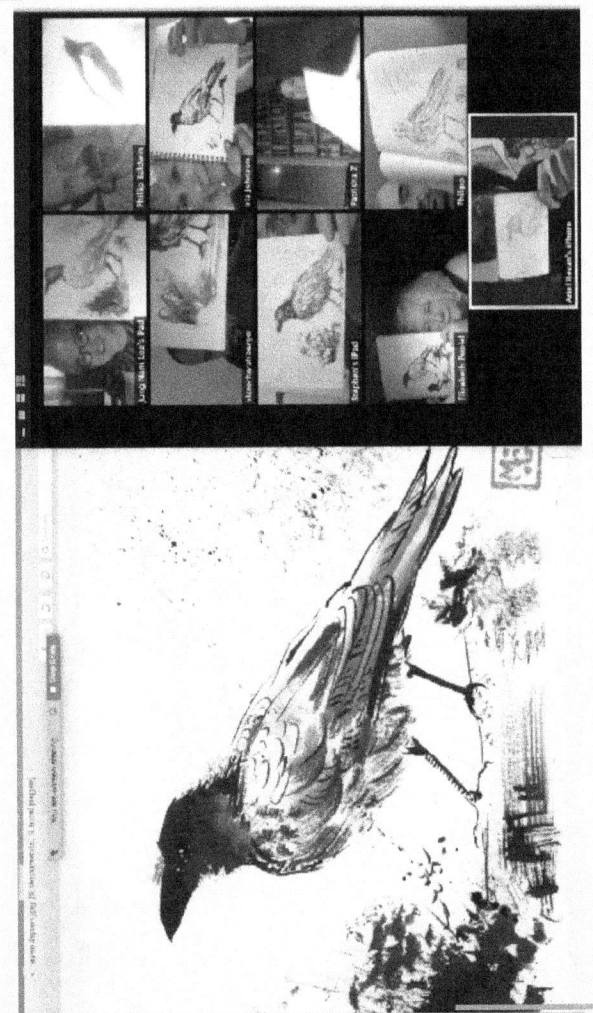

DRAWERS AND CRAWLERS PLAGUE BOOK

PHILLIP.BALDWIN@GMAIL.COM

CHELSEA CRAWL CREW

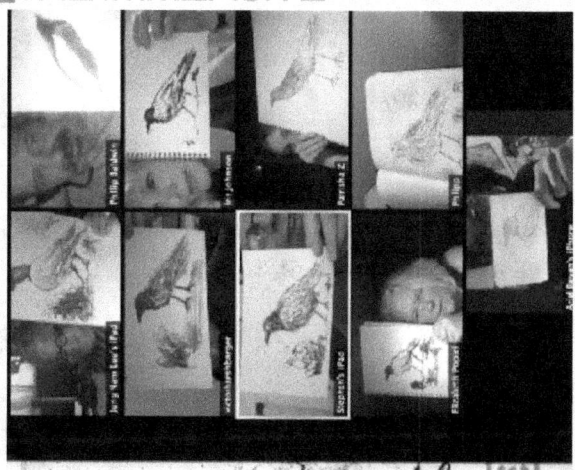

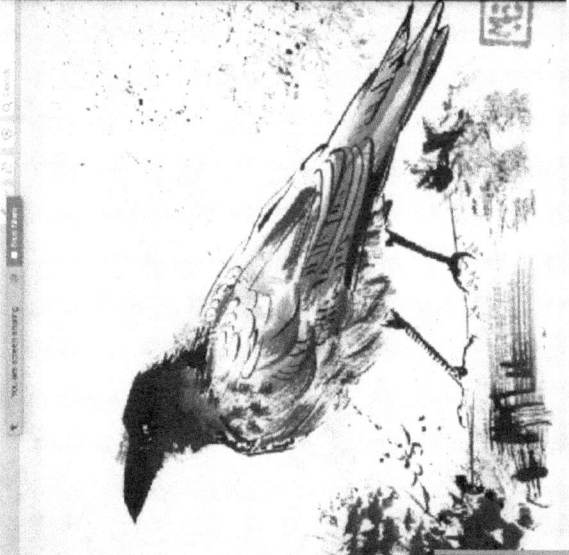

DRAWERS AND CRAWLERS PLAGUE BOOK

PHILLIPBALDWIN@GMAIL.COM

CHELSEA CRAWL CREW

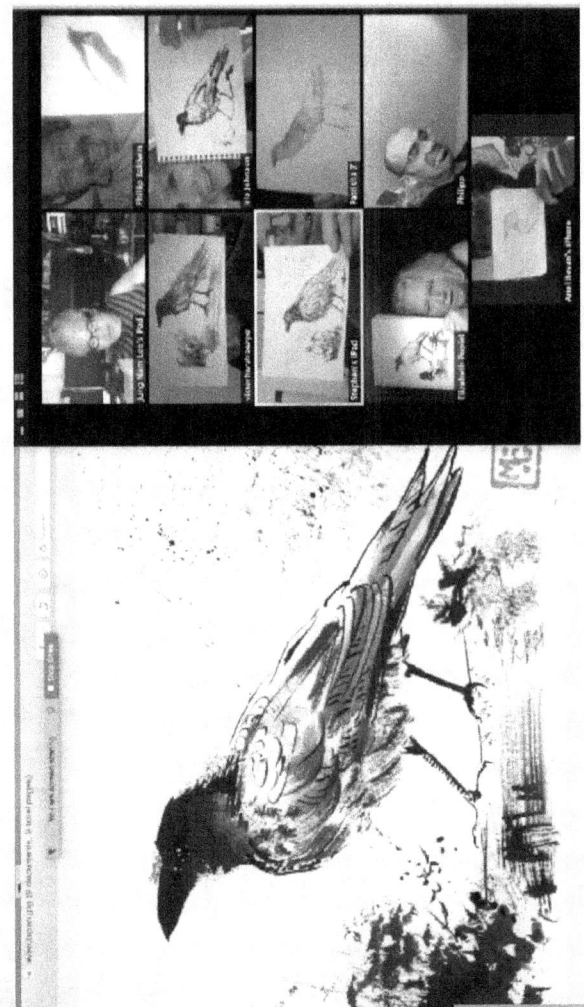

DRAWERS AND CRAWLERS PLAGUE BOOK
PHILLIP.BALDWIN@GMAIL.COM
CHELSEA CRAWL CREW

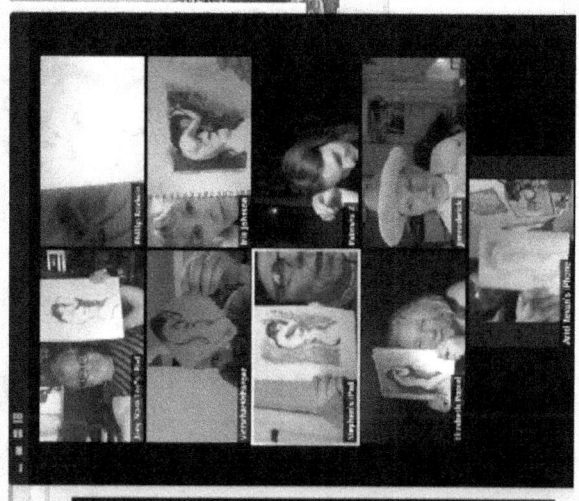

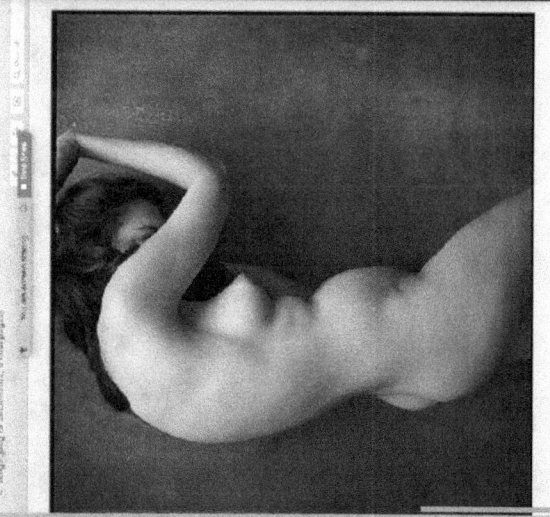

DRAWERS AND CRAWLERS PLAGUE BOOK

PHILLIPBALDWIN@GMAIL.COM CHELSEA CRAWL CREW

SELF
THE IMMERSIVE

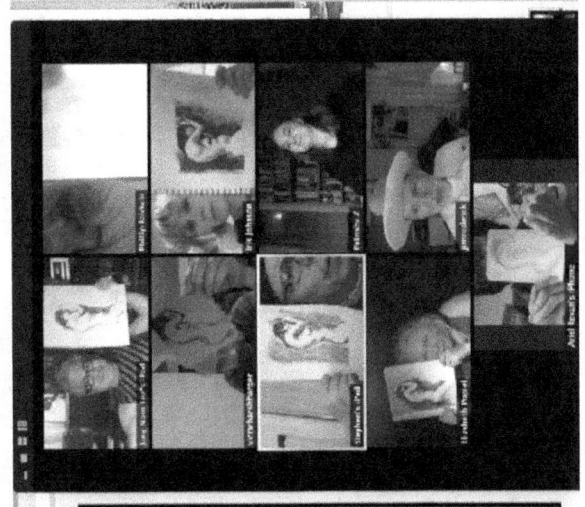

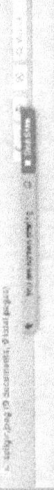
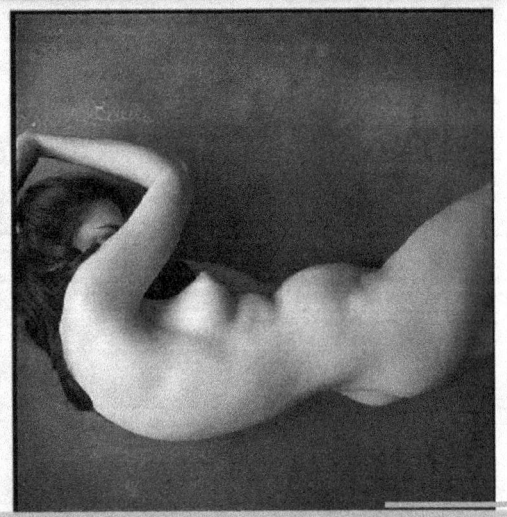

DRAWERS AND CRAWLERS PLAGUE BOOK
PHILLIPBALDWIN@GMAIL.COM

CHELSEA CRAWL CREW

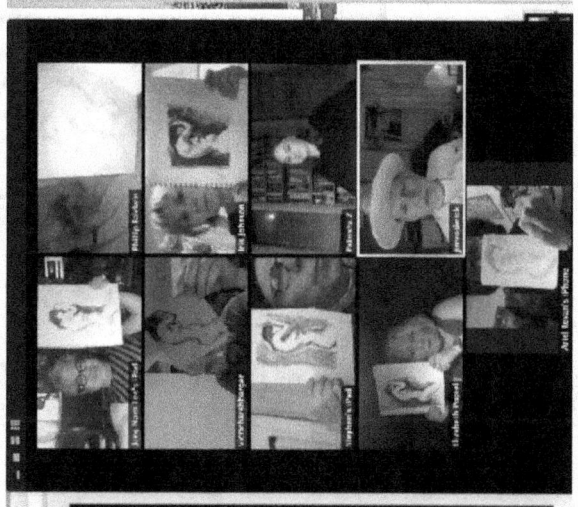

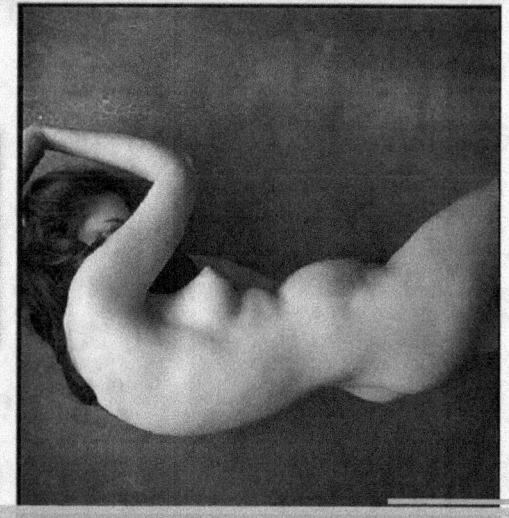

DRAWERS AND CRAWLERS PLAGUE BOOK

PHILLIP.BALDWIN@GMAIL.COM

CHELSEA CRAWL CREW

SELF
THE IMMERSIVE

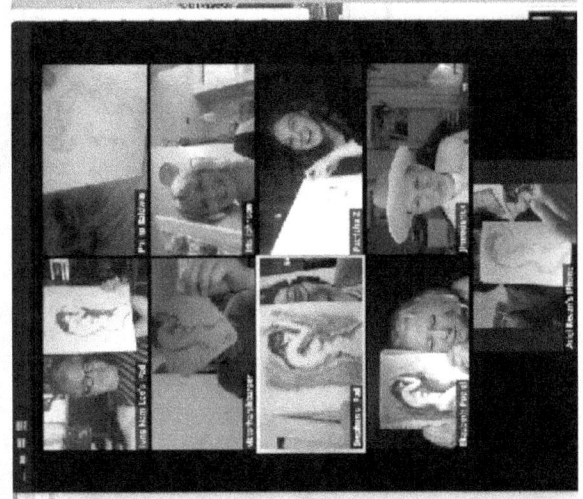

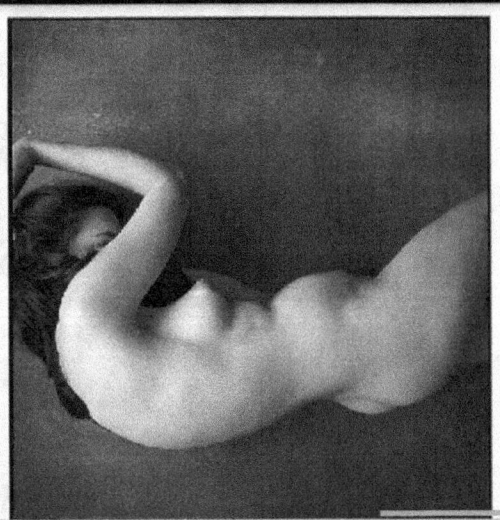

DRAWERS AND CRAWLERS PLAGUE BOOK
PHILLIPBALDWIN@GMAIL.COM

CHELSEA CRAWL CREW

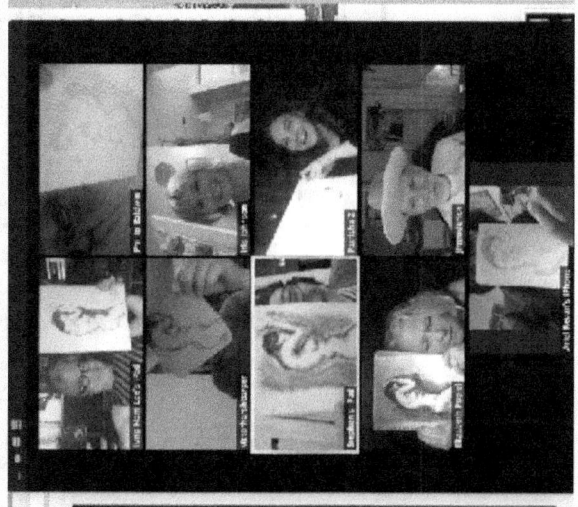

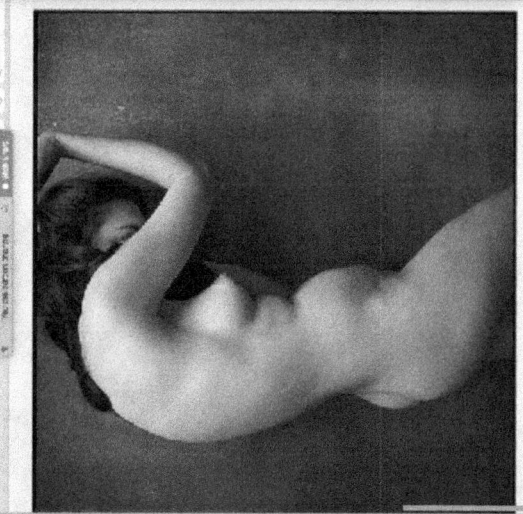

DRAWERS AND CRAWLERS PLAGUE BOOK
PHILLIP.BALDWIN@GMAIL.COM

CHELSEA CRAWL CREW

SELF
THE IMMERSIVE

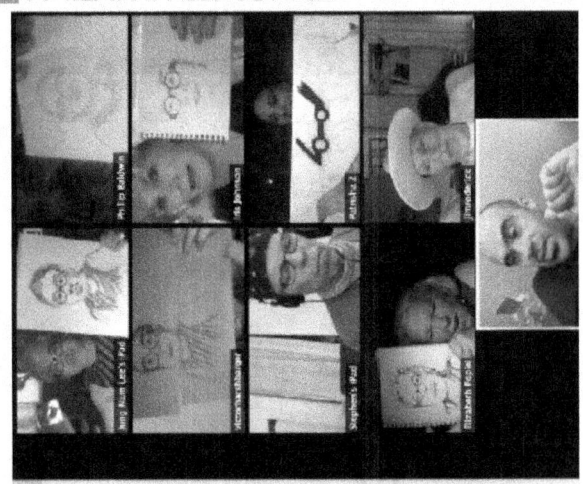

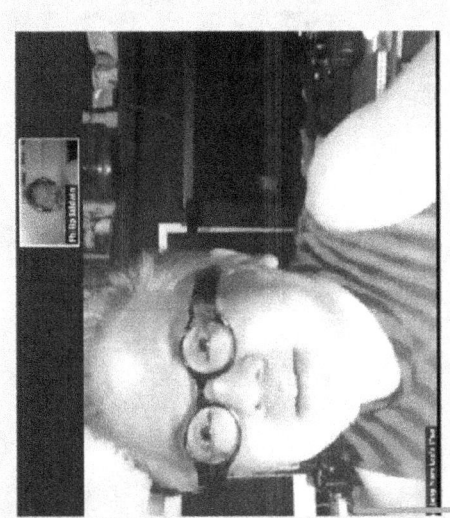

CHELSEA CRAWL CREW

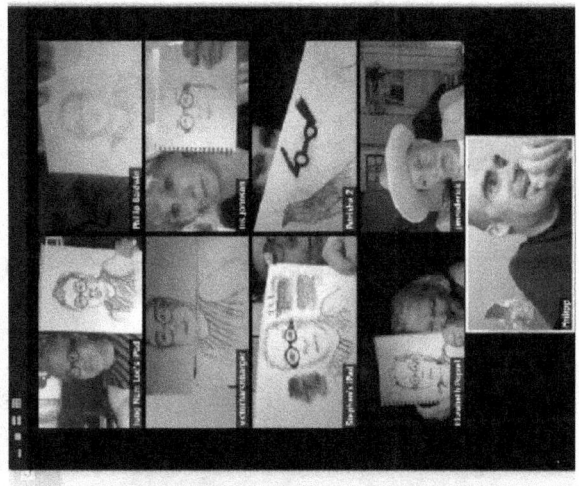

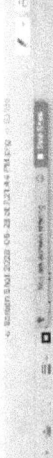

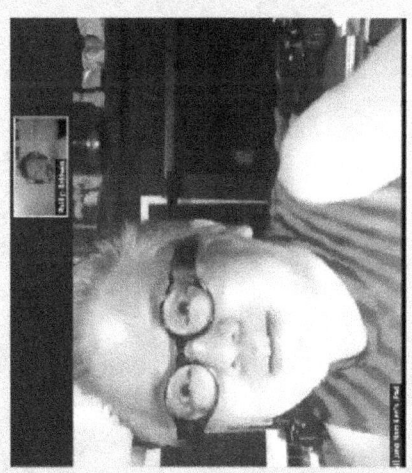

DRAWERS AND CRAWLERS PLAGUE BOOK
PHILLIP.BALDWIN@GMAIL.COM CHELSEA CRAWL CREW

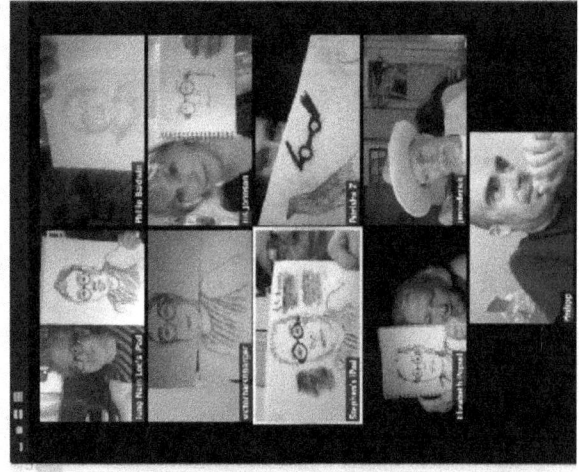

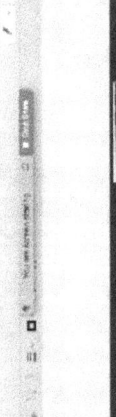

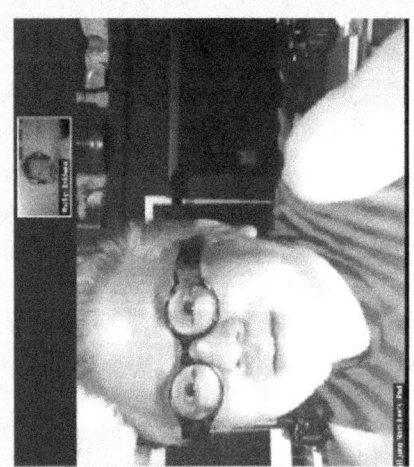

DRAWERS AND CRAWLERS PLAGUE BOOK
PHILLIP.BALDWIN@GMAIL.COM
CHELSEA CRAWL CREW

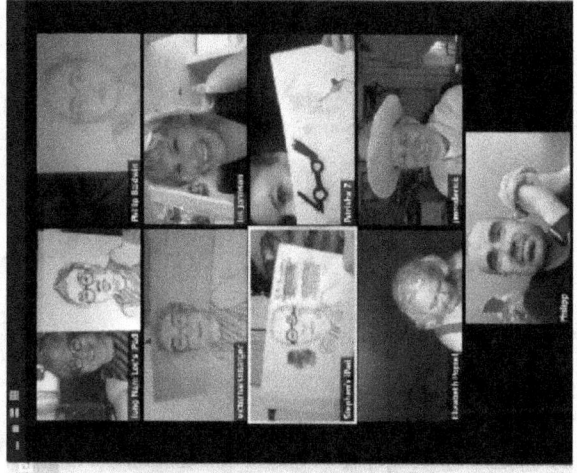

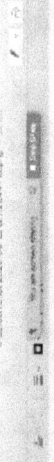

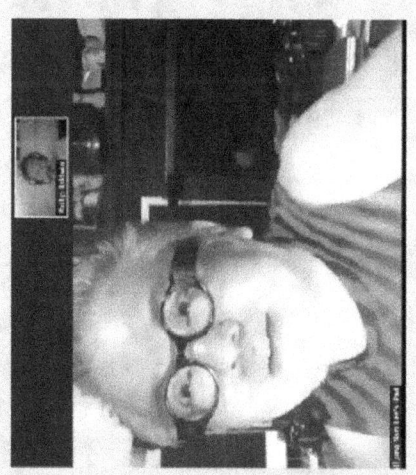

CHELSEA CRAWL CREW

SELF
THE IMMERSIVE

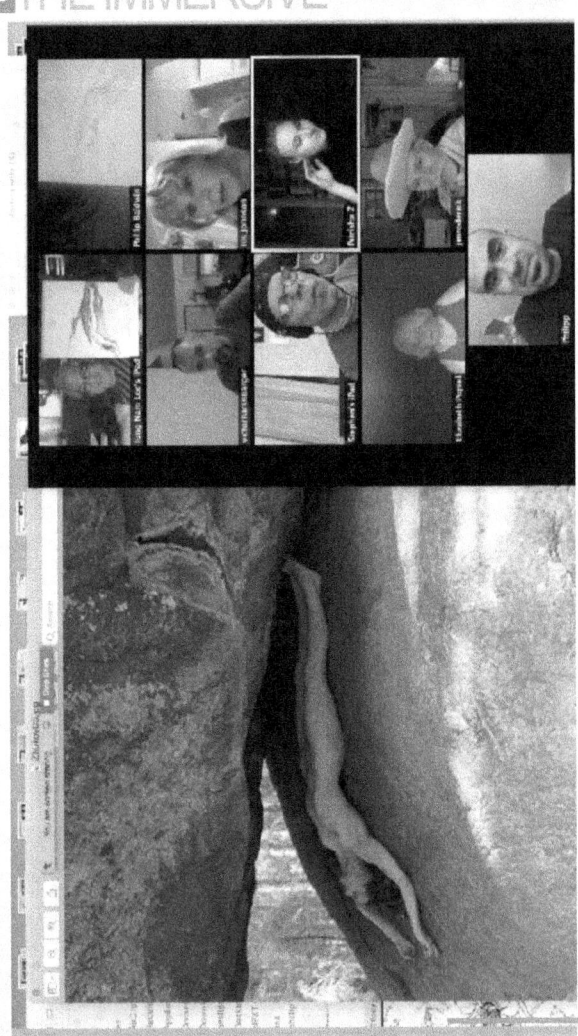

DRAWERS AND CRAWLERS PLAGUE BOOK
PHILLIPBALDWIN@GMAIL.COM

CHELSEA CRAWL CREW

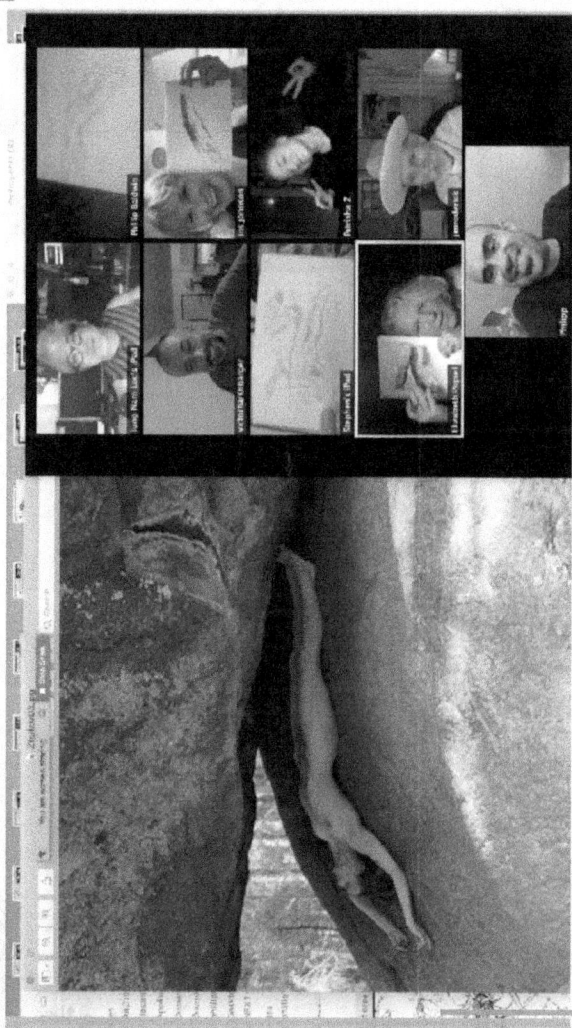

DRAWERS AND CRAWLERS PLAGUE BOOK
PHILLIP.BALDWIN@GMAIL.COM

CHELSEA CRAWL CREW

SELF
THE IMMERSIVE

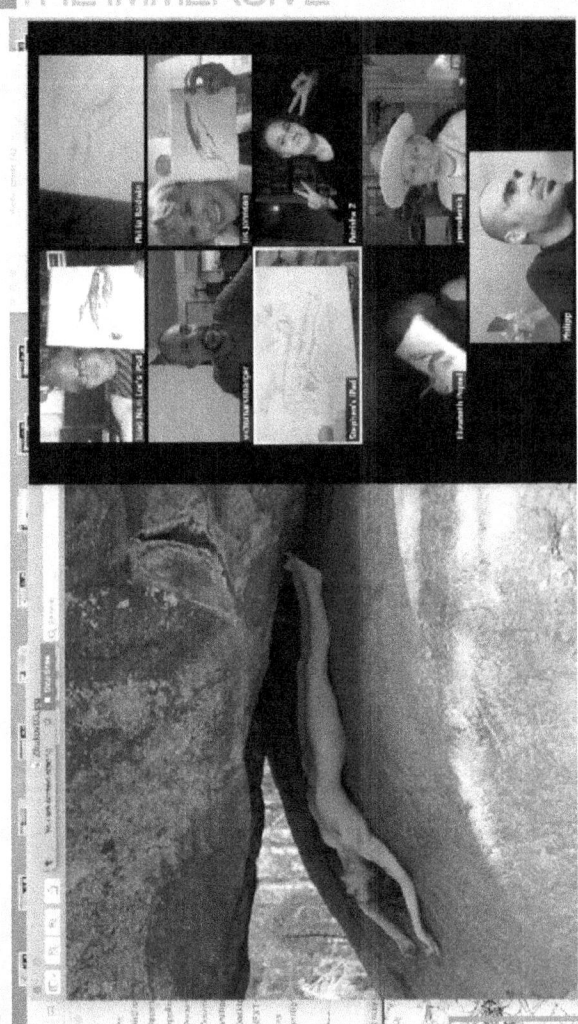

DRAWERS AND CRAWLERS PLAGUE BOOK
PHILLIPBALDWIN@GMAIL.COM CHELSEA CRAWL CREW

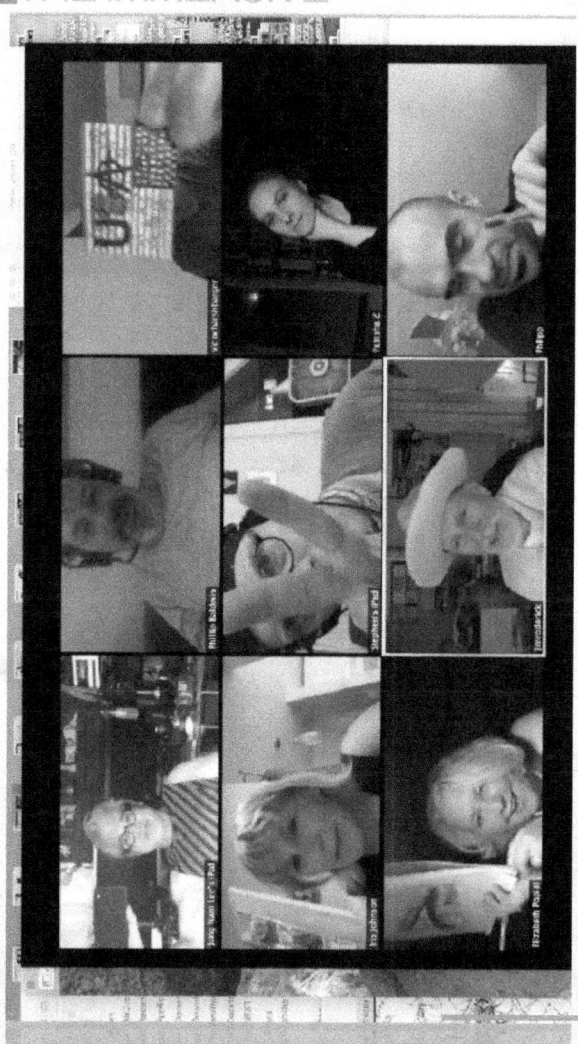

CHELSEA CRAWL CREW

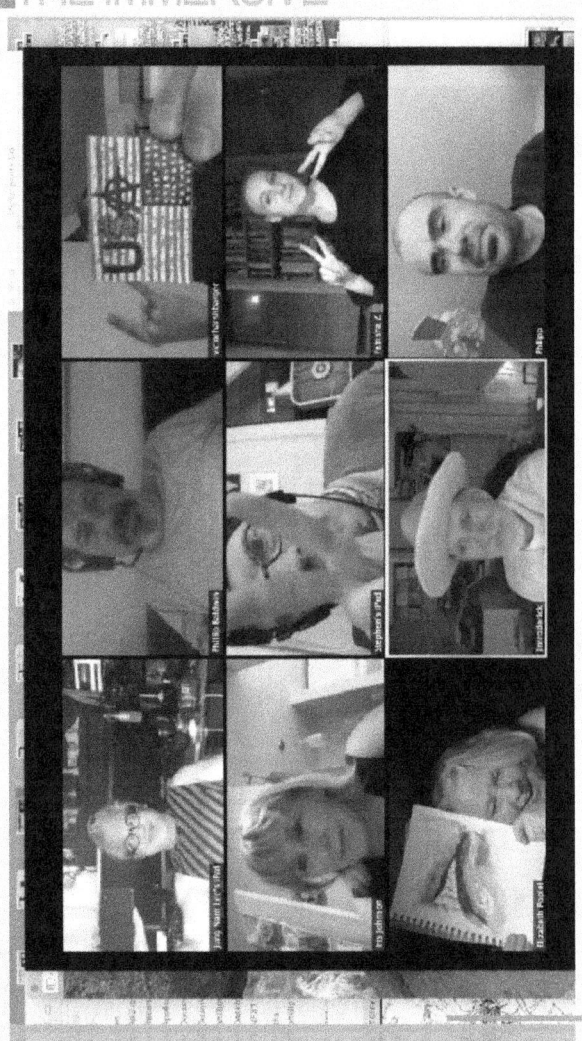

DRAWERS AND CRAWLERS PLAGUE BOOK
PHILLIP.BALDWIN@GMAIL.COM

CHELSEA CRAWL CREW

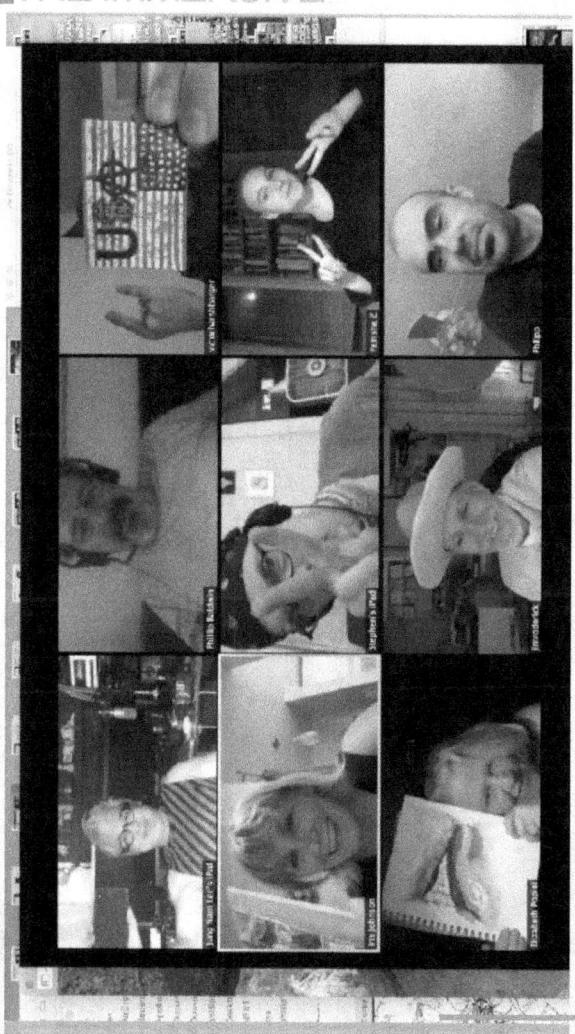

DRAWERS AND CRAWLERS PLAGUE BOOK
PHILLIP.BALDWIN@GMAIL.COM
CHELSEA CRAWL CREW

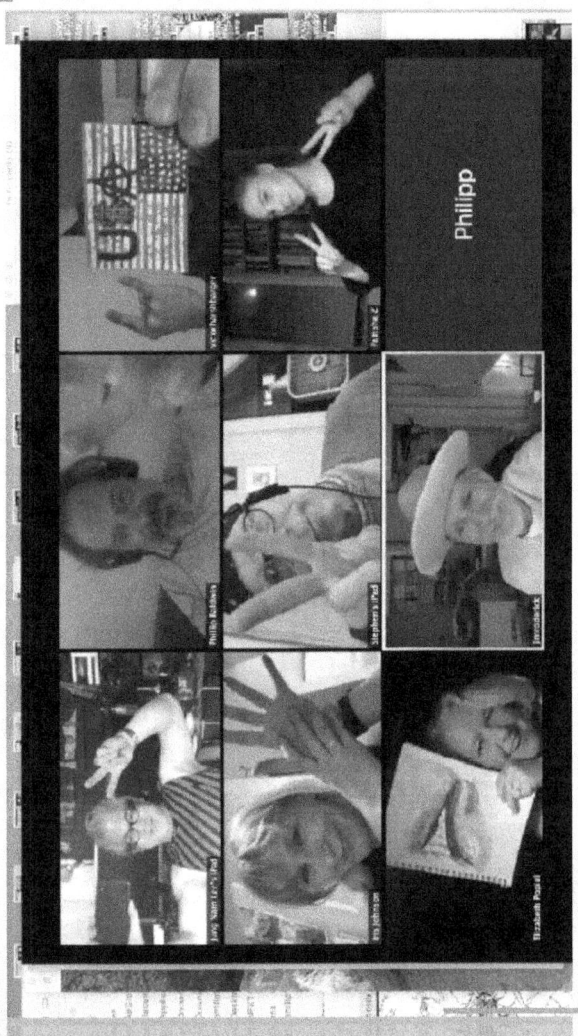

DRAWERS AND CRAWLERS
PLAGUE BOOK...

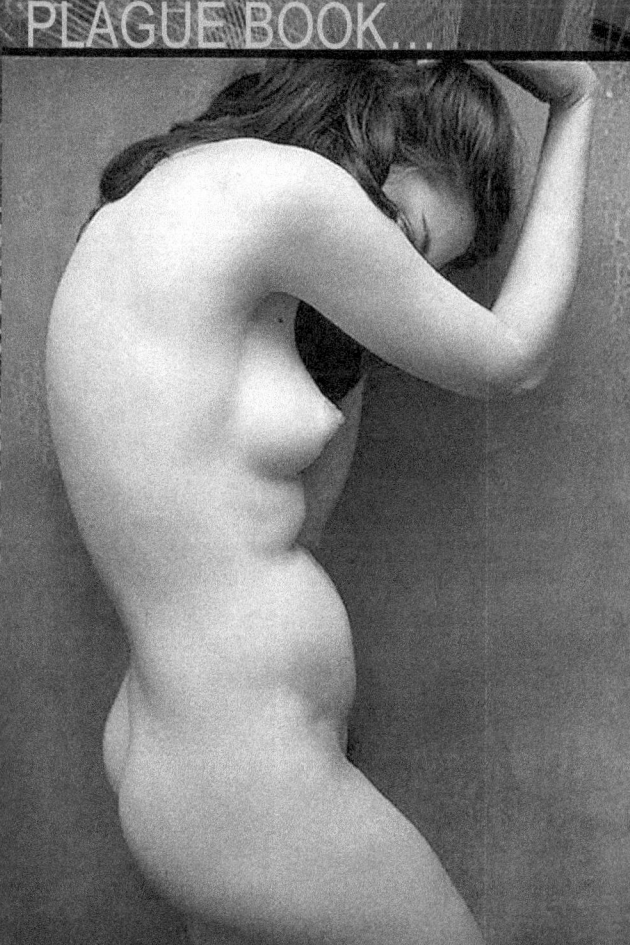

DRAWERS AND CRAWLERS
PLAGUE BOOK...

\\chelsea crawl crew...

DRAWERS AND CRAWLERS
PLAGUE BOOK...

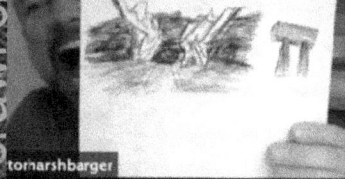

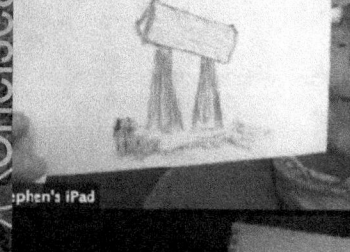

DRAWERS AND CRAWLER
PLAGUE BOOK...

Chelsea crawl crew...

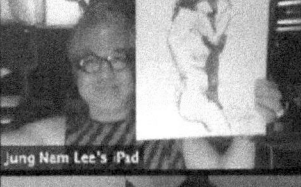

Jung Nam Lee's iPad | Phillip Baldwin

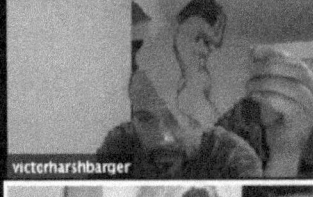

victorharshbarger | Iris Johnson

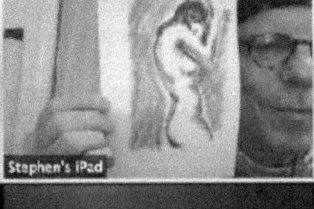

Stephen's iPad | Patrisha Z

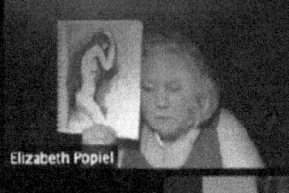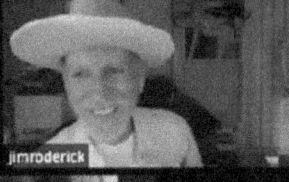

Elizabeth Popiel | jimroderick

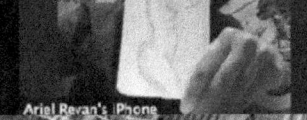

Ariel Revan's Phone

DRAWERS AND CRAWLERS
PLAGUE BOOK...

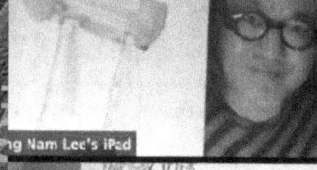

ng Nam Lee's iPad

Phillip Baldwin

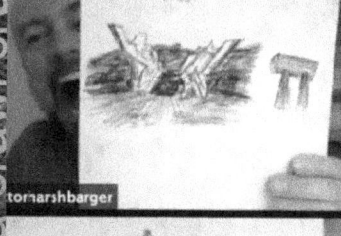

tomarshbarger

Iris Johnson

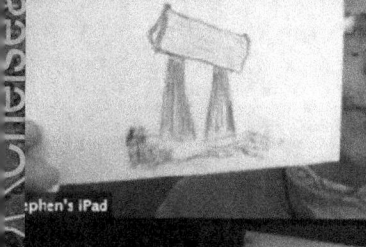

ephen's iPad

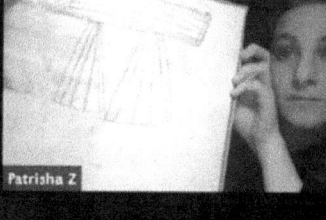

Patrisha Z

Elizabeth Popiel

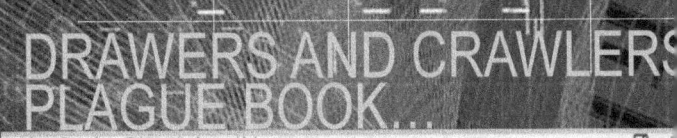
DRAWERS AND CRAWLERS
PLAGUE BOOK...

Chelsea crawl crew

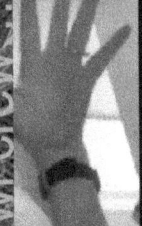
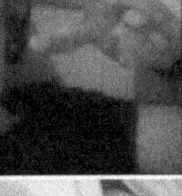
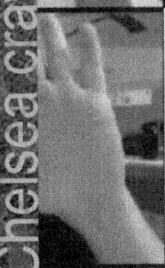
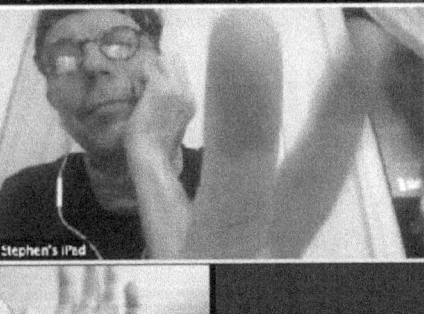
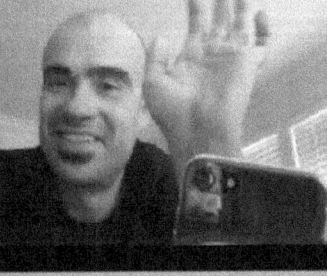

Phillip Baldwin

Elizabeth Popiel

Stephen's iPad

leahreid

Ariel Revan's iPho

DRAWERS AND CRAWLERS
PLAGUE BOOK...

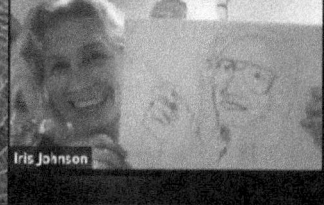

Iris Johnson

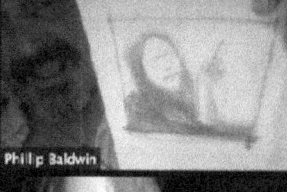

Philip Baldwin

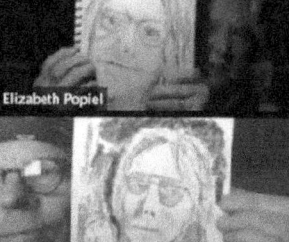

Elizabeth Popiel

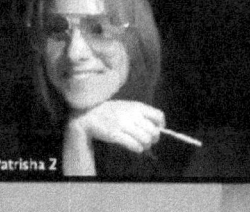

Patrisha 2

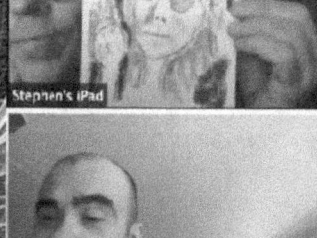

Stephen's iPad

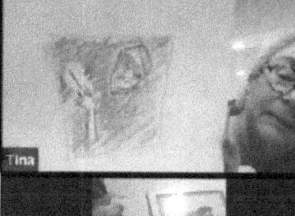

Tina

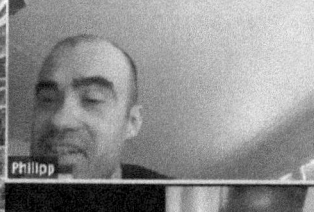

Philipp

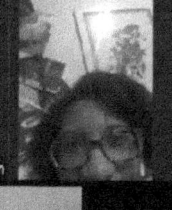

Ariel Revan

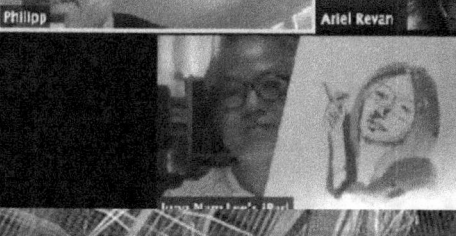

DRAWERS AND CRAWLERS
PLAGUE BOOK...

Chelsea crawl crew...

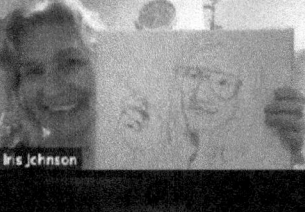

Iris Johnson

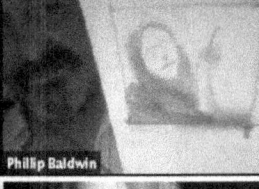

Phillip Baldwin

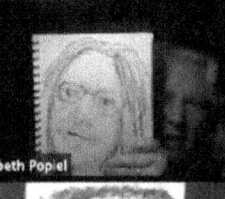

Elizabeth Popiel

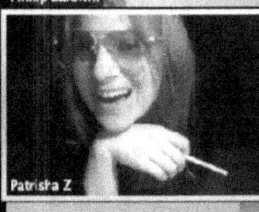

Patrisha Z

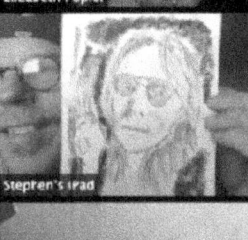

Stephen's iPad

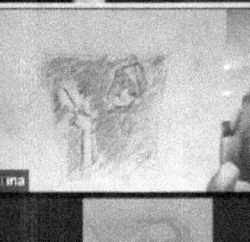

Tina

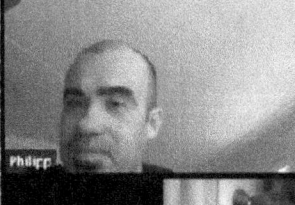

Philipp

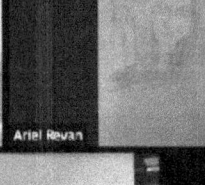

Ariel Revan

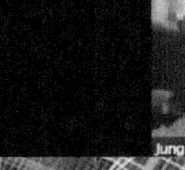

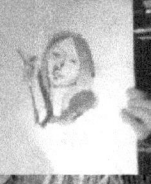

Jung Nam Lee's iPad

DRAWERS AND CRAWLERS
PLAGUE BOOK...

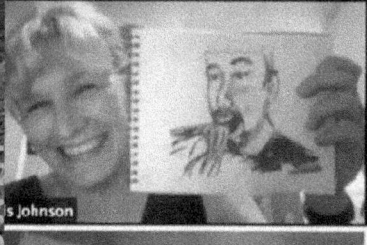

s Johnson

Phillip Baldwin

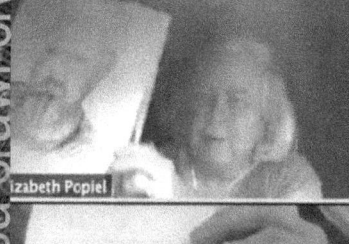

izabeth Popiel

victorharshbarger

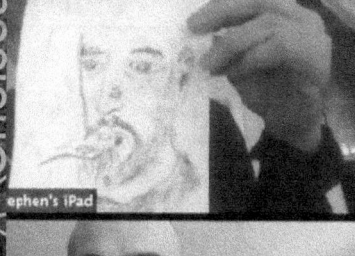

ephen's iPad

leahreid

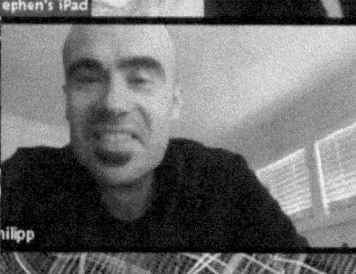

hilipp

Ariel Revan's iPho

DRAWERS AND CRAWLERS
PLAGUE BOOK...

Chelsea crawl crew

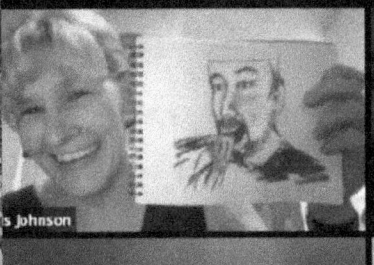

s Johnson

Phillip Baldwin

izabeth Popiel

victorharshbarger

ephen's iPad

leahreid

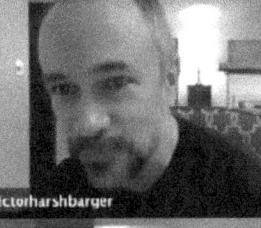

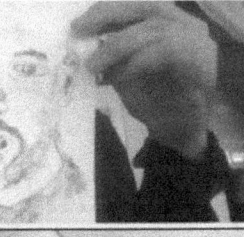

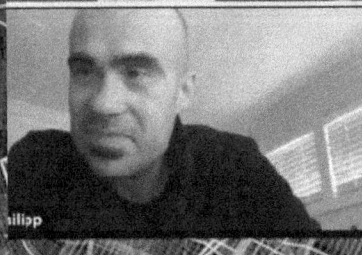

ilipp

Ariel Revan's iPh

DRAWERS AND CRAWLERS
PLAGUE BOOK...

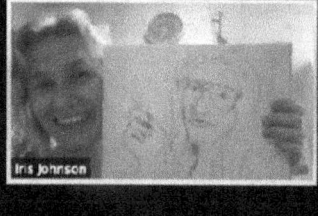

Iris Johnson

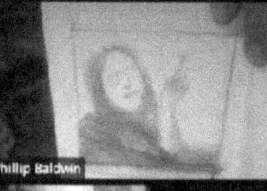

Phillip Baldwin

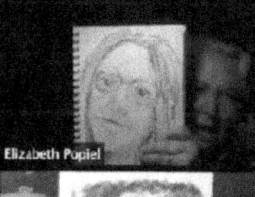

Elizabeth Popiel

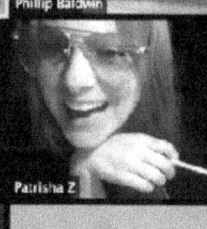

Patrisha Z

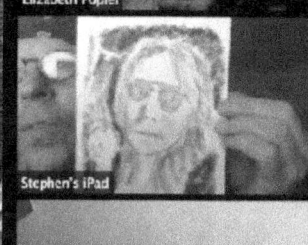

Stephen's iPad

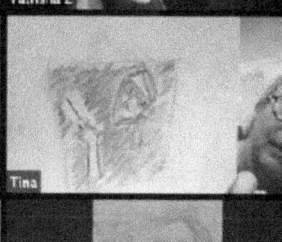

Tina

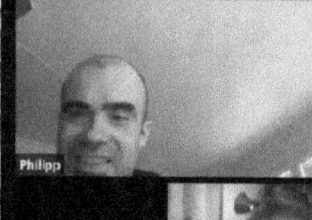

Philipp

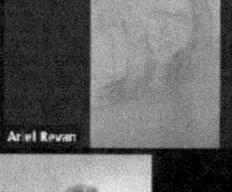

Ariel Revan

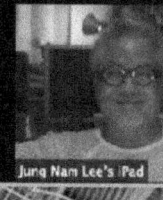

Jung Nam Lee's iPad

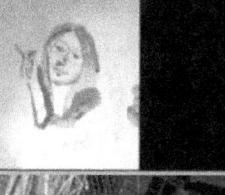

DRAWERS AND CRAWLERS PLAGUE BOOK...

Chelsea crawl crew...

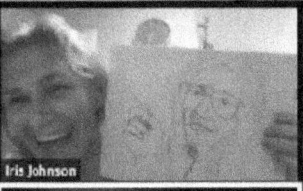

Iris Johnson

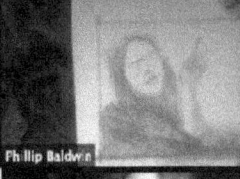

Phillip Baldwin

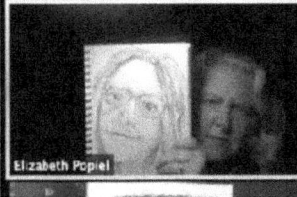

Elizabeth Popiel

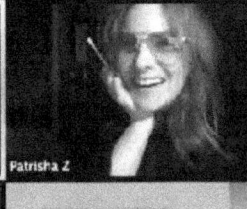

Patrisha Z

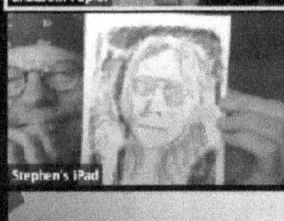

Stephen's iPad

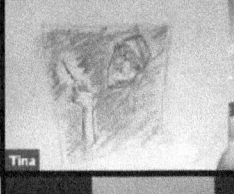

Tina

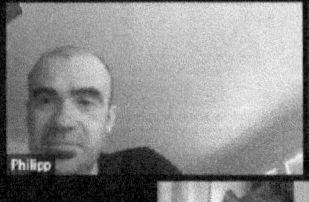

Philipp

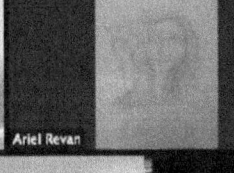

Ariel Revan

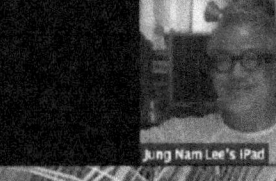

Jung Nam Lee's iPad

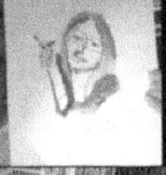

DRAWERS AND CRAWLERS
PLAGUE BOOK...

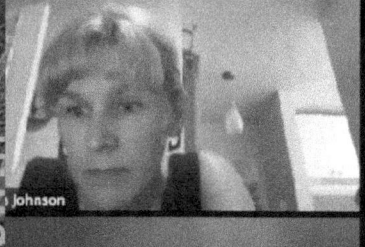

Johnson | Phillip Baldwin

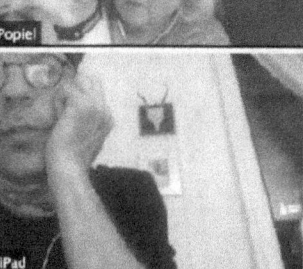

zabeth Popiel | victormarshbarger

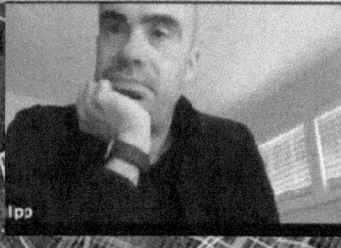

phen's iPad | leahreid

lpp | Ariel Revan's iPhon

DRAWERS AND CRAWLERS
PLAGUE BOOK...

Chelsea crawl crew

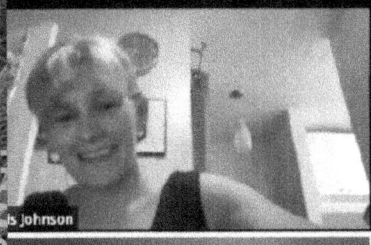

s johnson

Phillip Baldwin

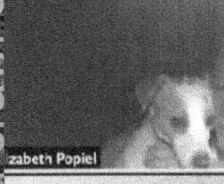

zabeth Popiel

victorkarshbarger

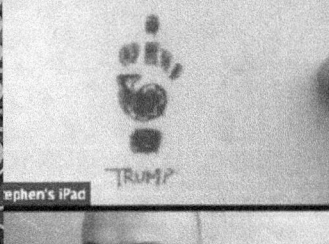

TRUMP?

ephen's iPad

leahreid

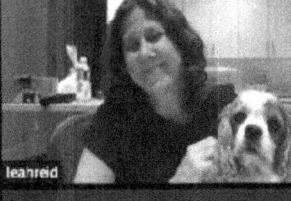

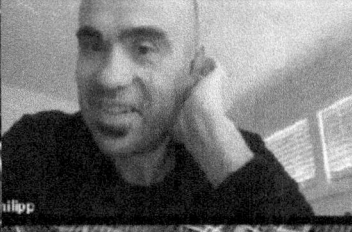

ilipp

Ariel Revan's iPh

DRAWERS AND CRAWLERS
PLAGUE BOOK...

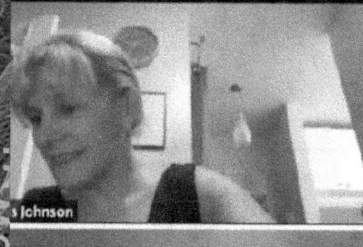

s Johnson

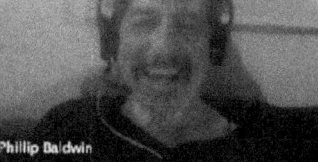

Phillip Baldwin

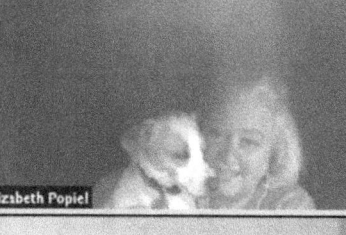

izabeth Popiel

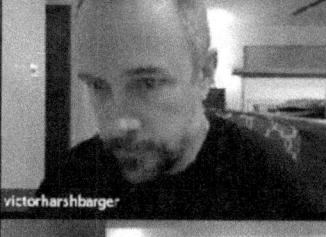

victorharshbarger

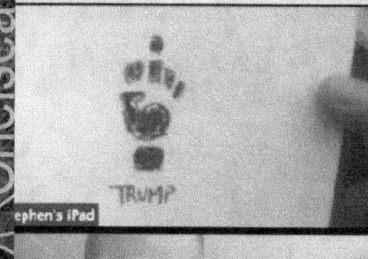

TRUMP

ephen's iPad

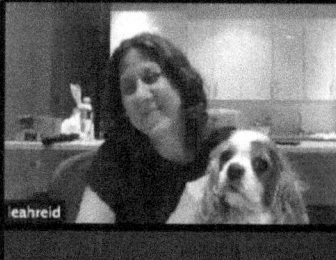

leahreid

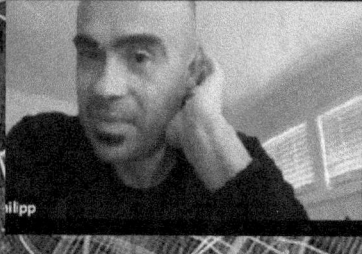

hilipp

Ariel Revan's iPhon

DRAWERS AND CRAWLERS
PLAGUE BOOK...

Chelsea crawl crew

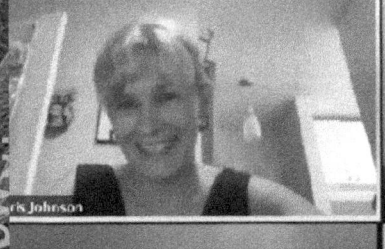

...s Johnson

Phillip Baldwin

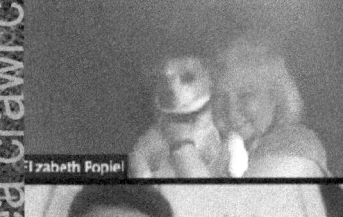

Elzabeth Popiel

victorharshbarger

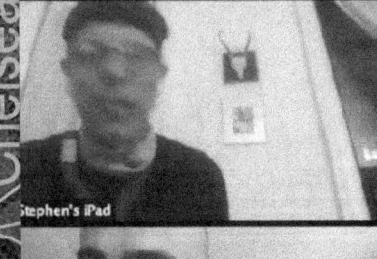

Stephen's iPad

leahreid

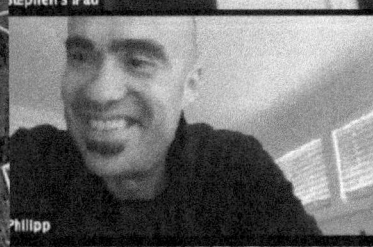

Philipp

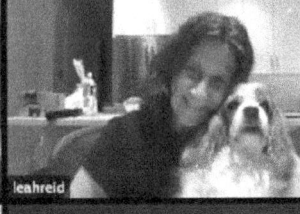

Ariel Revan's iPho

DRAWERS AND CRAWLERS
PLAGUE BOOK...

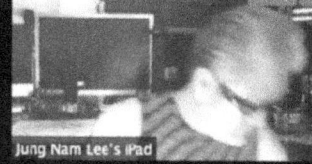

Jung Nam Lee's iPad

Phillip Baldwin

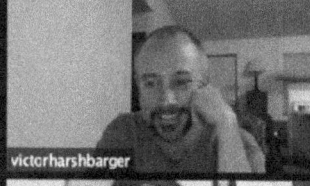

victorharshbarger

Iris Johnson

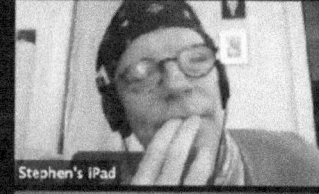

Stephen's iPad

Patrisha Z

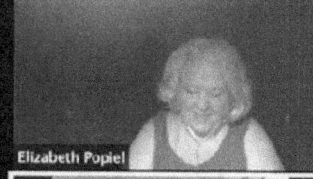

Elizabeth Popiel

jimroderick

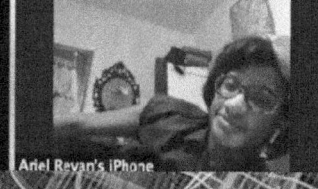

Ariel Revan's iPhone

Philipp

Connecting to audio...

A Chelsea Crawl-crew...

DRAWERS AND CRAWLERS
PLAGUE BOOK...

Phillip Baldwin

chelsea crawl crew

Jung Nam Lee's iPad

DRAWERS AND CRAWLERS
PLAGUE BOOK...

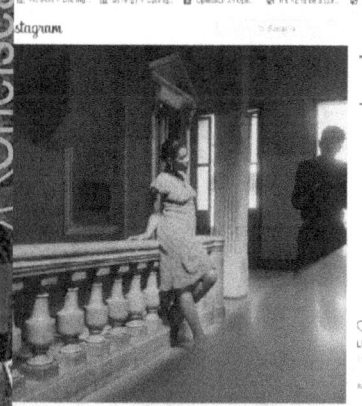

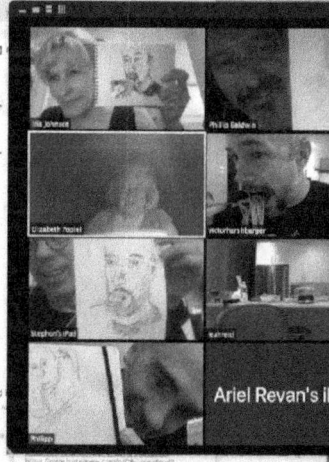

Ariel Revan's iPh

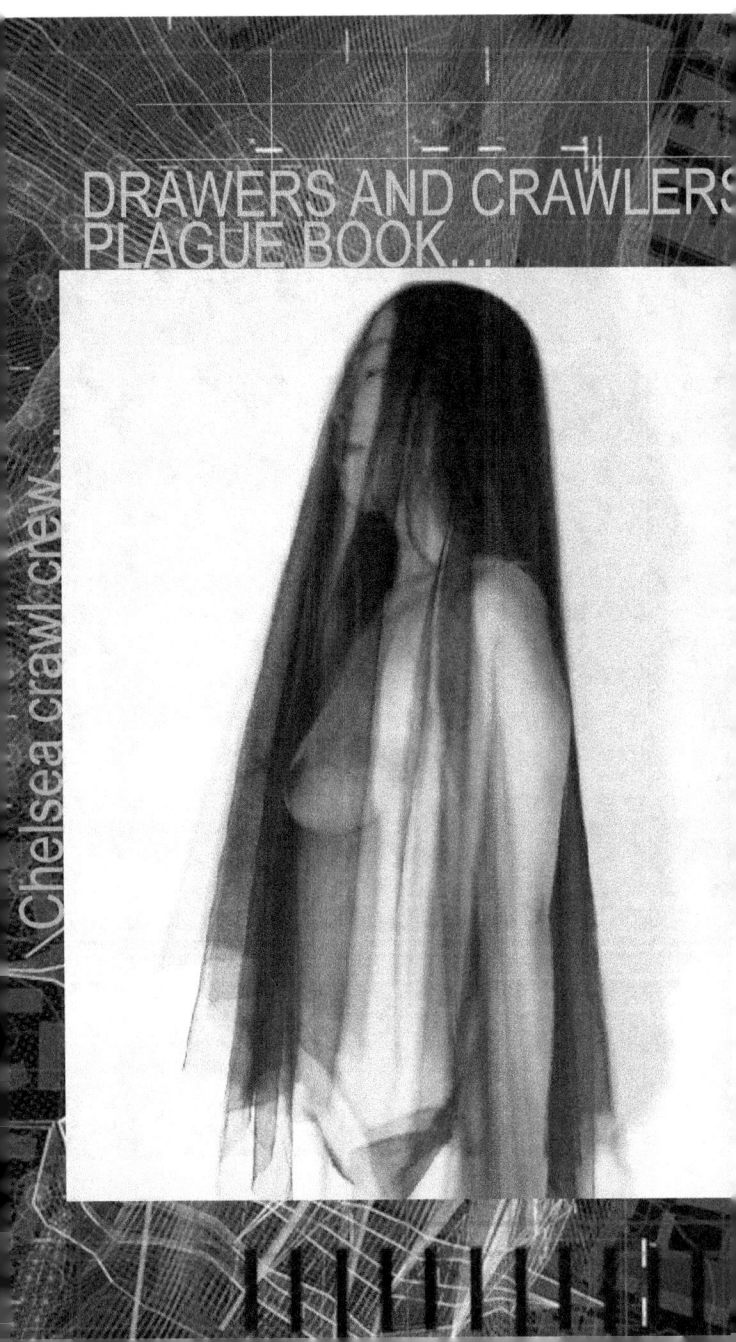

DRAWERS AND CRAWLERS
PLAGUE BOOK...

\\chelsea crawl crew

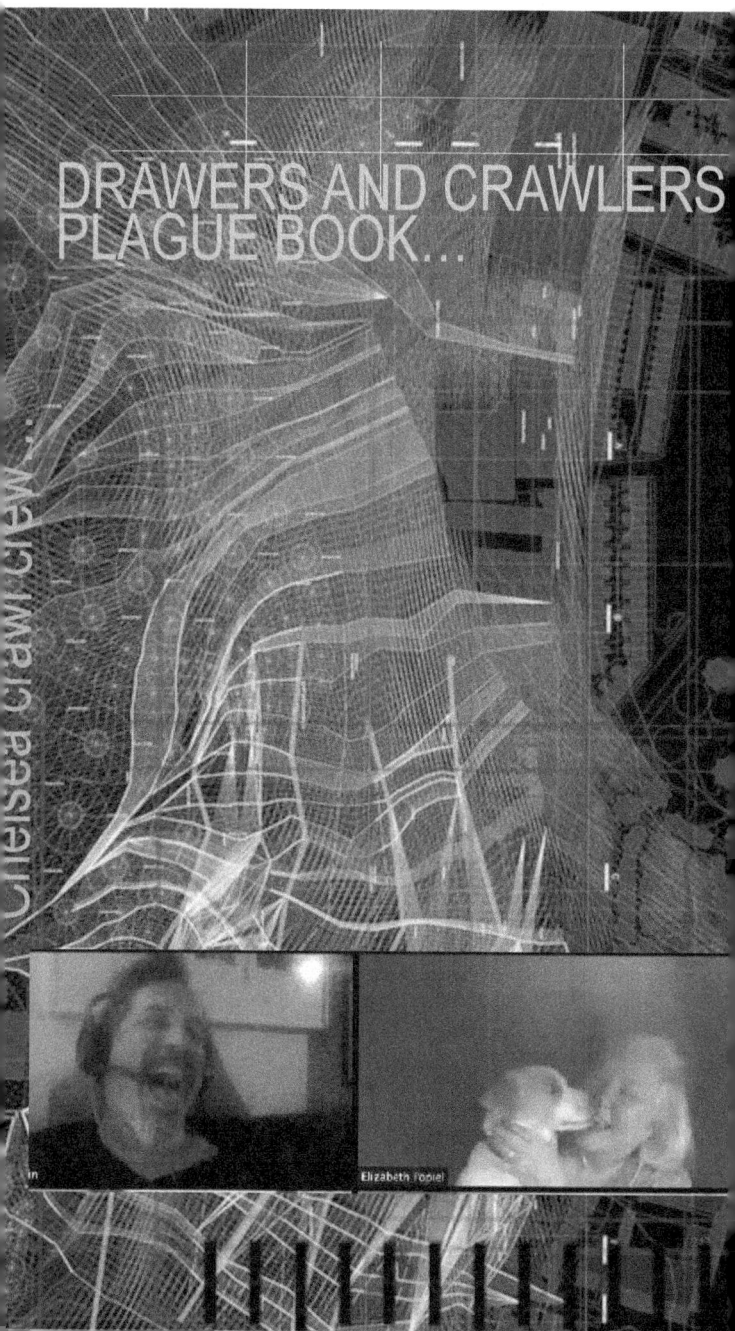

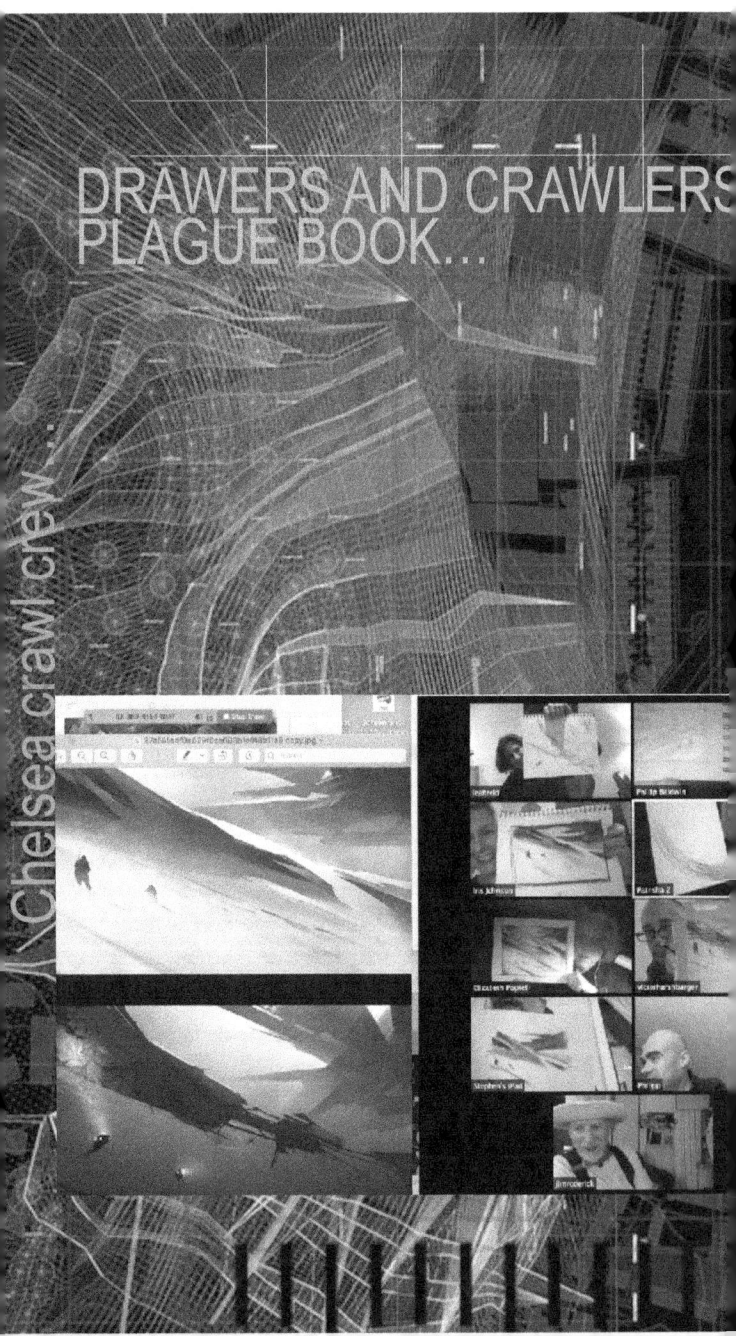

DRAWERS AND CRAWLERS
PLAGUE BOOK...

Chelsea crawl crew...

DRAWERS AND CRAWLERS
PLAGUE BOOK...

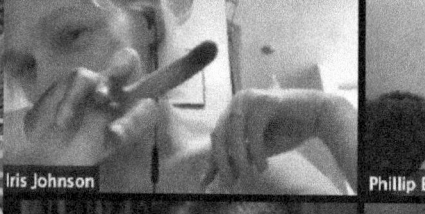 Iris Johnson

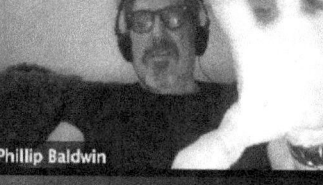 Phillip Baldwin

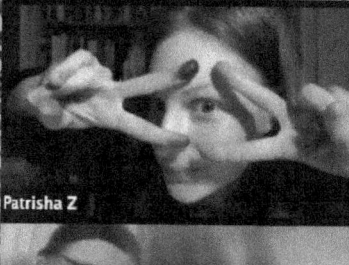 Patrisha Z

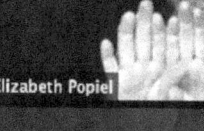 Elizabeth Popiel

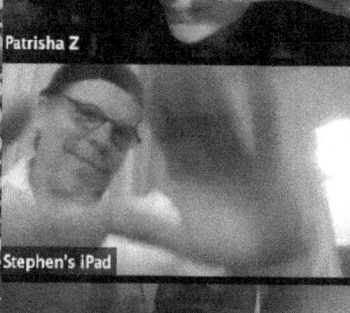 Stephen's iPad

 Philipp

 Sal Trapani

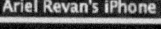 Ariel Revan's iPhone

DRAWERS AND CRAWLERS PLAGUE BOOK…

Chelsea crawl crew…

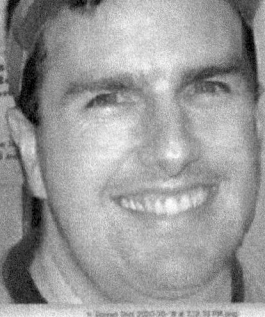

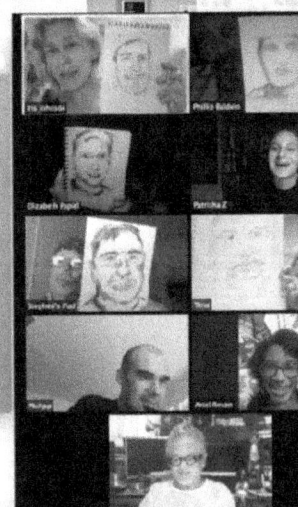

DRAWERS AND CRAWLERS
PLAGUE BOOK...

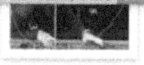

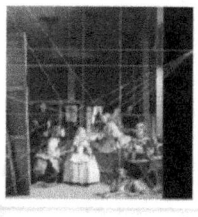

DRAWERS AND CRAWLERS
PLAGUE BOOK...

Chelsea crawl crew

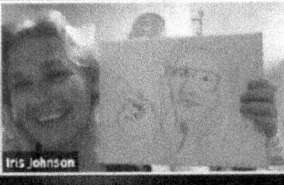

Iris Johnson

Philip Baldwin

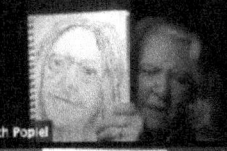

Elizabeth Popiel

Patrisha Z

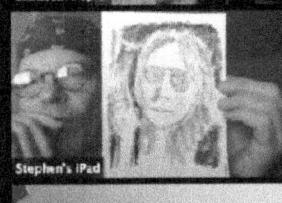

Stephen's iPad

Tina

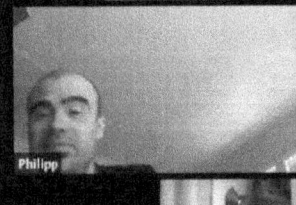

Philipp

Ariel Revan

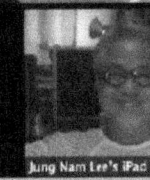

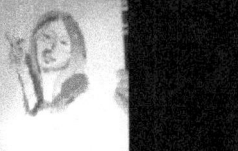

Jung Nam Lee's iPad

Participants (9)

Thu 9:34

Window   Help

AND CRAWLERS.AMERICAN BODY.NIGHTMARE OF SOLIPSISM.

Q Search

u are screen sharing   ■ Stop Share

f611=96b2fe15bder59124bc678ee2 jpg

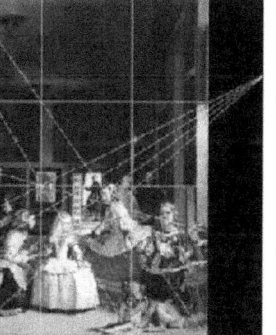

bf2189460217285 4cc3b66964d a .jpg

466 items. 10.51 GB available

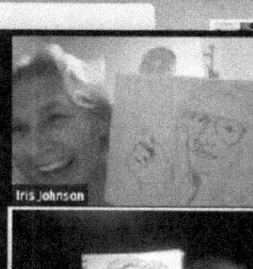

Iris Johnson

Elizabeth Popiel

Stephen's iPad

Philipp

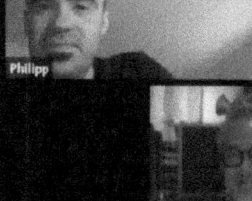

Jung Nam Lee's iPa

DRAWERS AND CRAWLERS
PLAGUE BOOK...

Chelsea crawl crew...

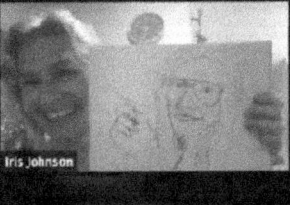
Iris Johnson

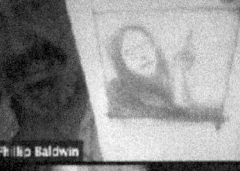
Phillip Baldwin

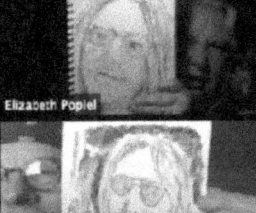
Elizabeth Popiel

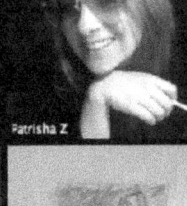
Patrisha Z

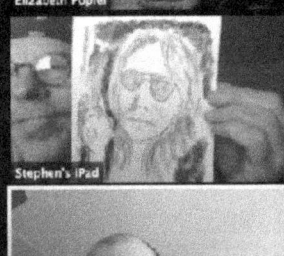
Stephen's iPad

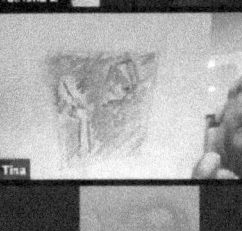
Tina

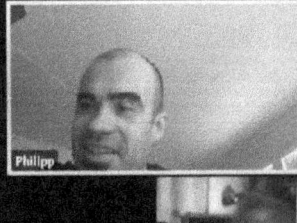
Philipp

Ariel Revan

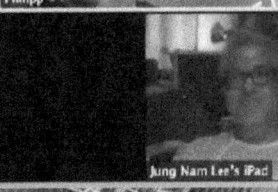

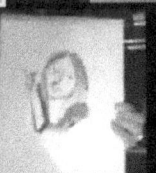
Jung Nam Lee's iPad